Dave Tate.

THE MISUSE OF ALCOHOL

THE MISUSE OF ALCOHOL

CRUCIAL ISSUES IN DEPENDENCE TREATMENT & PREVENTION

Edited by NICK HEATHER IAN ROBERTSON & PHIL DAVIES

on behalf of New Directions
in the Study of Alcohol Group

CROOM HELM
London & Sydney

©1985 New Directions in the Study of Alcohol Group
Croom Helm Ltd, Provident House, Burrell Row,
Beckenham, Kent BR3 1AT
Croom Helm Australia Pty Ltd, First Floor, 139 King Street,
Sydney, NSW 2001, Australia

British Library Cataloguing in Publication Data

The misuse of alcohol : crucial issues in
   dependence, treatment and prevention.
   1. Alcoholic beverages — Physiological effect
   I. Heather, Nick II. Robertson, Ian, *1944-*
   III. Davies, Phil IV. New Directions in the
   Study of Alcohol Group
   613.8'1   RC565
   ISBN 0-7099-3755-5

Printed and bound in Great Britain
by Billing & Sons Limited, Worcester.

CONTENTS

This book is dedicated to the memory of D.L. Davies,

a friend to many of us and an inspiration to us all.

GENERAL INTRODUCTION

The New Directions in the Study of Alcohol Group (NDSAG) emerged from a series of symposia on the topic of 'resumed normal drinking' organised by Dr D.L. Davies and the Alcohol Education Centre in 1976 and 1977. These meetings were so successful in bringing together people with common interests in the alcoholism field in Britain that they became a regularly occurring event, although the scope of discussions soon widened from its originally narrow focus. Eventually it was decided, somewhat reluctantly, to form an organised group with a formal constitution, committee of management, membership fees and so on, and this has now been in existence for four years.

Membership is open to anyone who is actively engaged in treatment, education or research in the area of alcohol use and misuse. The Group holds an annual conference at different venues in Britain and publishes a booklet of members' papers twice a year. Local groups of members are beginning to spring up in various parts of the country. All the authors who have contributed to this volume are members of NDSAG.

It should be emphasised that the Group has no particular axe to grind and is able to encompass within its membership a wide variety of views, although it is probably true to say that the great majority of members are united by a common, general perspective on alcohol problems - perhaps best summarised negatively as a rejection of disease conceptions of alcoholism. However, as anyone who has attended an NDSAG meeting will attest, this still leaves plenty of room for disagreement and the self-appointed task of the Group is to explore the many and varied conceptual and empirical directions which become apparent once the myopic influence of the disease position is thoroughly renounced. The heterogeneity of views represented in the Group is amply demonstrated in these essays.

Another point to make is that NDSAG is not a lobby or a pressure group; we do not seek to bring about changes in the law of the land or directly to influence government policy with regard to alcohol misuse. We may as individuals be intensely interested in these things but, as a Group, we think they are best left to other organisations in the field. The reverse of this coin is that, like

1

another well-known fellowship in the alcoholism field, we are entirely financially self-supporting. This independence is regarded as essential if we are to express ourselves on controversial issues without fear or favour.

Neither are we a training organisation in the obvious sense of the term. Although we hope that anybody attending our conferences or reading our booklet will learn something, we are not in the business of delivering ex cathedra instruction on the nature of alcohol comsumption.

As to what we do actually engage in, this might best be summarised by saying that we are merely 'a talking shop'. In other words, we are primarily concerned with the stimulation, analysis and criticism of ideas about the use and misuse of beverage alcohol, with the encouragement of research in this area, and with the dissemination of the results of these endeavours. This does not mean that the ideas in question need be irrelevant to practical and immediate concerns, as the contributions published here clearly show. And although we are not a pressure group, this does not mean that we do not aspire to influence events in the long run by influencing society's understanding of drinking behaviour. Indeed, it is precisely to that end that this book is directed.

Like Caesar's Gaul, the book is divided into three parts and, as in that earlier partition, the territory encompassed by the misuse of alcohol has been exhaustively covered - in this case in the general areas of dependence, treatment and prevention. Each part has been given a question to serve as a title and to describe the basic issue around which the contributions in it converge. It has now become commonplace to say that the alcoholism field is undergoing a period of rapid change and crisis, and it was the intention of the editors of this book to identify the three crucial and controversial issues underlying the transition.

We suggest that the revolution in our thinking about alcohol misuse can be economically illustrated by considering: (i) changes at the basic explanatory level in how we conceive of harmful drinking behaviour; (ii) changes in our confidence that the drinking behaviour of individuals can be effectively modified in the traditional context of 'treatment'; and (iii) changes in how we imagine harmful drinking may effectively be prevented. It is to be expected that some thinkers will be more radical than others and will wish to sweep away more of the old foundations than their more conservative colleagues, and it is precisely at this point of disagreement that the three crucial issues which currently dominate the world of alcohol studies emerge.

It is apparent that the three areas covered are intimately linked and that changes in thinking at one level affect changes at the other two. For example, concepts of dependence have been clearly influenced by evidence from epidemiological studies designed primarily with treatment and prevention in mind; the way in which treatment is organised must obviously reflect how the condition to be treated is conceived and explained; the need for effective preventative policies is made more urgent by pessimism over the real effectiveness of treatment; and so on. In this sense, the method of division used in the book is artificial and this should be borne in mind by the percipient reader.

As well as a heterogeneity of opinion, the membership of NDSAG also includes a diversity of professional preocccupations, ranging all the way from pure researchers to practising clinicians and caseworkers, from ivory tower to grass roots. Some of the contributions to this volume are thus founded mostly in the extensive working experience of their authors, while others pay more attention to academic reviews and research findings, with about every combination of these two sorts of influence that it is possible to imagine. Wherever feasible, the results of new, hitherto unpublished research have been included.

It should also be noted that the contributions to the book come from several different professional disciplines - from psychiatry, psychology, sociology, social work and, in one case, economics. This is itself a sign of the times and reflects the growing influence of the social sciences in the response to alcohol misuse. It is often said that the world of alcohol studies is a relatively enclosed and parochial one, and this situation is sometimes lamented when failure to learn from developments in other problem areas is observed. Fortunately, it does have the advantage that people entering the field from varying academic and professional backgrounds soon come to speak a common language and are able to identify their points of agreement and disagreement with relative clarity. Thus it is for 'alcohologists' - to use that horrible expression - that the book is chiefly intended.

On behalf of the editors, I should like to thank Isabel Ormerod, Dorothy Petrie, Gillian Lawrence and Jackie Brisbane for typing the manuscript with speed and accuracy. We must also thank Tim Hardwick of Croom Helm for his help and patience during the compilation of the manuscript.

As far as intellectual influence is concerned, it is of course the entire membership of NDSAG, however senior or junior and however garrulous or reticent, which should be thanked and we do so here with great enthusiasm. Although we asked a sample of individual members to contribute chapters, these individuals would be the first to insist that their efforts be regarded as the fruits and distillations of the many debates, arguments and other exchanges of ideas in which the Group has engaged over the past few years.

Nick Heather
Chairman, NDSAG

PART ONE

IS THERE AN ALCOHOL DEPENDENCE SYNDROME?

INTRODUCTION

Nick Heather

As long as human beings have pondered the behaviour of their fellow creatures they have doubtless been puzzled why some of them persist in drinking alcoholic beverages in a way which obviously does them harm. This is perhaps the central theoretical problem in the study of the misuse of alcohol or of any other drug - the problem of accounting for the 'glue', as Robin Room (1972) has put it, which holds a drug taker to a repeated pattern of harmful use. One of the most recent and certainly one of the most influential solutions to have been proposed for this problem is to say that it is because the individual is suffering from the alcohol dependence syndrome. And it is to the value of this proposed solution that the contributions in this first part of the book are all addressed.

It was during that momentous epoch in human history, the closing years of the eighteenth century, that scientific explanations began to be proposed for this central theoretical problem - or, at least, explanations which appeared to be scientific in the intellectual climate of the period. Thus, for the first time, habitual drunkenness was seen as an addiction, and it is a surprising fact, in view of our current association of the concept of addiction primarily with hard drugs, that alcohol was seen as an inherently addicting substance quite some time before opium was so regarded (see Levine, 1978). The 'disease of the will' which was thought to result from drinking too much alcohol was described in terms startlingly similar to modern psychiatric accounts of 'loss of control' over drinking, and this way of thinking about addiction or dependence has played an essential part in medical thought on the subject, so some commentators would argue, right up to the present day.

Certainly, the term addiction was retained in the first formulation of a rediscovered disease concept of alcoholism by Jellinek (1952). Here the 'alcohol addict' was distinguished from other types of misuser by the superimposed process of loss of control and the phases of alcohol addiction described the course of a chronic and progressive disease. In Jellinek's (1960) later work, loss of control became identified with the 'physical dependence', involving increased tissue tolerance, adaptive cell metabolism, withdrawal symptoms and craving, which was thought to

7

characterise addiction to heroin and other hard drugs. At the same time, Jellinek described a purely psychological dependence, with reliance on the effects of alcohol to relieve emotional pain, which was not however to be regarded as a disease.

The abandonment during the 1950s of the term addiction and the emergence of the concept of dependence have been well described by Anthony Thorley (1981). Although 'addiction' may have been useful for the purposes of medical science, it had grave disadvantages for the public relations exercise involved in the attempt to improve the alcoholic's image and to get the disease of alcoholism recognised as one worthy of legitimate medical attention. This was because it too obviously suggested the antisocial and altogether obnoxious behaviour of that demon of the post-war period, 'the drug addict'.

The first occasion on which the term dependence seems to have been used was in the report of a WHO (World Health Organization) sub-committee, of which Jellinek himself was a prominent member, published in the same year as his 'phases of alcohol addiction' paper (WHO, 1952). This report contained the now famous definition of alcoholics as

> those excessive drinkers whose dependence upon alcohol has attained such a degree that it shows a noticeable mental disturbance or an interference with their bodily and mental health, their interpersonal relationships, and their smooth social and economic functioning, or who show prodromal signs of such developments.

Despite the fact that the sub-committee was non-committal as to the causes, as opposed to the effects, of the dependence in question, this definition led to the inclusion of alcoholism as a mental illness in the International Classification of Diseases (see Thorley, 1981).

There was a period during the 1950s when 'dependence' came to be seen principally in social and psychological terms and as involving a compulsion to drink alcohol which was more serious than mere 'habituation' but less serious than addiction or specifically physical dependence. Indeed, the tendency to think of 'dependence' as a somehow less serious relative of 'addiction' may still be encountered today. As was noticed earlier, the distinction between physical and psychological dependence became enshrined in Jellinek's (1960) classic delineation of the species of alcoholism. At this point it is worth observing that, although the creators of the syndrome idea (e.g. Edwards, 1977) insist that it is best conceived of as a complex psycho-physiological disorder in which the contribution of the two types of dependence is inseparable, its critics claim that it is essentially and effectively a predominantly biological and hence medically oriented conception (see Stan Shaw, Chapter 2). This is one of the issues on which the reader must make up his or her mind.

In relation to drug misuse of all kinds, the semantic confusion surrounding various terms like addiction, dependence and habituation became an object of concern for the WHO Expert Committee on Addiction-producing Drugs which reported in 1964 (see Eddy, Halbach, Isbell and Seevers, 1965). Recognising that some drugs which did not lead to physiological withdrawal and tolerance could sometimes be as harmful as those which did, the report recommended the final abandonment of both 'drug addiction' and 'drug habituation' and their replacement by the generic term 'drug dependence'. In 1969, in a definition which has not been revised, this was defined as follows:

> Drug dependence is a state - psychic and sometimes physical - resulting from the interaction between a living organism on a drug, characterised by behavioural and other responses that always include a compulsion to take the drug on a continuous or periodic basis in order to experience its psychic effects, and sometimes to avoid the discomfort of its absence. Tolerance may or may not be present. A person may be dependent on more than one drug. (WHO, 1969)

Quite apart from the work of Griffith Edwards which will be described later, the 1970s saw several important developments and refinements of the concepts of drug dependence in general and alcohol dependence in particular. In an important paper which has already been referred to, Room (1972) expanded the conventional twofold classification of dependence as either physical or psychological by suggesting that dependence could be located at any one of five general, analytical levels: the physiological; the psychological; the level of interaction in face-to-face groups; the level of subcultures and social worlds; and the cultural level. Dependence seated at one level may cause dependence at another, and the extinction of dependence at one level will not necessarily result in the disappearance of the dependent behaviour. The chief virtue of Room's analysis is that it takes thinking about dependence beyond the isolated individual into the realm of social forces. Symbolic definitions of their situation made by drug users themselves, definitions which are structured by cultural norms and expectations, are of considerable importance in determining drug-related behaviour. Social scientists like Coleman (1976) are highly critical of conceptualisations of addiction and dependence which ignore or underestimate these social factors. These considerations apply as much to the alcohol dependence syndrome as to any other conception of dependence.

Perhaps the major theme in the development of the concept of dependence has been a downgrading of the importance of the biological or somatic element and this process was accelerated by Russell's (1976) attempt to find a fundamental definition of dependence. Russell is critical of definitions giving prominence to continued drug use and to pharmacological factors. Instead, he argues that man can show a powerful dependence on behaviours, like

9

gambling or over-eating, in which physical withdrawal cannot be so surely implicated. Furthermore, it is not frequent or continued use which marks dependence, but the difficulty in refraining from the behaviour in question and the negative affect experienced in its absence. The degree of dependence, writes Russell (1976), 'can be equated with the amount of this negative affect which may range from mild discomfort to extreme distress, or it may be equated with the amount of difficulty or effort required to do without the drug, object etc.'.

This elimination of any pharmacological element from a definition of what is necessary and sufficient for dependent behaviour to occur marked a significant advance in the history of the concept. This advance has been recognised to some extent in the latest pronouncement of the WHO (see Edwards, Arif and Hodgson, 1982), which appeared well after the initial formulation of the alcohol dependence syndrome. This WHO Memorandum, as well as distinguishing between unsanctioned, hazardous, dysfunctional and harmful use of a drug, stresses that dependence is essentially a behavioural concept and suggests that the changes in neurophysiological functioning which were previously called physical dependence should now be termed simply 'neuroadaptation'. Despite this clear definitional distinction, however, dependence is considered to be 'a psycho-physiological-social syndrome', a view which is of course fully compatible with the published accounts of the alcohol dependence syndrome.

Thorley (1981) has also described the development of the concept of the alcohol dependence syndrome, a development which may be traced in the consistently clear and stimulating thought over the years of Griffith Edwards. The idea first makes an appearance in a paper by Edwards (1967) in which a key feature of the syndrome, that it exists by degrees and is not all-or-none, is first insisted upon. Although this appeal to continuity is attractive to modern thinking, it may be noted that it is not without difficulties, especially with regard to the question of a cut-off point on the continuum at which a special kind of dependence begins. Both Stan Shaw (Chapter 2) and Anthony Thorley (Chapter 5) have commented on this difficulty.

Also in this early paper, Edwards for the first time compares dependence to the interferences in volition found in obsessional neurosis. This he refers to as the central illness among alcohol problems, 'a man's developing a state in which drinking, rather than being a take-it-or-leave-it affair, appears to him to have become a dominating necessity, a dependence from which he cannot, without help, break' (Edwards, 1967, p. 72). This notion of a central illness or core pathology reappears in a series of papers by Edwards and his colleagues in the early 1970s (e.g. Edwards et al., 1972) in which an attempt is made to operationalise and measure dependence. In a significant positional statement, Edwards writes:

> what a dependence score aims, however, to measure is
> a core pathology rather than the (symptomatic) social,
> physical, or mental consequences which result from

that pathology - it asks about measles rather than about time missed from school. (p. 74)

As Thorley (1981) points out, 'much of the dispute over the utility of the alcohol dependence syndrome lies in the validity of this central assertion'.

As noted by Douglas Cameron in Chapter 4, the alcohol dependence syndrome itself has been described somewhat differently in the various published versions of it. The first formal description came in 1976 in a paper written by Edwards in collaboration with the distinguished American biomedical researcher, Milton Gross (Edwards and Gross, 1976). The seven separate elements of the syndrome are listed and discussed several times in the forthcoming essays (see, especially, Chapter 3 by Jonathan Chick) and need not be repeated here. Suffice it to say that the syndrome was presented as being provisional and based largely on clinical impression, although Stan Shaw suggests in Chapter 2 that this presentation was not as 'provisional' as its authors implied. Edwards and Gross also emphasise that by the term syndrome, they mean to imply no more than the concurrence of a set of phenomena, that the elements of the syndrome need not always be present nor be present with the same intensity, and that no assumptions need be made about cause or pathological process.

It is important to understand that, at the time they wrote their seminal paper, Edwards and Gross were members of a WHO committee charged with identifying and classifying disabilities related to alcohol consumption. The description of the alcohol dependence syndrome which emerged was included in the ninth revision of the <u>International Classification of Diseases</u>. This was approved by the WHO in 1976 and thus the <u>alcohol dependence syndrome</u> came into force as an official medical diagnosis (No. 303) in January 1979. The wording clearly follows the definition of drug dependence arrived at by the WHO (1969) Committee and quoted earlier:

> A state, psychic and also physical, resulting from taking alcohol, characterised by behavioural and other responses that always include a compulsion to take alcohol on a continuous or periodic basis in order to experience its psychic effects, and sometimes to avoid the discomfort of its absence; tolerance may or may not be present. A person may be dependent on alcohol or other drugs. (WHO, 1979)

The main emphasis in the report of the WHO Working Group (WHO, 1977) is upon the entire range of alcohol-related disabilities of which the disabilities resulting from the dependence syndrome form only a part. Moreover, social and psychological disabilities may exist without dependence and vice versa, and it is essential that medical and social concern should not be restricted to the syndrome. The description of the syndrome's components in the WHO document is very different from other versions. Rather than seven elements, it here has three postulated altered states: (i) altered behavioural state; (ii) altered subjective state; and (iii) altered psychobiological state. The evidence relating to the altered psychobiological state, which refers mainly to tolerance, withdrawal phenomena, relief and avoidance drinking, and reinstatement of dependence, is covered extensively in a separate article in the report by Milton Gross.

A further difference from other versions is in the identification of the 'leading symptom' of the syndrome; in the WHO (1977) report it is 'impaired control over intake of the drug ethyl alcohol', whereas in Edwards and Gross (1976) and in Edwards (1977) it is degree of physical dependence on alcohol which assumes the paramount place. However, this difference in emphasis notwithstanding, the reader must determine whether or not this prominence of psychobiological aspects of alcohol misuse renders the syndrome merely a disguised version of the traditional disease concept of alcoholism presented, for example, by Jellinek (1960), as the syndrome's critics strongly assert (see Chapter 2).

A further account of the syndrome, concentrating on its clinical usefulness, was given by Edwards (1977). This is expounded mainly in terms of a shared model of understanding to facilitate communication between therapist and patient and between medical and non-medical members of the treatment team. In particular, the degree of dependence assessed could form the basis for negotiating an appropriate treatment goal, whether abstinence or controlled drinking. The clinical usefulness of the syndrome concept is a topic addressed by all the contributors to this part of the book and is concentrated on by Anthony Thorley in Chapter 5. The medical aspects of the syndrome are prominent in yet another description of it in the report of the Royal College of Psychiatrists (1979) and it is also discussed in Edwards' (1982) recent guide to the treatment of drinking problems.

In a vital sense, it might be claimed that the question which serves as a title for this part of the book, 'Is There an Alcohol Dependence Syndrome?', is misguided. Two conflicting philosophical traditions determine the spirit in which scientific hypotheses, such as that of an alcohol dependence syndrome, are evaluated. The essentialist tradition assumes that our concepts, including scientific concepts, describe things which are really there in nature, and therefore, from this point of view, our question would be quite acceptable. The alternative view is the nominalist tradition which assumes that scientific concepts are merely names or labels used by human beings in order to organise their understanding of nature and to communicate with each other, but without any necessary correspondence to reality. The question is therefore meaningless from the nominalist position and must be translated into: 'Is it useful to speak of an alcohol dependence syndrome?'

It is important to understand which of these two positions supporters of the syndrome concept are claiming. In a typically clear statement, Edwards (1980) opts for the essentialist set of assumptions:

> Here then let us risk a guess. We may guess that
> somewhere within the range of behaviours that go by
> the name of alcoholism, there lies a condition which is
> not to be understood simply in terms of variation but
> rather in terms of state. We try today to catch its
> image descriptively in terms of the dependence
> syndrome while others before us have certainly been
> trying to perceive its outline in terms of 'alcoholism as
> disease'. We are guessing though that somewhere in
> that landscape there is a real beast to be described
> rather than an arbitrary cut on a continuum, a label,
> an abominable and mythical medicalisation. (p. 309)

Despite this bold conjecture, it is probably fair to say that it is
fashionable for the majority of contemporary scientists, particularly
social scientists and psychologists, to subscribe to the nominalist
position. This is certainly true of Hodgson and Stockwell whose
defence of the dependence model in Chapter 1 concludes
unequivocally with an appeal to its usefulness as a means of
generating testable hypotheses.

Of course, in evaluating the usefulness of the syndrome, there
are at least two senses in which this usefulness may be judged, a
scientific and a practical sense. The first, scientific sense of
usefulness is most directly addressed in Chapter 1 by Hodgson and
Stockwell, and by Chick in Chapter 3. However, in assessing the
evidence which bears upon the syndrome, it is essential to
distinguish three separate issues which are sometimes confused:

(1) The first issue is whether the actual properties of the
syndrome, as described for example by Edwards and Gross (1976),
are borne out by the evidence. For example, it is possible that a
syndrome may emerge but not include 'narrowing of the drinking
repertoire'. Or it may be found that the described characteristics of
problem drinkers do cluster together but not that they are
unidimensional. This empirical issue is the main focus of Chapter 3,
by Jonathan Chick.

(2) A more fundamental issue is whether any kind of syndrome of
dependence can be usefully said to exist at all, or whether the basic
assumption of a clustering or grouping of aspects of dependent
behaviour is simply unhelpful, as Shaw and Cameron would
undoubtedly argue. It must be pointed out here that an answer to
this question is not just a matter of empirical findings but must also
take into account a priori objections to alleged logical
inconsistencies and tautologies contained in the terms of the
syndrome concept, as shown particularly by Stan Shaw's
contribution, Chapter 2.

(3) At an even more fundamental level, the issue becomes, is the

concept of dependence itself a scientifically useful one? Thus, Hodgson and Stockwell begin Chapter 1 by carefully arguing for the utility of the basic concept and only then go on to support, in more qualified terms, the further development of a dependence syndrome.

In a similar fashion, Thorley in Chapter 5 describes the syndrome as a 'distillate' of the concept of dependence. It is at this level that Douglas Cameron mainly pitches Chapter 4. His answer to the question of whether a dependence syndrome can be usefully said to exist is, 'No, because the concept of dependence is simply another device for use in the social control of deviant drinkers'. Again, it is quite possible that the kinds of evidence cited in the other chapters are strictly irrelevant to an evaluation of Cameron's arguments because these are directed at the basic, ideological assumptions on which the syndrome idea is founded.

A second and quite different sense of the usefulness of the syndrome is the one employed by Edwards himself in his 1977 article and which forms the basis of Anthony Thorley's contribution, Chapter 5. This is whether it is useful for the practising clinician or caseworker in his or her attempts to help problem drinkers. That this issue may be regarded as separate from an assessment of the scientific evidence for or against a syndrome of dependence is shown by the fact that Thorley has no doubts as to its clinical reality but has considerable reservations, as does Stan Shaw, about its ability to assist the treatment process.

Thorley is also concerned with the somewhat wider but related area of the best way to organise the nation's response to drinking problems. He sees the syndrome as very limited in this respect because, quite simply, he wishes to see some form of demedicalisation of services, and thinks that the promulgation of the syndrome concept can only retard this development.

Mention of the demedicalisation of services leads on to what is perhaps the most heated aspect of the controversy surrounding the syndrome - the charge (attributed to, but disclaimed by, Stan Shaw) that the syndrome is at bottom simply a plot 'to keep medical men in business'. It is ironical, in view of this charge, that the principal supporters of the syndrome in this book are both psychologists, while the positions of the medically qualified contributors range from Chick's critical approval, through Thorley's sceptical pragmatism to Cameron's open hostility!

Nevertheless, there is a serious question here concerned with the desirability of medical dominance of the response to problem drinking, and with the extent to which, and how fast, this should be encouraged to change over the coming decades. Despite Griffith Edwards' earlier equivocation on the subject (see, e.g. Edwards, 1977, p. 137), there can be little doubt that the alcohol dependence syndrome is an essentially disease-oriented and medically based conception of problem drinking. But this is not _ipso facto_ a bad thing! After all, as Edwards (1970) has himself observed, 'to have persuaded society to shift a particular type of deviancy from the bad role to the sick role could ..., whatever the logic, whatever the science, prove to be an event of importance' (p. 161). If this view is regarded as too complacent, the task still remains of deciding whether the alcohol dependence syndrome does in fact support the status quo of medical dominance or whether it can allow a satisfactory degree of participation in treatment and prevention by other professional groups.

One thing is certain, and that is that we live in a time when our understanding of harmful drinking is rapidly changing. Seen in this context, the alcohol dependence syndrome can be characterised, perhaps crudely, in one of two ways - synthesis or compromise. Is it a synthesis of the best of the scientific findings and clinical wisdom of the past, which fully incorporates and combines with sound medical knowledge the important recent developments in the fields of psychology and sociology? Or is it basically a compromise designed to take into account the disturbing findings and criticisms of the disease theory of the past 20 years, but at the same time retain its major assumptions and implications for the organisation of treatment services? It is hoped that the following pages will provide enough information and discussion for this decision to be made, or at least more closely approached.

REFERENCES

Coleman, J.W. (1976) 'The myth of addiction', Journal of Drug Issues, 6, 135-41

Eddy, W.B., Halbach, H., Isbell, H. and Seevers, M.H. (1965) 'Drug dependence: its significance and characteristics', Bulletin of the World Health Organisation, 32, 721-3

Edwards, G. (1967) 'The meaning and treatment of alcohol dependence', Hospital Medicine, December, 272-80

____ (1970) 'The status of alcoholism as a disease', in R.V. Phillipson (ed.), Modern Trends in Drug Dependence and Alcoholism, London: Butterworths

____ (1977) 'The alcohol dependence syndrome: usefulness of an idea' in G. Edwards and M. Grant (eds), Alcoholism: New Knowledge and New Responses, London: Croom Helm

____ (1980) 'Alcoholism treatment: between guesswork and certainty' in G. Edwards and M. Grant (eds), Alcoholism Treatment in Transition, London: Croom Helm

____ (1982) The Treatment of Drinking Problems: A Guide for the Helping Professions, London: Grant McIntyre Medical and Scientific

____ and Gross, M. (1976) 'Alcohol dependence: provisional description of a clinical syndrome', British Medical Journal, i, 1058-61

Chandler, J. and Hensman, C. (1972) 'Drinking in a London suburb. I Correlates of normal drinking', Quarterly Journal of Studies on Alcohol, Supplement No. 6, 69-93

___ Arif, A. and Hodgson, R. (1982) 'Nomenclature and classification of drug- and alcohol-related problems: a shortened version of a WHO Memorandum', British Journal of Addiction, 77, 3-20

Jellinek, E.M. (1952) 'Phases of alcohol addiction', Quarterly Journal of Studies on Alcohol, 7, 673-84

___ (1960) The Disease Concept of Alcoholism, New Haven: Hillhouse Press

Levine, H.G. (1978) 'The discovery of addiction: changing conceptions of habitual drunkenness in America', Journal of Studies on Alcohol, 39, 143-74

Room, R. (1972) 'The social psychology of drug dependence' in The Epidemiology of Drug Dependence. Report on a Conference, London, 1972, Copenhagen: WHO

Royal College of Psychiatrists (1979) Alcohol and Alcoholism, London: Tavistock

Russell, M.A.H. (1976) 'What is dependence?' in G. Edwards, M.A.H. Russell, D. Hawks and M. MacCafferty (eds), Drugs and Drug Dependence, London: Lexington Books

Thorley, A. (1981) 'Alcohol dependence and the alcohol dependence syndrome', New Directions in the Study of Alcohol Group, Members' Booklet No. 1

WHO (1952) Report of Expert Committee on Mental Health: Alcoholism Sub-Committee, Geneva: WHO Technical Report Series, No. 48

___ (1969) Report of Expert Committee on Addiction-producing Drugs, Geneva: WHO Technical Report Series, No. 407

___ (1977) Alcohol Related Disabilities, Geneva: WHO Offset Publications, No. 32

___ (1979) International Classification of Diseases, Geneva: WHO Offset Publications

THE THEORETICAL AND EMPIRICAL BASIS OF THE ALCOHOL DEPENDENCE MODEL: A SOCIAL LEARNING PERSPECTIVE

Ray Hodgson and Tim Stockwell

Problem drinking is one of those sensitive areas, like politics and religion, where protagonists holding irreconcilable views take great pleasure in lampooning straw men and mauling the carcasses of dogs long since dead. Moreover, we have discovered that our own tentative model of problem drinking draws fire from both camps, since, on the one hand, we believe that the notion of alcohol dependence is indispensable and, on the other, have adopted the working hypothesis that it is essentially a learned behaviour which can be unlearned. In order to provide a clear picture of our position, we have decided, therefore, to begin by briefly describing the social learning model which guides our approach to research and treatment.

SOCIAL LEARNING AND ALCOHOL DEPENDENCE
During the last 50 years several schools of psychology and many conflicting theories of human behaviour have looked for popular support. In their time, psychoanalysis, behaviourism, biological psychology and gestalt psychology have all held sway. More recently, social learning theory has emerged, not as a school or a creed, but as a developing set of concepts which are relevant to all human behaviour, whether normal or abnormal, moderate or excessive (e.g. Bandura, 1977; Hodgson, 1984). When problem drinking is viewed from a social learning perspective, the following assumptions or working hypotheses are made:

(1) Drinking Alcohol is Mainly Functional
Alcohol is consumed by the social drinker and the problem drinker because of the expectation that a pleasant consequence will follow, or an unpleasant consequence will be avoided. Pleasant effects could be feeling 'high', a pleasant glow, verbal fluency and sociability, getting to sleep, or simply relaxation. Unpleasant effects, which alcohol can reduce or allay, include anxiety, frustration and

17

withdrawal symptoms. The particular functional significance of a drink or a drinking session will depend upon the set and the setting, including specific thoughts and feelings, expectations and plans, social situations and drinking companions. A person's cognitive appraisal of these antecedent events, whether they be mood states or environmental cues, is a crucial element in the chain of events. For example, withdrawal symptoms might not lead to drink on a Sunday morning when no visitors are expected, but suffering withdrawal symptoms on a work day without turning to drink might be out of the question.

One method of carrying out a functional analysis of a particular drinking session is, therefore, to assess the expected consequences associated with both drinking and resisting drink. A balance sheet or pay-off matrix (e.g. Orford, 1977) would include both short-term and long-term expected consequences, and would assess both the probability and the value of the event (Mausner and Platt, 1977). For example, a problem drinker might know that alcohol can lead to liver cirrhosis and places a high value on his health, but believe that, in his case, cirrhosis is unlikely because his heavy-drinking father lived to be 80. On the other hand, he is sure that divorce will result if he continues to drink, but he doesn't really care. Without a number of additional assumptions, this model is a much too rational account of heavy drinking, which sometimes appears to be irrational, mindless and beyond all reason. For example, a drinking binge of several days' duration is often accompanied by increasing anxiety and general mood disturbance (e.g. Hodgson, Stockwell and Rankin, 1979b; Stockwell, Hodgson and Rankin, 1982b). How can such an experience reward heavy drinking? This is just another instance of the 'neurotic paradox' which has been discussed for a number of years (e.g. Mowrer, 1960). A number of possible explanations have been proposed. First, short-term consequences tend to influence behaviour more powerfully than long-term consequences. Second, pleasant effects which occur only intermittently can have a powerful influence on behaviour. The one-armed bandit is a good example of an intermittent reinforcer which, nevertheless, encourages hopeful expectations. Third, expected consequences are always relative. An increase in anxiety as a result of drinking will be tolerated if the alternative is even worse. Fourth, behaviour is influenced by expected consequences which might be very different from the actual consequences. Finally, some consequences might be ignored or repressed if thinking about them is too distressing (Bandura, 1977).

(2) Drinking is Learned

Through observational learning and communications, we learn about drinking from parents, peers, books, films and the media. Some of the expected consequences of drinking will be learned in this way. Others are learned through direct experience. The likelihood that a person will have direct experience of heavy drinking will depend upon a wide range of psychosocial factors, including occupation, personality, subculture, price and availability.

Learning to drink heavily is the result of numerous experiences, some of them powerful and others more subtle. Reducing and avoiding anxiety is one of the most frequently reported effects (e.g. Edwards, 1972; Litman, Eiser, Rawson and Oppenheim, 1979), even though there has been some controversy about the Tension-Reduction Theory (Cappell and Herman, 1972; Hodgson et al., 1979b). Quickly passing from an agitated state of withdrawal back to normality is also a powerful direct experience which must have a reinforcing effect if we are to believe any of the basic learning theory concepts (e.g. Brown and Herrnstein, 1975). Frustration is a state that human beings try to avoid. Holding back anger, waiting for a meal and resisting temptation can be unpleasant experiences, and our actions are sometimes simply desperate attempts to avoid frustration. Experiencing the frustration of resisting drink and then the relief of drinking leads to a habit which some would call functionally autonomous (Walton and Mather, 1963).

So the desire to drink is linked through learning to a variety of psychological and social cues. If it is a strong desire, then craving would seem to be an appropriate label, whether its functional significance is to achieve intoxication, reduce anxiety or avoid withdrawal symptoms. Many other learning processes have been implicated, including cue generalisation, secondary reinforcement, faulty inference, and misattribution (e.g. Marlatt, 1978; Hodgson, 1983). Learning to drink heavily is also influenced by those compensatory adaptive processes which lead to tolerance and withdrawal symptoms.

(3)   Learning to Drink Heavily Will Be Influenced by Compensatory Adaptive Processes

Since alcohol alters the state of the central nervous system, it has been suggested that an adaptive or homeostatic process gradually develops in order to counteract alcohol's effects (Kalant, Leblanc and Gibbins, 1971; Solomon, 1977; Gross, 1977). It has also been proposed that this homeostatic process, or neuroadaptation (Edwards, Arif and Hodgson, 1981), results in both tolerance and withdrawal symptoms (Kalant, 1973). In the face of a massive body of research there can now be no doubt that some such adaptive processes are involved in problem drinking, and future debate will be about their exact contribution to dependence. At what point in a drinking career are these processes involved? Can they be reversed? To what extent are learning and conditioning involved in the development of compensatory adaptive processes?

Although tolerance and withdrawal must be included in a comprehensive model, some traditional conceptions will have to be modified as a result of recent research evidence in this area. Consider, for example, the popular distinction between psychological and physical dependence, which implies that a person starts to drink for psychological reasons, but ends up drinking to avoid physical symptoms. There is now a great deal of evidence to suggest that such a dichotomy is too simple. First, it has been demonstrated that minimal physical signs of withdrawal are present in social drinkers who volunteer to drink heavily for a few days (Zilm, Kaplan and Cappell, 1981). Second, we cannot ignore psychological processes such as learned helplessness (Seligman, 1976), conditioned withdrawal (O'Brien, 1976), and behavioural tolerance (Siegel, 1979), which are present in the most severely 'addicted' individuals. A dimensional approach which postulates a variable relationship between the psychological, biological and behavioural phenomena would appear to be a sensible alternative conception.

(4) A Learned Habit Can Become a Learned Compulsion

If a heavy drinker begins to experience problems to do with health, finance, personal relationships, self-esteem, mood swings, or any of the wide variety of unpleasant consequences associated with alcohol, then a set of negative expectations will develop. These will become part of the balance sheet or pay-off matrix, so that the drinker has strong reasons to want alcohol and also strong reasons to resist. For some people, this change will lead to moderation or abstinence and few further problems. For others, the expected negative consequences will not be considered to be strong enough reasons to make any changes at all. Between these two extremes, the only people who ask for help are the 'dissonant drinkers' who want to drink and yet don't want to drink. They have developed an approach-avoidance conflict which will then be experienced as a compulsion. To say that some heavy drinking appears to be a learned compulsion is simply to put a label upon this process.

(5) Cognitive Control Will Tend to be Impaired

In the field of alcohol problems, the very word 'control' has special connotations. Put forward as one of the first rank symptoms of alcoholism, the concept of 'loss of control' has been rightly criticised from all sides because it is simplistic, redundant, all-or-none, and associated with disease models (Mello, 1975; Merry, 1966; Keller, 1972a).

Within a social learning perspective, however, great emphasis is placed upon the development of cognitive control skills and the ways in which such an ability can be impaired (e.g. Bandura, 1977; Hodgson, 1984). The gardener, writer and problem drinker will make plans, set both short-term and long-term goals, and make pledges or commitments. They will think about the future consequences of their actions and will deliberately attempt to achieve desirable objectives. Sometimes, however, a state of 'learned helplessness' afflicts the gardener, the writer and the problem drinker, as a result of repeated failures (Seligman, 1976). In this state, motivation is sapped, emotionality heightened and pessimism prevails. Problem drinkers often describe such a state both before and after starting a drinking binge, when no attempt is made to stop because they have learned from past experience that it is futile to try.

Bearing in mind the particular psychological framework which guides our own thinking, we believe that learned helplessness varies from a little to a lot and involves an impairment in cognitive control, that is the ability to regulate drinking by thinking, planning, goal-setting and making commitments. This approach to impaired control is very similar to the abstinence violation effect proposed by Marlatt (1978) to explain the cognitive and behavioural effects of a few drinks on some problem drinkers.

(6) The Nature of the Relapse Process Will Change as Drinking Progresses

Although relapse is a continuous process, it can be arbitrarily divided into three phases. Phase 1 involves mainly psychosocial cues such as arguments, anxiety, criticism, social pressure and frustration (Litman et al., 1979; Marlatt and Gordon, 1980). Phase 2 involves the person's reactions to taking just a few drinks. We can make the prediction from a learning-theory model that a few drinks will prime a desire for more (Hodgson et al., 1979a) and also that learned helplessness will tend to be experienced. Finally, phase 3 will clearly involve the expectation of withdrawal symptoms and drinking which is motivated by desire to escape from or avoid them. From a purely theoretical point of view, we can make the prediction that phase 1 is involved for all problem drinkers, but that phases 2 and 3 become increasingly involved as drinking becomes more and more excessive.

Having briefly described one approach to problem drinking, we can now move on to the concept of dependence and the notion of an alcohol dependence syndrome.

ALCOHOL DEPENDENCE: A STATE AND A DISPOSITION

If a social learning model of dependence is not totally misguided, then some of the phenomena that have been described will tend to emerge and co-vary as a person drinks more heavily and repeatedly. The functional significance of drink will change and the pay-off matrix for each drinking decision will involve more negative consequences. The desire to drink will tend to increase across a wide range of sets and settings. Withdrawal symptoms and functional tolerance will be experienced, along with behavioural tolerance and conditioned withdrawal symptoms. A variety of cognitive changes are predicted from this model: for example, a diffuse state of arousal associated with drinking is more likely to be labelled as a withdrawal state. Cognitive control will tend to be impaired when drink is involved, and a feeling of compulsion will be experienced. The drinker's confidence that he can resist drink - his 'perceived self-efficacy' - will be reduced (Bandura, 1977). Controlled or moderate drinking will be less likely and relapse will tend to involve priming effects, learned helplessness and the rapid reinstatement of withdrawal symptomatology.

According to this view, the experience of severe withdrawal symptoms and withdrawal-relief drinking are certainly components of dependence, but they should not be considered to be the only cardinal symptoms. The relative weights that need to be assigned to the various dependence phenomena are a matter for research rather than speculation.

Dependence, like anxiety, is not an entity, a lesion or a lump, but a multidimensional construct involving a system of subjective, behavioural, physiological and biochemical phenomena (Rachman and Hodgson, 1974, 1980; Hodgson and Rachman, 1974). Actually, our own view of dependence can be made a little clearer by drawing out the analogy between dependence and anxiety. First, it is evident that anxiety varies from day to day. An anxiety state is not a fixed characteristic of a person, but fluctuates according to sets and settings. Second, it does make some sense, nevertheless, to speak of an anxious person. This person might be fishing or swimming and showing no signs of an anxiety state, but he is more likely to manifest anxiety across a wide range of situations than is a person with low trait anxiety. It would appear that alcohol dependence can also be viewed as either a state or a learned disposition. As with anxiety states, it is common knowledge that people move in and out of problem drinking and dependence states (Cahalan, 1970; Vaillant and Milofsky, 1982). To what extent the dependence disposition can be reversed and how this is achieved is, of course, the question that tends to separate the learning from the disease conceptions.

FACTOR ANALYTICAL STUDIES OF DEPENDENCE

There is now good evidence from interview and questionnaire studies to show that the main components of dependence can be reliably assessed (Chick, 1980a; Stockwell, Murphy and Hodgson, 1983a) and that some of them do hang together to form a core construct. Stockwell, Hodgson, Edwards, Taylor and Rankin (1979) designed a self-completion questionnaire (the SADQ) to assess psycho-physiological state first thing in the morning during a typical heavy drinking period. They found that intensity of withdrawal symptoms, drinking to escape and avoid withdrawal, and reinstatement after a period of abstinence all correlated with level of consumption and formed a first component accounting for more than 50 per cent of the total variance. Polich, Armor and Braiker (1980) questioned 389 alcoholics about their experience of tremors, morning drinking, loss of control, blackouts, missing meals and long periods of continuous drinking. They also found that one dimension accounted for about 50 per cent of the total variance. Similar results were obtained by Polich and Orvis (1979) in a study of a heterogeneous general population sample. Chick's investigation of dependence (1980b) was specifically designed to test the model proposed by Edwards and Gross (1976). He concluded that, 'if a unidimensional syndrome exists, it comprises Withdrawal; Subjective Need; Aspects of Salience; and probably Relief Drinking and Increased Tolerance.' At least with his particular form of questioning, 'impaired control' and 'narrowing of drinking repertoire' were not part of the core construct. Skinner and Allen (1982) carried out a factor analytical study of the Alcohol Use Inventory, and identified a first factor which is clearly very similar to the provisional clinical description of the alcohol dependence syndrome given by Edwards and Gross (1976). Alcoholics obtaining a high score on this factor tended to drink large quantities in a compulsive manner and report loss of control. Withdrawal symptoms had been experienced, and drinking bouts were associated with depression, worry and fear. High scorers had a history of seeking help and had experienced social consequences as a result of their drinking such as lost jobs, imprisonment for a drunkenness offence and lack of family involvement. Skinner's 'alcohol dependence' factor correlated with scores on the Michigan Alcoholism Screening Test (MAST).

Another recent factor-analytic study not only indicated an alcohol dependence factor, but also demonstrated that the construct was roughly the same in American and French patients being treated for drinking problems (Meyer et al., 1985). As can be seen in Table 1.1, 85 per cent of the items which loaded most heavily on the major factor of 'alcohol dependence' for one sample are shared by the other.

These results suggest that a brief interview or self-completion questionnaire is sufficient to assess a dimension which could reasonably be labelled severity of dependence, and that this dimension is defined by a number of physiological, subjective and behavioural components, including withdrawal symptoms, drinking to relieve and avoid withdrawal symptoms, subjective need, salience, increased tolerance, as well as level of consumption.

CORRELATES OF ALCOHOL DEPENDENCE
From the previous section it can be seen that there are a number of different approaches to the measurement of dependence and although we have developed a questionnaire that seems to be both reliable and valid (Stockwell et al., 1979, 1983), we intend to keep an open mind on which approach is the best. On the one hand, we have argued that dependence involves a broad range of phenomena, but then, paradoxically, our method of assessment has tended to rely upon the presence and severity of withdrawal symptoms and withdrawal-relief drinking. Actually, no paradox is involved. We have simply assumed that these phenomena can be assessed more reliably than other phenomena such as impairment of control, learned helplessness, compulsion or craving. Furthermore, they appear to be key components of dependence, since every attempt to pin down the dependence phenomena has identified items such as tremors and morning drinking. It would seem reasonable to suppose, therefore, that our method of assessing dependence cannot be faulted on the grounds that we are assessing a trivial component.

One of the earliest indications that a history of withdrawal and withdrawal-relief drinking might be a powerful predictor of other behaviour was the study carried out by Orford, Oppenheimer and Edwards (1976). The progress of 100 problem drinkers was assessed two years after attendance at the Maudsley Hospital, London, the major finding being that a seven-item scale concerned with morning drinking, tremor, nausea, loss of control, passing out when drunk and hallucinations prior to attendance predicted very closely the type of 'good' drinking outcomes that were observed two years later. Those who were controlling their drinking within defined

Table 1.1: Varimax Rotated Factors and Major Factor Loadings Obtained from American (N=148) and French (N=248) Questionnaire Responses (Meyer et al., 1985)

1. Factor Name: Alcohol Dependence

American Patients		French Patients	
Variable (Item)	Loading	Variable	Loading
Difficult to stop before completely intoxicated	0.72	Took a few quick ones before going out to a party	0.71
Unable to remember things done while drinking	0.69	Drank more than friends	0.67
Difficult to stop, even for a single day	0.68	Drink first thing in the morning	0.64
Drank more than friends	0.65	Needed more and more alcohol to get same effect	0.63
Failed to do what was normally expected, because of drinking	0.65	Difficult to stop, even for a single day	0.62
Got drunk at times or places which later regretted	0.63	Unable to remember things done while drinking	0.62
Consumed as many as ten drinks in one sitting	0.60	Had the 'shakes'	0.59
Drink first thing in the morning	0.59	Tended to perspire when sleeping at night	0.58
Needed more and more alcohol to get same effect	0.58	Difficult to stop before completely intoxicated	0.56
Tend to perspire when sleeping at night	0.56	Need to have a drink after several hours of abstinence	0.56
Took a few quick ones before going out to a party	0.55	Failed to do what was normally expected, because of drinking	0.55
Drink for the effect of alcohol	0.54	Gulp drinks	0.55
Gulp drinks	0.52	Tended to get directions wrong	0.52
Need to have a drink after several hours of abstinence	0.52	Tend to overreact when touched	0.50
Spend money on alcohol needed for essentials	0.51	Consumed as many as ten drinks in one sitting	0.50
Had the 'shakes'	0.50	Spent money on alcohol needed for essentials	0.47
Had to do things slowly to avoid making mistakes	0.50	Had to do things slowly to avoid making mistakes	0.47
Consumed as many as six drinks without appearing drunk	0.45	Consumed as many as six drinks without appearing drunk	0.44
Sneaked drinks when no one was looking	0.44	Drink for the effect of alcohol	0.42
Family complained about money spent on alcohol	0.41	Became annoyed and irritated	0.42

limits tended to have had three or fewer of these symptoms (eight out of eleven) while abstainers were mainly those with four or more symptoms (eight out of ten). A similar relationship between severity of such drinking symptoms and the likelihood of a controlled-drinking outcome was also subsequently noted by Polich et al. (1980) and by Vaillant and Milofsky (1982). Polich and his colleagues found that older men (over 40) with severe dependence on admission had lower relapse rates at four years if they had been abstaining at the 18th-month follow-up point; those who were drinking in a non-problem way were more likely to relapse. For younger moderately dependent men the situation was reversed: those who were abstaining at 18 months had higher relapse rates at four years than those who were drinking in a non-problem way at 18 months. Marital status and unemployment were also predictive of differential risks associated with abstinence and normal drinking. Vaillant and Milofsky (1982) carried out a prospective study of 110 'alcohol abusers'. Only four of the 71 men with more than six problems on a 'problem drinking scale' ever returned to controlled drinking for more than one year, but 43 achieved at least one year's abstention. For those men with fewer than six problems, a return to social drinking was five times more likely than abstinence. In a ten-year follow-up study Edwards (1984) noted that eight out of 68 patients seemed to be engaging in 'social drinking', and that seven of them had been only moderately dependent as assessed by the SADQ.

Why should it be that severely dependent drinkers are less likely to be able to return to normal drinking styles than to complete abstinence? We have noted that 'learned helplessness' or 'perceived self-efficacy' are probably implicated, but could it also be that a couple of drinks for such individuals increase their desire for more, or for the experience of intoxication? There has been a steady stream of experimental work concerned with the possibility that small amounts of alcohol can 'prime' an alcoholic's desire for drink (e.g. Merry, 1966; Marlatt et al., 1973). Interestingly, few such priming effects were found until subjects' severity of alcohol dependence was assessed (Hodgson et al., 1979a). We compared eleven problem drinkers designated as 'severely dependent' upon the basis of reporting several months of almost daily withdrawal, relief-type drinking and a 'narrowed drinking repertoire' with nine 'moderately dependent' who had experienced less extensive withdrawal experiences. All were in-patients of the Bethlem Royal Hospital Treatment Unit while participating in the study. Three hours after a relatively high priming dose (150 ml vodka), the severely dependent group consumed available alcoholic drinks faster than after a small (15 ml vodka) priming dose or no priming dose. The reverse was the case for moderately dependent drinkers, and the contrast between the two groups was highly significant. No result would have emerged at all had degree of dependence not been assessed. A more recent study of priming effects has confirmed this finding, and demonstrated that the actual alcoholic content of the priming dose overrides the subject's belief as to its content for severely, but not moderately, dependent drinkers (Stockwell,

Hodgson and Rankin, 1982a).

The latter study also found evidence that severely dependent drinkers experience a greater overall disposition or motivation to consume alcohol, in that they drank alcohol faster and reported more desire to drink in all conditions than moderately dependent subjects. Since Jellinek (1960) simplistically proposed 'loss of control' over drinking as the hallmark of true alcohol addiction, there has been much interest in and speculation about possible priming effects. Recognising the dimension of severity of alcohol dependence has proved critical in demonstrating their existence.

We will briefly mention three further studies which incline us increasingly to propose that 'Keller's Law' of alcoholism (Keller, 1972b) can usefully be reworked as follows: for an attribute or variable accessible to social, psychological or biological research, an alcoholic either has more or less of this, as a function of his degree of dependence, than non-alcoholics. The first example comes from personality research. The role of antisocial characteristics both as antecedents to and consequences of alcoholism has frequently been discussed (e.g. Robins, Bates and O'Neal, 1962). Employing the SADQ as a measure of alcohol dependence, Rankin, Stockwell and Hodgson (1982) discovered a highly significant and positive correlation between degree of dependence and the P-scale of the Eysenck Personality Questionnaire (Eysenck and Eysenck, 1975). This scale is thought to assess antisocial and impulsive personality attributes. The second example comes from a quite different area of enquiry: the biochemistry of alcohol metabolism and withdrawal states. Topham (1983) studied the excretion of a tetrahydroiso-quiniline (TIQ), salsolinol, in the urine of alcoholics during the first four days of withdrawal from alcohol. It has been postulated that TIQ's may have an important role in the development of dependence on alcohol and other drugs of abuse (Davis and Walsh, 1970). Topham found a linear trend for increasing release of salsolinol over the withdrawal period that was more pronounced in severely than in moderately dependent subjects, dependence being measured by the SADQ.

Our final example is provided by a recent study of fears and phobias among alcoholic in-patients and the relationship of these to severity of alcohol dependence (Stockwell, Smail, Hodgson and Canter, 1984). Out of a total sample of 60, 42 subjects reported having one or more fears on Matthews' and Marks' Fear Questionnaire (Matthews, 1979). This sub-group were asked the simple question, 'Do your fears get worse after a period of very heavy drinking?'. Those subjects replying in the affirmative had significantly higher SADQ scores than those who denied having this experience. The phemomenon of heavy drinking increasing anxiety levels and worsening mood has been the subject of much debate and speculation (e.g. Mendelson and Mello, 1979; Stockwell et al, 1982b). This finding suggests that the experience of 'Tension Induction' during heavy drinking is related to severity of alcohol dependence. It was also found that for subjects who were assessed as having a significant phobic anxiety state, past fluctuations in the severity of this were highly concordant with fluctuations in an individual drinker's degree of dependence.

In this and the previous sections we have gathered together a great deal of evidence to show that alcohol dependence refers to a circumscribed set of co-varying phenomena. Furthermore, the measurement of dependence is not a trivial exercise but has cognitive, behavioural, physiological and biochemical implications. Having argued that the concept is indispensible, are we entitled to elevate the idea to that of a 'syndrome' as suggested by Edwards and Gross (1976)? We will critically examine the evidence and logic behind such a move in the next section.

Is there an Alcohol Dependence Syndrome?

According to Edwards (1977), by 'syndrome' is meant 'an observable coincidence of phenomena. Not all the phenomena need always be present or present in the same degree'. Those phenomena which were provisionally claimed to coincide in this way to constitute the syndrome of alcohol dependence are (under brief headings): a narrowed repertoire of drinking with respect to both time and context, high salience of drink-seeking over other behaviours, increased tolerance to alcohol, repeated withdrawal symptoms, drinking to escape or avoid these symptoms, awareness of a compulsion to drink or 'impairment of control' over drinking, and a rapid reinstatement of all these features if drinking takes place after a period of abstinence. These elements are described as 'markers', each capable of variation in the extent and/or intensity of their presentation, and which jointly indicate the degree of a 'heightened drive state' (Edwards, 1977). Other stated overall features of the proposed syndrome are its existence in different degrees of severity and its distinctness from other alcohol-related disabilities.

One straightforward approach to the question posed at the head of this section is simply to ask: if the elements of this proposed syndrome are measured, will they tend to correlate with each other in a population of problem drinkers? Our reading of the literature here generates the even more straightforward answer: 'Yes'; and this conclusion is based upon the following evidence.

The proposition that a strong disposition to drink alcohol is associated with an extensive history of daily withdrawal-relief drinking received strong confirmation from the experimental studies concerned with priming effects outlined above. Other indications of a strong disposition to drink emerge from the factor-analytic studies discussed earlier: items such as 'difficult to stop before completely intoxicated', 'difficult to stop, even for a single day', 'need to have a drink after several hours of abstinence' (Meyer et al., 1983) and 'can't think of anything else than drinking' (Chick, 1980b) have been found to correlate very well with those concerning withdrawal and withdrawal relief. It should be noted, however, that it can be hard to operationalise such subjective aspects of drinking behaviour. The notion of 'impaired control' is particularly problematic. For example, Chick's subjects were perplexed by questions about

27

whether they were ever 'unable to keep to a limit' or found it 'difficult to stop getting drunk'. It was hard to decide whether the subject intended to keep to a limit or not get drunk. Further, if he often did fail in this intention, was this due to simply 'changing his mind' or due to forces within him and 'beyond his control'? This semantic problem may account for Chick's study failing to find associations between measures of 'impaired control' and withdrawal history.

The claim that the alcohol dependence syndrome can be present in different degrees of severity is born out by the wealth of data showing important differences between moderately and severely dependent drinkers discussed in the last section. Further, this distinction can be made reliably both by clinician's ratings and questionnaire responses (Stockwell et al, 1979; Stockwell et al, 1983). The proposed crucial distinction between dependence and other alcohol-related disabilities is certainly quite clear conceptually. It has also been borne out in a community survey of drinking habits that dependence symptoms and various social and medical problems associated with heavy drinking do not always present jointly (Cartwright, Shaw and Spratley, 1975). Meyer et al, (1983), in their study of French and American problem drinkers, identified two different factors which were obviously to do with 'alcohol dependence' and 'alcohol-related disabilities'. Wodak, Saunders, Ewusi-Mensah, Davis and Williams (1983) employed the SADQ to assess the degree of dependence among patients with a diagnosis of alcoholic liver disease, and discovered only a very low incidence of severe dependence in this group. Furthermore, no significant correlation emerged between degree of alcohol dependence and the severity of liver damage.

There have been conflicting findings with regard to the status of a 'narrowed drinking repertoire' as a correlate of alcohol dependence. Chick (1980a; 1980b) failed to find an association between a recent narrowing of repertoire (withing the last three months), with respect to both days of the week and in response to 'mood' cues, and other aspects of dependence. Stockwell et al. (1983), however, found that the variability of drinking patterns both between days and within a drinking day correlated negatively with degree of dependence measured by SADQ scores. Certainly, the concept of the alcohol dependence syndrome does not require the recent narrowing of repertoire which Chick attempted to identify. The second study provides confirmation of narrowness, if not narrowing, of repertoire for quantity and frequency of intake if not for drinking in response to mood cues

The concept of 'rapidity of reinstatement' of dependence as a function of severity of dependence is very relevant in the context of controlled drinking versus abstinence goals and relapse-prevention generally. Topham (1983) provides further evidence that a future relapse into drinking and dependence is related to current levels of drinking and dependence. She carried out a six-month follow-up study designed to assess the predictive validity of the SADQ and demonstrated that those problem drinkers who are severely dependent when referred to treatment relapsed more quickly, consumed more during their first drinking session, and were less likely to report single drinking days. One drinking day tended to lead to another for the severely dependent. This phenomenon may simply reflect the unremarkable tendency for an individual's drinking behaviour to be consistent over time (e.g. Gottheil, Murphy, Skoloda and Corbett, 1972) - thus very heavy drinkers will almost immediately revert to very heavy drinking after a period of abstinence. However, the model we are advancing here proposes that specific psycho-physiological and learning mechanisms underlie this observed consistency: namely, learned helplessness, learned compulsion, the rapid reinstatement of withdrawal symptoms, and the urge to drink in order to minimise these. In another study we found significant early morning withdrawal symptoms after only one day of heavy drinking by dependent drinkers already withdrawn from alcohol in hospital (Stockwell et al., 1982b). This phenomenon may well contribute to the severely dependent drinker's difficulty in returning to controlled alcohol use.

So far, there are quite strong grounds for supporting the major claims of the proposed syndrome as provisionally described by Edwards and Gross (1976). A remaining doubt is whether the term 'syndrome' is justified given the dimensional nature of dependence and the clear medical connotations of the term.

There can be no doubt that 'syndrome' is a medical term - Chamber's Twentieth Century Dictionary provides the definition 'concurrence; especially of symptoms'. This might suggest a disease entity comprising a fixed constellation of symptoms. An individual presents with all or none of them. While the authors of the concept of the alcohol dependence syndrome have explicitly stated that this syndrome is quite different in each of these respects, it is arguably still an incorrect use of language.

Nevertheless, alternatives are hard to find that roll easily off the tongue and that are neither too narrow nor so vague as to have no meaning at all. If the term syndrome is to be used then it is necessary to repeatedly explain its special usage in connection with alcohol dependence. Specifically, when present the syndrome of alcohol dependence:

(a) may exist in varying degrees of severity;
(b) may not comprise all the recognisable elements provisionally proposed by Edwards and Gross in every instance;
(c) may be reversible to some degree, possibly even completely;
(d) has been acquired as a consequence of both learning and compensatory adaptive processes; and
(e) is both empirically and conceptually distinct from other alcohol-related disabilities.

Clinical Usefulness of the Syndrome Concept

It has sometimes been suggested that an assessment of the presence and degree of the proposed syndrome can never usefully inform treatment decisions concerning individual patients. Even the frequently made claim that such as assessment is crucial in advising on the choice of abstinence or moderate drinking goals has not escaped criticism (Thorley, 1981). Our main concern in this chapter has been to defend the syndrome concept both as an accurate description of genuinely co-varying phenomena and as a theoretical construct providing some important insights into etiological processes. We do not believe the utility of the syndrome idea necessarily stands or falls according to its relevance to current clinical practice. Successful intervention strategies of the future, however, may well be informed by the dependence processes we have discussed here. For example, behavioural and/or pharmacological methods may be developed to weaken the severely dependent drinker's compulsion to drink following a priming dose of alcohol or while experiencing minimal withdrawal symptoms. Possibly, techniques to prevent the reinstatement of the withdrawal experience and to reduce tolerance may also be developed and applied within a broader treatment programme.

With respect to current clinical practice, the evidence we have outlined so far strongly suggests that assessment of severity of alcohol dependence is highly relevant to several common management decisions. As acknowledged in several major reviews (e.g. Miller and Hester, 1980; Heather and Robertson, 1981), degree of dependence is one of several predictors of whether an individual is more likely to succeed at abstinence or controlled drinking. Other considerations include the extent of previous controlled drinking, social supports for either treatment goal and severity of medical conditions which might preclude any alcohol use. A clear prediction from this model also related to choice of treatment goal is that a longer period of initial abstinence may be needed by the more severely dependent before attempting controlled drinking. Another treatment implication stemming from an assessment of degree of alcohol dependence concerns the timing of interventions for drinkers who present with phobic anxiety states - a fairly common occurrence in 'alcoholic' populations (Mullaney and Trippett, 1979; Smail, Stockwell, Canter and Hodgson 1984). Since the severity of the phobic complaint is very likely to subside following a few weeks abstinence for a severely dependent drinker, it would seem unwise to rush in earlier with time-consuming and intensive behavioural interventions (Marks, 1977). Similar considerations may well apply to the timing of any treatment procedure concerned with an affective disorder accompanying alcohol dependence.

The usefulness of the dependence model might not seem obvious if our main concern is to help a person to solve a wide range of personal problems. It is undoubtedly useful, however, when the focus is upon understanding the career of a problem drinker, developing a framework within which to think about one type of excessive drinking and about future treatment approaches. The paradigm that we have described does lead to testable hypotheses. As Kuhn (1970) has noted, when discussing the usefulness of a model or paradigm: 'In the absence of a paradigm all of the facts that could possibly pertain to the development of a given science are likely to seem equally relevant' (p. 15). At the very least a social learning model of dependence directs attention towards a number of specific questions that need to be answered.

REFERENCES

Bandura, A. (1977) 'Self-efficacy: Toward a unifying theory of behavior change'. Psychological Review, 84, 191-225

Brown, R. and Herrnstein, R.J. (1975) Psychology, New York: Methuen

Cahalan, D. (1970) Problem Drinkers, San Francisco: Jossey-Bass

Cappell, H. and Herman, C.B. (1972) 'Alcohol and tension reduction: a review', Quarterly Journal of Studies on Alcohol, 33, 33-64

Cartwright, A.K.J., Shaw, S.J. and Spratley, T.A. (1975) Paper presented at 21st International Institute on the Prevention and Treatment of Alcoholism, Helsinki

Chick, J. (1980a) 'Alcohol dependence: methodological issues in its measurement: reliability of the criteria', British Journal of Addiction, 75, 175-86

___ (1980b) 'Is there a unidimensional alcohol dependence syndrome?', British Journal of Addiction, 75, 265-80

Davis, V.E. and Walsh, M.J. (1970) 'Alcohol, amines and alkaloids; a possible biochemical basis for alcohol addiction', Science 167, 1005-6

Edwards, G. (1972) 'Motivation for drinking among men: survey of a London suburb', Psychological Medicine, 2, 260-71

___ (1977) 'The alcohol dependence syndrome: Usefulness of an idea' in G. Edwards and M. Grant (eds), Alcoholism: New Knowledge and New Responses, London: Croom Helm

___ (1984) 'Drinking in a longitudinal perspective', British Journal of Addiction, 79, 175-83

___ and Gross, M.M. (1976) 'Alcohol dependence: provisional description of a clinical syndrome', British Medical Journal, 1, 1058-61

___ Arif, A. and Hodgson, R. (1981) 'Diagnosis and classification of drug- and alcohol-related problems: a WHO Memorandum', WHO Bulletin 3865, Geneva: WHO

Eysenck, H.J. and Eysenck, S.B.G. (1975) Manual of the Eysenck Personality Questionnaire, London: Hodder & Stoughton

Gottheil, E., Murphy, B.F., Skoloda, T.E. and Corbett, L.L. (1972) 'Fixed interval drinking decisions. II. Drinking and discomfort in 25 alcoholics', Quarterly Journal of Studies on Alcohol, 33, 325-40

Gross, M.M. (1977) 'Psychobiological contributions to the alcohol dependence syndrome: a selective review of recent research' in Edwards et al. (eds), Alcohol Related Disabilities, Geneva: WHO

Heather, N. and Robertson, I. (1981) Controlled Drinking, London: Methuen

Hodgson, R.J. (1984) 'Social learning theory' in P. McGuffin, M. Shanks and R.J. Hodgson (eds), The Scientific Principles of Psychopathology, London: Academic Press

____ and Rachman, S. (1974) 'Desynchrony in measures of fear', Behaviour Research and Therapy, 12, 319-26

____ Rankin, H. and Stockwell, T.R. (1979a) 'Alcohol dependence and the priming effect', Behaviour Research and Therapy, 17, 379-87

____ Stockwell, T.R. and Rankin, H.J. (1979b) 'Can alcohol reduce tension?', Behaviour Research and Therapy, 17, 459-66

Jellinek, E.M. (1960) The Disease Concept of Alcoholism, New Brunswick: Hillhouse Press

Kalant, H. (1973) 'Biological models of alcohol tolerance and physical dependence' in M.M. Gross (ed.), Alcohol Intoxication and Withdrawal: Experimental Studies, New York: Plenum Press

____ LeBlanc, A.E. and Gibbins, R.J. (1971) 'Tolerance to and dependence on some non-opiate psychotropic drugs', Pharmacological Review, 23, 135-91

Keller, M. (1972a) 'On the loss of control phenomenon in alcoholism', British Journal of Addiction, 67, 153-66

____ (1972b) 'The oddities of alcoholics', Quarterly Journal of Studies on Alcohol, 33, 1147-8

Kuhn, T.S. (1970) The Structure of Scientific Revolutions (2nd edition), Chicago: University of Chicago Press

Litman, G.K. Eiser, J.R., Rawson, N.S.B. and Oppenheim, A.N. (1979) 'Differences in relapse precipitants and coping behaviours between alcoholic relapsers and survivors', Behaviour Research and Therapy, 17, 89-94

Marks, I. (1977) 'Phobias and obsessions: Clinical phenomena in search of a laboratory model' in J.D. Maser and M.E.P. Seligman (eds), Psychopathology: Experimental Models, San Francisco: Freeman

Marlatt, G.A. (1978) 'Craving for alcohol, loss of control and relapse: a cognitive-behavioral analysis' in P.E. Nathan, G.A. Marlatt and T. Loberg (eds), Alcoholism: New Directions in Behavioural Research and Treatment, New York: Plenum Press

____ Demming, B. and Reid, J.B. (1973) 'Loss of control drinking in alcoholics: and experimental analogue', Journal of Abnormal Psychology, 81, 233-41

____ and Gordon, J.R. (1980) 'Determinants of relapse: Implications for the maintenance of behaviour change' in P.O. Davidson and Sheena M. Davidson (eds), Behavioural Medicine: Changing Health Lifestyles, New York: Brunner/Mazel

Matthews, A.M. (1979) 'Brief standard self-rating for phobic patients', Behaviour Research and Therapy, 17, 263-7

Mausner, B. and Platt, E.S. (1977) Smoking: A Behavioral Analysis, New York: Pergamon

Mello, N.K. (1975) 'A semantic aspect of alcoholism' in H.D. Cappell and A.E. LeBlanc (eds), Biological and Behavioral

Approaches to Drug Dependence, Ontario: Addiction Research Foundation

Mendelson, J.H. and Mello, N.K. (1979) 'One unanswered question about alcoholism', British Journal of Addiction, 74, 11-14

Merry, J. (1966) 'The loss of control myth', The Lancet, 1, 1257-8

Meyer, R.E., Babor, T.F., Hesselbrock, M., Hesselbrock, V. and Kaplan, R. (1985) 'New directions in the assessment of the alcohol patient' in L. Towle (ed.), Proceedings: NIAAA-WHO Collaborating Center Designation Meeting and Alcohol Research Center, Rockville Md: NIAAA (in press)

Miller, W.R. and Hester, R.K. (1980) 'Treating the problem drinker: modern approaches' in W.R. Miller (ed.), The Addictive Behaviours, New York and Oxford: Pergamon

Mowrer, O.H. (1960) Learning Theory and Behaviour, New York: Wiley

Mullaney, J.A. and Trippett, C.J. (1979) 'Alcohol dependence and phobias: clinical description and relevance', British Journal of Psychiatry, 135, 565-73

O'Brien, C.P. (1976) 'Experimental analysis of conditioning factors in human narcotic addiction', Pharmacological Review, 27, 533-43

Orford, J. (1977) 'Alcoholism: New Knowledge and New Responses. London: Croom Helm

____ Oppenheimer, E. and Edwards, G. (1976) 'Abstinence or control: the outcome for excessive drinkers two years after consultation', Behaviour Research and Therapy, 14, 409-18

Polich, J.M. and Orvis, B.R. (1979) Alcohol Problems: Patterns and Prevalence in the US Air Force, Santa Monica: Rand Corporation

____ Armor, D.J. and Braiker, H.B. (1980) The Course of Alcoholism: Four Years after Treatment, New York: Wiley

Rachman, S. and Hodgson, R.J. (1974) 'Synchrony and desynchrony in fear and avoidance', Behaviour Research and Therapy, 12, 311-18

____ (1980) Obsessions and Compulsions, Englewood Cliffs, NJ: Prentice Hall

Rankin, H.J., Stockwell, T.R. and Hodgson, R.J. (1982) 'Personality and alcohol dependence', Personality and Individual Differences, 3, 145-51

____ Hodgson, R.J. and Stockwell, T.R. (1980) 'The behavioural measurement of dependence', British Journal of Addiction, 75, 43-7

Robins, L., Bates, W. and O'Neal, P. (1962) 'Adult drinking patterns of former children' in D. Pitman and C.J. Sneider (eds), Society, Culture and Drinking Patterns, New York: Wiley

Seligman, M.E.P. (1976) 'Learned helplessness and depression in animals and men' in Spence et al. (eds), Behavioural Approaches to Therapy, General Learning Press

Siegel, S. (1979) 'The role of conditioning in drug tolerance and addiction' in J.D. Keehn (ed.), Psychopathology in Animals: Research and Clinical Applications, New York: Academic Press

Skinner, H.A. and Allen, B.A. (1982) 'Alcohol Dependence Syndrome: measurement and validation', Journal of Abnormal Psychology, 91, 199-209

Smail, P., Stockwell, T., Canter, S. and Hodgson, R. (1984) 'Alcohol dependence and phobic anxiety states I: A prevalence survey', British Journal of Psychiatry, 144, 53-7

Solomon, R.L. (1977) 'An opponent process theory of acquired motivation. The effective dynamics of addiction' in J.D. Maser and M.E.P. Seligman (eds), Psychopathology: Experimental Models, San Francisco: Freeman

Stockwell, T.R., Hodgson, R.J., Edwards, G., Taylor, C. and Rankin, H.J. (1979) 'The development of a questionnaire to measure severity of alcohol dependence', British Journal of Addiction, 74, 79-87

_____ and Rankin, H.J. (1982a) 'Alcohol dependence, beliefs and the priming effect', Behaviour Research and Therapy, 20, 513-22

_____ and Rankin, H.J. (1982b) 'Tension reduction and the effects of prolonged alcohol consumption', British Journal of Addiction, 77, 65-73

_____ Murphy, D. and Hodgson, R. (1983) 'The severity of alcohol dependence questionnaire: its use, reliability and validity', British Journal of Addiction, 78, 145-55

_____ Smail, P., Hodgson, R. and Canter, S. (1984) 'Alcohol dependence and phobic anxiety states II: a retrospective study', British Journal of Psychiatry, 144, 58-63

Thorley, A. (1981) 'Alcohol dependence and the alcohol dependence syndrome', in New Directions in the Study of Alcohol Group, Booklet No. 1, January

Topham, A. (1983) Alcohol Dependence and Craving, unpublished PhD thesis, University of London

Vaillant, G.E. and Milofsky, E.S. (1982) 'Natural history of male alcoholism. IV. Paths to recovery', Archives of General Psychiatry, 39, 127-33

Walton, D. and Mather, M.D. (1963) 'The application of learning principles to the treatment of obsessive compulsive states', Behaviour Research and Therapy, 1, 163-74

Wodak, A.D., Saunders, J.B. Ewusi-Mensah, I., Davis, M. and Williams, R. (1983) 'Assessment of alcohol dependence in patients with alcoholic liver disease', British Medical Journal, 287, 1420-22

Zilm, D.H., Kaplan, H.L. and Capell, H. (1981) 'Electro-encephalographic tolerance and abstinence phenomena during repeated alcohol ingestion by non-alcoholics', Science, 212, 1175-7

Chapter 2

THE DISEASE CONCEPT OF DEPENDENCE

Stan Shaw

A few years ago I proffered a critique of the concept of the alcohol dependence syndrome (Shaw, 1979). It was, I thought, written in a reasonably polite and dispassionate manner, which unfortunately cannot be said of some of the correspondence I received in reply! Interestingly, very little of this attempted to refute my two major criticisms of the syndrome idea that (1) only part of the concept, namely psychobiological alterations due to alcohol, could be confirmed from scientific evidence, and that (2) its use in research and treatment would be at best superfluous but more probably misleading and confusing. Rather, what seemed to make the fur fly was my conclusion that since this idea, lacking therapeutic or full empirical justification, had been adopted into the International Classification of Diseases with almost indecent haste, this must have been primarily a political decision rather than an academic one. By this, even in Ray Hodgson's (1980) balanced reply, I was assumed to be making only the crude assertion that the syndrome idea was invented 'to keep medical men in business'. Hodgson also claimed that various parts of my case were 'stereotyped', 'over-stated' and 'very wide of the mark'.

I feel somewhat disposed, then, to reply to all this in a fairly blunt manner, but will not. Instead, I hope to proceed to make more constructive comments and argue that a preoccupation with the syndrome concept would sell short the potential response of medically based research and treatment as much as that of any other approach.

A SYNDROME OF AMBIVALENCE?
But to begin with brass tacks. The definition of the alcohol dependence syndrome was approved by the World Health Assembly in the same year in which Edwards and Gross (1976) said that 'a definitive description of this syndrome will be premature' (p. 1058)! This seems to me entirely typical of this episode; the supporters of

the syndrome idea want to have their cake and eat it. Edwards (1977) said that 'what can be put forward is only a partly informed series of conjectures' (p. 142), but was also leading author of a WHO publication (Edwards, Gross, Keller, Moser and Room, 1977) claiming that 'the reality and significance of this syndrome seemed to be well supported by a review of present evidence' (p. 6). This latter document also claimed that 'the syndrome of alcohol dependence is not all or none', but then clearly implicated a cut-off point to exist between 'dependent' and 'non-dependent' persons (see Shaw, 1979). Depending on which image of the dependence syndrome is required for a particular argument, it can be presented, even in the same article, as either a 'multidimensional construct involving a system of subjective, behavioural, psychological and biochemical phenomena' or alternatively 'a core construct' (essentially the psychobiological part of the syndrome) which accounts for over 50 per cent of the variance in factor-analytical studies (see Chapter 1).

Moreover, when criticisms are lodged against the syndrome it miraculously acquires new properties. In 1979, I put the view that the supposed 'leading symptom' of the syndrome, namely 'impaired control', was a weak idea both conceptually and empirically. In fact, Chick's (1980) later study was predictably unable to link the construct of 'impaired control' to other aspects of the syndrome. However, Hodgson's reply was that I 'embraced the equally biased view that priming effects do not occur at all' (Hodgson, 1980, p. 258). Certainly, I never mentioned 'priming effects' - for the simple reason they had never been mentioned before as part of the justification of the syndrome in the WHO documents or Edwards' writings. Nevertheless, the 'priming' idea fits in with these latter justifications; that is, it represents another attempt to find some internal trigger to explain excessive consumption - what the definition of the syndrome refers to as a 'compulsion', what Alcoholics Anonymous call a 'craving' and speculated might be due to an 'allergy'. Indeed, Keller (1976) has speculated that Gross' work (see Gross, 1977) might lead to the discovery of 'an alcoholismic lesion'. The fashionable jargon of 'impaired control' and 'priming' is exactly the same as 'craving', and 'loss of control' in this crucial respect - the experience of wanting more alcoholic drink - is taken to be the reason in itself why more drinking occurs. But although these subjective experiences are very real to those who feel them, they must be composed of various motivations for and against drinking, partly unconscious and partly explicit, partly learned and partly inherent. It is the interplay between these motivations, and not their mere resulting manifestation, which should be the target of alcohol research and treatment. The dependence syndrome idea, like its forebears, denies the underlying complexities and is attracted like the other moths to the flame of one major universal causative pathology. Since it confuses motivations for drinking with the experience of feeling these motivations, it is prone to tautology; indeed, since the experiences are imputed to be causative in themselves, the whole edifice is a circular argument.

A SYNDROME OF TAUTOLOGY?

Consider the experiments to prove that 'priming effects' occur (e.g. Hodgson, Rankin and Stockwell, 1979). A group of people are defined as more 'dependent' than others on the grounds that they have had more severe withdrawals, engaged in more relief drinking and more general drinking than another 'moderately dependent' group. When given drink, the group who usually drink more anyway not surprisingly report more desire for drink, and indeed drink more than the other group. This is taken to demonstrate 'priming' and the severity of 'impaired control'. The 'prediction', however, is self-fulfilling. The degree of construct (a), dependence, with a supposed leading symptom of impaired control, is defined in terms of its constituent constructs, (b) relief drinking, (c) withdrawal symptoms etc. By admission, dependence is nothing other than the combination of the levels of (b) plus (c) plus (d) etc. However, experimental exhibitions of (b) (c) etc. relating to levels of (a) are then taken to prove the validity of (a). This has predictive validity, but not the more important types of validation such as logical concurrent or construct validation, since it is logically impossible for the level of (a) to be high when the levels of (b) (c) (d) etc. are low. In other words, there are no dependent and independent variables. It is like saying a cake is made up of sugar, eggs, flour and so on. The higher the measures of these ingredients, the bigger the cake. It cannot be otherwise. The predictive validity of the dependence syndrome has been rightly cited by Hodgson (1980), but this is the weakest form of validity (and there are various chestnuts from the history of epidemiology to illustrate that). It may be, for example, that although construct (a) correlates with (b) and (c), there is actually some extraneous causative factor x, such as, say, genetic predisposition to heavy alcohol consumption, which actually determines the levels of both (a) and of (b) and (c).

This might also be said of the correlations found between the different sections of the Severity of Alcohol Dependence Questionnaire (Stockwell, Murphy and Hodgson, 1983), but here the more simple commonsense interpretation would be that correlations must be logically expected anyway. It would surely be very peculiar if people who reported experiencing severe withdrawal symptoms did not report drinking heavily, or if people reported a reinstatement of symptoms without having had the symptoms in the first place, or if they reported drinking to relieve withdrawal symptoms but then did not report having had withdrawal symptoms. Of course, all these factors correlate with each other; it is logically impossible for them not to. Ultimately, this is all the supposed validations of the dependence syndrome have to offer as 'proof' that there is a relationship between excessive drinking, withdrawal, relief drinking and associated psychic experiences. But this is hardly news. A major part of my argument against the disease concept of alcoholism in the mid '70s (see Shaw, Cartwright, Spratley and Harwin, 1978) was that the concept did not specify the critical roles of increasing tolerance, increasing withdrawal and rapid rein-statement. Equally, I said then and have consistently maintained since, that there is absolutely no need for a superfluous umbrella concept of dependence, particularly when it grafts onto these well-documented phenomena other completely tenuous and speculative ideas about 'behavioural alterations' and 'drink-centred mentation', for which the evidence of what Gross (1977) called 'the withdrawal syndrome' is offered as bogus proof. As far as I can see, there is no evidence at all that there is one syndrome across all individuals and cultures. I argue that the amount of variance accounted for by a single factor in the questionnaire studies is purely a reflection of how far the questionnaire items restrict themselves to the psychobiological factors. Indeed, the strongest correlations of all are found if items are restricted to experience of withdrawal symptoms and relief drinking. In the history of questionnaire studies of alcoholism, the key items usually turned out to be shakes and morning drinking. However, if a questionnaire were designed to measure correlations between the range of psychobiological alterations and the other two component parts of the triad of the dependence syndrome described by Edwards, i.e. the subjective and behavioural, then the strengths of the correlations would decline markedly.

Moreover, even when one considers the interrelations between the psychobiological factors in more detail than is possible in questionnaire-based studies, the relationships are more complex than the mere fact of correlation can indicate. One of Gross' own studies (Gross, Kierzenbaum and Lewis, 1975) suggested that there is no linear relationship between severity of withdrawal and desire for drink, but that when withdrawal becomes particularly severe, the feelings of craving can be replaced by self-disgust and a wish for treatment. Mello and Mendelson have also noted the possibility of severe withdrawal as a negative reinforcement (Mendelson, Mello and Soloman, 1968; Mello and Mendelson, 1972) and, possibly, the AA concept of reaching 'rock bottom' may partly be an experiential version of this.

DEPENDENCE AS CORE PATHOLOGY
Furthermore, the centrality of psychobiological alterations as the key aspect of dependence is not a view shared by all shades of medical opinion. For example, Russell (1971) would argue that 'dependence' might not necessarily include either physical withdrawal or its relief by more consumption, but that the key item of dependence on a drug is 'negative affect experienced in its absence'. Others, such as Davies (1974), have also envisaged dependence in a wider context and on a longer continuum than that represented in the alcohol dependence syndrome idea. It would therefore be paranoid to believe that the patronage of the syndrome idea was some sort of fiendish plot by Griffith Edwards to reclaim the alcohol field for the medical profession. Rather, Edwards supports this particular version of the idea of dependence because, as Anthony Thorley (1981) has perspicaciously drawn out, he genuinely believes that it is at the root of alcohol problems. Thorley put the debate in a nutshell when he wrote

the crucial proposition which appears to emerge in Edwards thinking is that dependence is the measles, the core pathology leading to alcohol problems. Much of the dispute over the utility of the alcohol dependence syndrome lies in the validity of this central assertion (p. 6).

I would further specify that Edwards believes the psychobiological factors in particular to be the measles, rather than the factors of altered feeling and behaviour. For it is the psychobiological core which appears to fulfil the criteria for a universal pathology of problem drinking. How else could he write that the syndrome might 'look different in France and Utah', but imply it is actually identical (Edwards, 1977). If this is indeed what is meant, it is a more dogmatic view than, say, Jellinek's (1960) view of the alcoholisms which posited that in some important aspects the experience of becoming an alcoholic in these two societies was qualitatively different. Of course, questionnaire studies such as those cited by Hodgson (Meyer, 1985; and see Chapter 1) will find a similar 'alcohol dependence factor' in the two societies. But the idea of a unitary dependence syndrome beneath apparent surface variations glosses over the qualifications and specific mechanisms reported by Gross (1977). His interpretation of the evidence was that some effects included within his withdrawal syndrome were more related to blood alcohol concentration than others, and he noted that cultural drinking patterns would determine the continuity of blood alcohol concentration and thus affect how particular withdrawal syndromes developed.

There is perhaps here a certain irony in noting the influences of both Jellinek's and Gross' work. Jellinek's collection of data on alcoholics became, partly against his better judgement, a scientific veneer of a simple popular version of the disease concept of alcoholism. Similarly, many of the variations in the phenomena of tolerance, withdrawal, relief drinking, reinstatement and so on, and the relationships between them, carefully detailed by Gross, seem to be disregarded in favour of a less detailed and thus more popularly acceptable concept of dependence. Perhaps this is inevitable, since a one-core-cause theory is always more politically and psychologically powerful than continually dealing with the reality of complexity and variation.

A DISEASE CONCEPT OF DEPENDENCE?
Indeed, there has already developed what could be called a disease concept of dependence - i.e. a simple cause, symptom and treatment concept which is not a detailed view of the factors involved or even a representative account of all medical views of the concept of dependence. It should be remembered that the disease concept of alcoholism became not only popularly accepted, but also accepted amongst those involved in research and treatment, even though its theoretical and factual flaws now seem obvious. Although there

were historical factors which made it very likely that the disease concept of alcoholism would dominate over other views of drinking problems during the 1930s and '40s (see Shaw, 1982), a disease concept of dependence today might still achieve some degree of popular acceptance and would inhibit research and treatment accordingly. Consider the similarities between the disease concept of alcoholism and what could be called the disease concept of dependence.

Just as supporters of the dependence syndrome have suggested that beneath individual and cultural variations in drinking problems lies an underlying similarity of dependence, so the 'Big Book' of Alcoholics Anonymous (1939) observed that alcoholics seemed very varied on the surface but were, so the argument ran, all linked by one thing:

> Alcoholics ... have one symptom in common ... they cannot start drinking without developing the phenomenon of craving. This phenomenon ... may be the manifestation of an allergy ... it has never been, by any treatment with which we are familiar, permanently eradicated. The only relief we have to suggest is entire abstinence ... (p. 55).

The disease concept of dependence says that people who have the alcohol dependence syndrome may 'look different in France and Utah' (Edwards, 1977) but actually 'always' have a 'compulsion to take alcohol' (WHO, 1977). They have a 'leading symptom' of 'impaired control' (Edwards et al., 1977), and once they start drinking priming effects are likely to occur (Hodgson, 1980). There are basically two treatment goals depending on the severity of the syndrome. If dependence is severe, the patient should be abstinent, but 'if the syndrome is only minimally developed ... then a social drinking goal should be considered very possible' (Edwards, 1977, p. 147-8). The disease concept of dependence, then, is essentially a less dogmatic version of the disease concept of alcoholism. Because of its self-fulfilling internal logic it can assume itself to be dealing with the core pathology and that other etiological factors are peripheral and thus largely incidental to research and treatment. I do not believe that the evidence justifies this, and it is here that a fundamental difference in perspective arises. The most common criticism made of my writings on dependence is that I 'don't understand' that 'once a person is dependent' their original reasons for drinking do not matter and the psychobiological factors have taken over. Of course, this is what happens for a certain period in many cases. But it would be an incomplete and inconsequential diagnosis to explain cases purely in terms of withdrawal, relief drinking, reinstatement and psychic experience of these, without analytically distinguishing variations between these phenomena or taking into account other important etiological factors. The phenomena of psychobiological alterations, by themselves, cannot explain why people become excessive drinkers, and more importantly for treatment, they cannot explain why people stop being problem drinkers. The disease concept of alcoholism became eventually untenable because AA's views that 'allergic types can never safely use alcohol in any form at all' (Alcoholics Anonymous, 1939) was contradicted in practice and it became clear that the allergy/craving theory was not the best working explanation. There is a similar flaw in the disease concept of dependence. If its internal logic held, and if the psychobiological factors were the be-all and end-all, the drinker would be inextricably trapped in the cycle of high consumption, withdrawal, relief drinking and rapid reinstatement. Indeed this is what is sometimes supposed. For example, Madden (1979) claimed that I 'overlooked' that 'alcohol dependence (whatever its etiology in a given subject) becomes an ongoing and self-perpetuating entity that overshadows its causes and continues when they are no longer operative' (p. 350). This is exactly the sort of dogmatic statement which I predicted the dependence syndrome idea would encourage. It is simply not true that these psychobiological factors are 'self-perpetuating', as indeed they are not in the cases of addictions to other drugs. Gross (1977) specifically stated that the dependence syndrome was not self-perpetuating, and that it was usually eventually overruled by other factors.

> The foundation is set for the progression of the alcohol dependence syndrome by virtue of its biologically intensifying itself. One would think that, once caught up in the process, the individual could not be extricated. However, and for reasons poorly under-stood, the reality is otherwise. Many, perhaps most, do free themselves (p.120).

It seems plain to me, then, that factors extraneous to those included within the framework of the dependence syndrome must actually be more important in determining the natural history of a drinking career. This confirms the possible fallacy in the causal theory of the syndrome. It might be, to give a simplistic example, that there are extraneous factors x and y, say difficult family relationships and stress at work, which become linked with heavy drinking and cause the development of factors a, b and c (high tolerance, withdrawal, relief drinking etc.). For a while, a, b and c may indeed account for most of an individual's consumption and, indeed, may continue to do so even if x and y are no longer operative. However, if x and y were no longer causally important, the individual could eventually free himself from the vicious circle of factors a, b and c. But this would appear unlikely as long as factors x and y remained unresolved, and their relationship to the individual's drinking remained. In this latter situation, however, a, b and c would still appear to be the crucial etiological factors, even though by themselves they were not the crucial determinants of how long the person remained a problem drinker.

The disease concept of dependence is thus theoretically weak in exactly the same two connected areas as the disease concept of alcoholism. It (1) either underestimates or ignores the etiological importance of factors other than those contained within its own framework and, therefore, (2) it is at a loss to explain why the syndrome does not go on 'biologically intensifying itself'. The dependence syndrome idea is not comfortable in explaining change, because it does not readily perceive the development and recession of tolerance and withdrawal in a dynamic context with other motivations for drinking or not drinking. Indeed, it is significant that the phenomenon of tolerance, which received extensive attention from Gross, is rarely mentioned in more recent writings on the syndrome. This is probably because tolerance is important only in terms of motivations for drinking; without desires or drives for considerable repetitive drinking, tolerance would not noticeably increase. Supporters of the dependence syndrome idea, such as Hodgson, who do appreciate the importance of other etiological processes, are left vacillating between using the evidence of the withdrawal syndrome as the core of dependence, and at other times appearing to imply that the whole gamut of behavioural learning is somehow a justification of the syndrome concept.

BEST AND WORST EFFECTS OF THE SYNDROME IDEA

Whether the dependence syndrome is meant to be a core psychobiological construct, or an everything-included, multi-dimensional construct does not really matter, since whichever is the focus of interest, the concept of dependence is superfluous in either case. Or rather, at best, the idea of dependence is superfluous. At worst, it would blinker research and treatment in the same way as the disease concept of alcoholism did - and it would blinker medical contributions as much as any others, since it would continue to devalue the importance of research into the etiology of problem drinking, the importance of prevention, and therapeutic contributions which were not linked to the assessment of severity of psychobiological alterations. Even when considering purely psycho-biological factors, to label someone as severely or moderately dependent is not a precise diagnosis. The precise diagnosis would assess the degree of development of tolerance, withdrawal symptoms, relief drinking, the likelihood of reinstatement, associated psychic experiences, the reasons for non-withdrawal induced drinking, and the individual relationships between these various factors. At best the umbrella label of dependence would be unnecessary; at worst it would mystify the situation and detract attention away from other important causes which interact with psychobiological phenomena.

In assessing the possible best and worst consequences of the popular usage of the dependence syndrome, one has unfortunately to expect the worst, since sophisticated accounts of complex problems have a nasty habit of becoming oversimplified dogma once they achieve political status. For all these reasons, I cannot agree with Edwards view that 'perhaps it would be best in our particular society and at the present time to look on alcohol dependence as a disease, but with the added insistence that society has to take an informed rather than a mechanical view of what is meant by that statement' (Royal College of Psychiatrists, 1979, p.56). How can society be expected to take an informed view of a disease concept of dependence when even people in the field of alcohol research and treatment do not? As a concluding comment on the disease concept of dependence, I can do no better than to paraphrase Davies' (1974) remarks on how the disease concept of alcoholism came to be counterproductive in practice. One merely has to substitute the concept of the alcohol dependence syndrome for the concept of alcoholism.

> To call the alcohol dependence syndrome a disease does not do justice to the complexities of the problem, and, by ordering medical thought along the lines of symptoms and signs, it [would be] largely to blame for the late recognition of the condition. It militates against the shift of emphasis to the non-disease state of (harmless) dependence, where preventative measures of a social kind may be most effective in the long run. Two other unfortunate consequences of the disease concept might be mentioned. One is the way research into the alcohol dependence syndrome tends to focus on the metabolic processes rather than on the social and psychological conditions which favour high consumption of alcohol. The other is that it needlessly confuses the non-medical, professional people, who are concerned with helping alcoholics. (p.132)

REFERENCES

Alcoholics Anonymous (1939) The Story of How Many Thousands of Men and Women have Recovered from Alcoholism, New York: Alcoholics Anonymous, World Services Incorporated

Chick, J. (1980) 'Is there a unidimensional alcohol dependence syndrome?', British Journal of Addiction, 75, 265-80

Davies, D.L. (1974) 'Alcoholism as a disease', Psychological Medicine, 4, 130-2

Edwards, G. (1977) 'The Alcohol Dependence Syndrome: usefulness of an idea' in G. Edwards and M. Grant (eds), Alcoholism: New Knowledge and New Responses, London: Croom Helm

____ and Gross, M.M. (1976) 'Alcohol dependence: provisional description of a clinical syndrome', British Medical Journal, 1, 1058-61

____ Gross, M.M., Keller, M., Moser, J. and Room, R. (1977) Alcohol-Related Disabilities, Geneva: WHO Offset Publication 32

Gross, M.M. (1977) 'Psychobiological contributions to the Alcohol Dependence Syndrome: a selective review of recent research' in G. Edwards, M.M. Gross, M. Keller, J. Moser and R. Room (eds), Alcohol-Related Disabilities, Geneva: WHO Offset Publications 32

____ Kierzenbaum, H. and Lewis, E. (1975) 'The desire to drink: relationship to age, blood alcohol concentration and severity of the withdrawal syndrome on admission for detoxification', paper presented on 6th Annual Medical Scientific Session, National Council of Alcoholism, April

Hodgson, R. (1980) 'The Alcohol Dependence Syndrome: a step in the wrong direction?', British Journal of Addiction, 75, 255-63

____ Rankin, H.J. and Stockwell, T.R. (1979) 'Alcohol dependence and the priming effect', Behaviour Research and Therapy, 17, 379-87

Jellinek, E.M. (1960) The Disease Concept of Alcoholism, New Haven: Hillhouse Press

Keller, M. (1976) 'The disease concept of alcoholism revisited', Journal of Studies on Alcohol, 37, 1694-717

Madden, J.S. (1979) 'Commentary on Shaw', British Journal of Addiction, 74, 349-52

Mello, N.K. and Mendelson, J.H. (1972) 'Drinking patterns during work-contingent and non-contingent alcohol acquisition', Psychosomatic Medicine, 34, 139-64

Mendelson, J.H., Mello, N.K. and Soloman, P. (1968) 'Small group drinking behaviour: an experimental study of chronic alcoholics' in A. Wikler (ed.), The Addictive States, Baltimore: Williams & Wilkins

Meyer, R.E., Babor, T.F., Hesselbrock, M., Hesselbrock, V. and Kaplan, R. (1985) 'New directions in the assessment of the alcoholic patient' in L. Towle (ed.), Proceedings: NIAAA-WHO Collaborating Designation Meeting and Alcohol Research Center, Rockville, Md: NIAAA (in press)

Royal College of Psychiatrists (1979) Alcohol and Alcoholism, London: Tavistock

Russell, M.A.H. (1971) 'Cigarette smoking: natural history of a dependence disorder', British Journal of Medical Psychology, 44, 1-16

Shaw, S.J. (1979) 'A critique of the concept of the Alcohol Dependence Syndrome', British Journal of Addiction, 74, 339-48

____ (1982) 'What is problem drinking?' in M. Plant (ed.), Drinking and Problem Drinking, London: Junction Books

____ Cartwright, A.K.J., Spratley, T.A. and Harwin, J. (1978) Responding to Drinking Problems, London: Croom Helm

Stockwell, T., Murphy, D. and Hodgson, R. (1983) 'The severity of alcohol dependence questionnaire: its use, reliability and validity', British Journal of Addiction, 78, 145-55

Thorley, A. (1981) 'Alcohol Dependence and the Alcohol Dependence Syndrome', New Directions in the Study of Alcohol Group: Members' Booklet No. 1, January

World Health Organisation (1977) International Classification of Diseases, Geneva: WHO Offset Publication

Chapter 3

SOME REQUIREMENTS OF AN ALCOHOL DEPENDENCE SYNDROME

Jonathan Chick

We are bound to try to tame the wild profusion of our subject by categorisation, but there are mysterious influences on the choice of surfaces and planes by which categorisation proceeds. Here is a taxonomy from 'a certain Chinese encyclopaedia' (Foucault, 1970), dividing animals into: (a) belonging to the Emperor; (b) embalmed; (c) tame; (d) sucking pigs; (e) sirens; (f) fabulous; (g) stray dogs; (h) included in the present classification; (i) frenzied; (j) innumerable; (k) drawn with a fine camel-hair brush; (l) etcetera; (m) having just broken the water pitcher; (n) that from a long way off look like flies.

The medical profession's love of syndrome categories is so great that sometimes scientific considerations have been suspended. Even the most fundamental attribute of a syndrome, that the phenomena comprising the syndrome should occur more frequently together in the same individual than can be accounted for by chance association, has not always been met (Cochrane, 1965). For example, an old favourite of medical school teachers, the Paterson-Kelly or Plummer-Vinson syndrome supposedly of difficulty swallowing in middle-aged women accompanied by iron deficiency anaemia, 'identified' by several groups of workers amongst hospital patients, cannot be detected in the general population (Elwood, Jacobs, Pitman and Entwhistle, 1964). Even the syndrome of migraine (unilateral headache, preceded by an aura such as perceptual disturbance, accompanied by nausea) falls apart if examined under the exacting conditions of epidemiology (Waters, 1973).

Edwards and Gross (1976) abstracted from the conglomerate 'alcoholism' the concept of a syndrome of alcohol dependence. The elements of this proposed syndrome were to be:

(1) Narrowing of the drinking repertoire.
(2) Salience of drinking (the increasing importance of alcohol in the everyday life of the individual).
(3) Subjective awareness of compulsion to drink. This comprised two elements: (a) a feeling of 'needing' to drink; (b) impaired control of drinking.

(4)   Increased tolerance to alcohol.
(5)   Repeated withdrawal symptoms.
(6)   Relief drinking.
(7)   Reinstatement after abstinence - the above syndrome returns with great rapidity when drinking recommences after a period of abstinence from alcohol.

Edwards and Gross proposed this as a working hypothesis. This chapter will present some tests of that hypothesis and review some of the data on its utility, including published and unpublished data collected at the Royal Edinburgh Hospital. Here are four important attributes of a syndrome and these will be used to structure the ensuing discussion:

(i)   It has elements which can be defined and reliably assessed;
(ii)   Its elements should be seen to go together more than can be accounted for by chance association. This cohesiveness should occur not only in one or two specialised populations, such as hospital in-patients, but should occur in other populations or in the population at large;
(iii) 'It enables predictions about treatment and/or prognosis;
(iv) It improves communication with colleagues and/or patients.

OPERATIONAL DEFINITIONS AND RELIABILITY OF ASSESSMENT OF THE ELEMENTS OF THE ALCOHOL DEPENDENCE SYNDROME

Most of the elements in the Edwards and Gross description can be operationalised simply, that is, put into the form of a question which a patient can answer using one or two words. 'Reinstatement after abstinence' has perhaps been the hardest to capture, and I did not find a reliable question to include in a structured interview measuring alcohol dependence (Chick, 1980a). Stockwell, Hodgson, Edwards, Taylor and Rankin (1979) in a self-completion questionnaire used an 'imagine if' question. 'Imagine the following situation, (1) you have been completely off drink for a few days, (2) then you drink very heavily for a few days. How would you feel the morning after those two days of heavy drinking?'. (The subject is asked to rate whether he would start to sweat, would have shaking hands or body, or would be craving for a drink.)

The concept of reinstatement after abstinence has recently been subjected to careful laboratory study in clinics where it has not been regarded as unethical to give large amounts of alcohol, or alcohol over successive days, to abstinent alcoholics. In newly abstinent alcoholics a dose of alcohol can be shown to increase the desire to drink (Funderburk and Allen, 1977; Hodgson, Rankin and Stockwell, 1979; Stockwell, Murphy and Hodgson, 1983). Dose and exposure have not been sufficient to actually produce a withdrawal syndrome, though a day of drinking alcohol in newly abstinent dependent drinkers leads to increased heart rate and tremor detectable by instruments on the 'morning after'. This effect is greater in more severely dependent patients (Stockwell, Hodgson and Rankin, 1982a). A model of reinstatement of physical dependence after abstinence has also been demonstrated in mice and rats - the tendency to withdrawal phenomena is more easily evoked in animals who have previously already been made physically dependent (Goldstein, 1979; Tang and Falk, 1983).

There are, of course, other theories why abstinent alcoholics relapse into physical dependence on recommencing drinking. There is a view that, if a patient believes that one drink necessarily will lead to harmful drinking, this is a self-fulfilling prophecy which gives rise immediately to very heavy consumption (Donovan and Marlatt, 1980). It could simply be argued, however, that alcoholics tend to resume the style of drinking that they have known best in recent months, rather than take up a totally new style. This often means immediately drinking large quantities, and clinicians recognise that in some of these individuals the syndrome of physical dependence re-emerges very rapidly.

Impaired control is difficult to operationalise because the experience can only occur in people who have tried to limit their drinking and subjects find it difficult to recall how hard they were trying. Four items were used:

(a) (within drinking occasions)
    (i)   'set a limit but completely unable to keep to it'
    (ii)   'difficult to stop yourself from getting what you would call drunk ... or specially intended to avoid being drunk but could not control it'
    (iii)   'drinking to the point where you passed out in public'
(b) (overall intentions)
    'tried to cut down but found it difficult'

The first two items proved very time-consuming to employ reliably because of specifying the meaning of 'drunk' and of setting limits. This is partly why they were omitted from research with samples of working men reported below. The third item, on passing out in public, was also omitted because of its comparative rarity even in clinic patients.

Stockwell, Hodgson, Edwards, Taylor and Rankin (1979), and Stockwell et al. (1983) in their self-completion questionnaire rely on the patient recalling a recent month when he or she was drinking heavily in a way which 'for you was fairly typical of a heavy drinking period'. If patients are reminded which month they have selected, they can recall fairly consistently the sorts of symptoms they experienced in that period when tested two weeks apart. There may be problems in the patient knowing which month to choose; consumption elicited by this procedure correlates rather poorly with blood tests known to be affected by heavy recent consumption (Stockwell et al., 1983), and this suggests either that they tend to answer about a month two or three months ago, or that the method is not very reliable.

COHESIVENESS OF THE PHENOMENA OF THE ALCOHOL DEPENDENCE SYNDROME

One trap in testing whether the elements of the alcohol dependence syndrome hang together is that many alcoholics come to adopt a certain view of themselves, relabelling their behaviour in order to conform with the stereotype of the alcoholic to which they may have been exposed during treatment. Jellinek (1960) points this out with respect to members of Alcoholics Anonymous. A robust, reliable instrument is necessary.

Stockwell et al. (1979), in a sample of moderately and severely dependent patients, found that responses to their questionnaire yielded a strong general factor indicating that the aspects of the syndrome reflected a unitary phenomenon. They did not measure 'salience of drink-seeking behaviour', or some features of 'subjective awareness of compulsion to drink'. Neither was 'narrowness of drinking repertoire' measured, but a subsequent study enabled a reconstruction to be made of the variability in a patient's daily pattern, and lack of variability correlated with severity on the main scale of dependence (Stockwell et al., 1983).

A questionnaire allows room for a patient to bias his responses according to his views of himself, whereas in an interview, when an individual acknowledges a particular item, he is required to give a detailed example before a rating is made. When the unitariness of the syndrome was tested using such a structured interview, factor analysis of the responses of 109 patients accounted for a disappointingly low proportion of the total variance - 24 per cent. The items loading on this factor were salience, need, withdrawal, relief drinking (Chick, 1980b). Impaired control on single drinking occasions - can't keep to a limit, difficulty in avoiding getting drunk - formed a separate dimension. Difficulty in cutting down loaded weakly but equally on both first and second factors. Narrowing of repertoire formed a further, separate factor.

Though strictly speaking factor analysis does not allow one to speak of clusters of individuals, I think that in a clinic such as ours we see a sizeable group of patients who have little in the way of dependence, but who have problems associated with repeated drunkenness on single occasions. We have another finding indicating that impaired control on single drinking occasions is not central to the syndrome of alcohol dependence. We found that when a patient acknowledges impaired control on single drinking occasions, he tends to place it at the beginning of his drinking career, not late on at the phase of addiction as in Jellinek's (1960) Alcoholics Anonymous sample. Table 3.1 shows the results of a study of sequencing of symptoms (Chick and Duffy, 1979). However, this sequence is 'an average'; there are individuals who only began regularly to lose control at a late stage.

Clark and Cahalan (1976) examined the relationship between symptoms reported in a general population survey in 1967 and symptoms reported at a follow-up interview five years later. Individuals who acknowledged 'loss of control' did indeed go on to report continuing social and interpersonal problems associated with

Table 3.1:   The 'Typical' Developmental Sequence of 21 Symptoms
in Males Admitted to an Alcohol Problems Clinic

Completely Unable to Keep to a Limit

Needing More Than Companions

Difficulty Preventing Getting Drunk

Spending More Time Drinking

Missing Meals

Amnesias

Difficulty Cutting Down

Giving Up Interests

Restless Without

Change to Drinking Same on a Work Day as a Weekend

Organising Day to Ensure Supply

Tense on Waking

Passing Out While Drinking

Trembling

Can't Think of Anything Else

Retching

Sweating

Morning Drinks

Decreased Tolerance

Waking Feeling Frightened

Hallucinations

Source: From Chick and Duffy (1979). (All subjects do not have all
symptoms, but if they have a given symptom, it is likely to have
occurred in the position indicated.)

their drinking at the follow-up interview. However, the correlation between loss of control at time 1 and symptomatic drinking at time 2 was both significant and fairly high (0.36). This suggests that loss of control can be a forerunner of dependent drinking, as we found (Chick and Duffy, 1979). Dependent drinking at time 1 did not predict loss of control at time 2 (correlation 0.04).

The above led us to omit impaired control on single drinking occasions when we examined alcohol dependence symptoms in a community survey. We also omitted narrowing of repertoire because, as already stated, it did not appear to belong to the core of dependence, in so far as we had operationalised it. Our survey sample comprised two groups of men from high risk occupations: company directors in a variety of commercial and financial institutions; and manual workers in alcohol production firms. We wanted to see whether, like the elements of the syndrome of migraine, the elements of the alcohol dependence syndrome would fall apart when examined in a community-based sample amongst people who had not been near treatment agencies and had not had their view of their symptoms influenced by the ideology of the treatment agency. The data to be reported have not been published, but other results from this survey appear in Chick, Kreitman and Duffy (1981). In this survey we did not use every item that had previously been used to operationalise the elements of salience, need, withdrawal and relief drinking in our original work. Table 3.2 shows the interrelations between symptoms amongst the distillery workers. Ignoring the infrequently scored item, 'Gave up interest because of drinking', there are many significant inter-correlations. There is a first factor which runs through these five symptoms accounting for 41 per cent of the total variance. Among company directors (Table 3.3), there is poor inter-correlation, which is partly due to the low incidence of symptoms. (There was, however, no shortage of heavy drinkers - 25 per cent of the directors had a gamma GT over 50 units per litre, and a further 4 per cent had an MCV (mean cell volume) of 98fl. or over. Both these blood tests indicate heavy drinking (Chick et al. 1981).)

Thus, amongst patients and certainly among heavy-drinking manual workers, the items go tolerably well together but the place of impaired control remains controversial. Few studies have separately analysed the relationship between impaired control and withdrawal symptoms, relief drinking, feelings of need and salience. Vaillant, Gale and Milofsky (1982) looked at the relationship between different diagnostic dimensions in a 33-year prospective community study of some 400 men. One diagnostic approach used was that of DSM III (American Psychiatric Association, 1980). Here alcohol dependence is defined as 'abuse of alcohol' - broadly speaking, social or occupational problems and 'pathological use'- plus 'tolerance' or 'withdrawal'. Of the 68 subjects who met the criteria of alcohol dependence at some point during the study period, 90 per cent 'admitted problems controlling alcohol use'. However, so also did 72 per cent of the 110 men who reached the criteria of 'alcohol abuse', but fell short of dependence. This suggests that problems of

Table 3.2: Inter-correlations of Symptoms of Alcohol Dependence in Distillery Workers (n = 248)

	Frequency %	Morning relief drink	Restless without	Spending more time drinking	Gave up interests	Difficult to cut down	Alcohol intake (past 7 days)
Tremor	21	.37	.39	.17	n.s	.22	.48
Morning relief drink	22		.36	.17	n.s	.16	.60
Restless without alcohol	6			.24	n.s	.26	.43
Spending more time drinking	18				n.s	.23	.44
Gave up interests because of drinking	5					n.s.	n.s
Difficult to cut down	7						.29

Notes: $\geq$ .2 is sig. at 0.001 level $\geq$ .16 is sig. at 0.005 level

Table 3.3: Inter-correlations of Symptoms of Alcohol Dependence in Company Directors (n = 298)

	Frequency %	Morning relief drink	Restless without	Spending more time drinking	Gave up interests	Difficult to cut down	Alcohol intake (past 7 days)
Tremor	9	n.s	n.s	n.s	n.s	.15	.19
Morning relief drink	3		.19	n.s	n.s	n.s	.15
Restless without alcohol	9			n.s	.35	.15	.17
Spending more time drinking	12				n.s	.20	.16
Gave up interests because of drinking	1					.46	n.s
Difficult to cut down	7						.26

Notes: $\geq$ .18 is sig. at 0.001 level $\geq$ .15 is sig. at 0.005 level control are not diagnostic of alcohol dependence. Further, the definition of alcohol dependence required the subject to have already attained the criteria for alcohol abuse, and thus did not include people who were dependent with no other social problems.

My own view is that poor control may be the reason why some drinkers started drinking heavily enough to become dependent, but some drinkers are dependent and have good control, at least within single occasions. This position has an echo of Jellinek's (1960) distinction between those alcoholics who 'lose control' and those who 'are unable to abstain'.

PREDICTIVE UTILITY OF THE ALCOHOL DEPENDENCE SYNDROME
Predicting the Natural History
Ojesjo (1981) reported on the follow-up in 1972 of a population of problem drinkers originally identified in a general population survey in 1957. Of 29 patients who in 1957 were drinkers with physical dependence symptoms, only 4 were in remission in 1972. Among people who at time 1 were classified only as 'abusers' (drinking heavily as well as having repeated acute medical and social adverse consequences), 25 out of 49 were in remission.

Figure 3.1: Classification of the Lundby (1957) (Time 1) Male Alcoholic Population by Outcome at Follow-up (1972) (Time 2) (Ojesjo 1981)

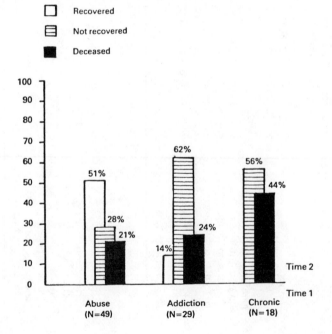

In Ojesjo's study the younger problem drinkers had a better prognosis. This may contaminate the relation between physical dependence and having a poor outcome. He does not report the mean age of his groups but it is possible that the dependent subjects were on average older than the 'abusers'.

Clark and Cahalan (1976) discussed the outcome of a general population sample re-interviewed in 1972, five years after an initial survey interview in 1967. Half of the 21 subjects who could be classified as alcohol dependent ('symptomatic drinking' in their terminology) were still alcohol dependent at the follow-up. Of these individuals 76 per cent had one or more social or interpersonal problems due to alcohol at follow-up. To have simply any social or interpersonal problem at time 1 predicted a 66 per cent probability of having some problem at time 2. Thus, to have dependence symptoms (or to be drinking enough to have them) reduces the likelihood that an individual in the general population will completely shake off all alcohol problems, but does not make it impossible.

Predicting Associated Problems

In a prison population, Edwards, Gattoni and Hensman (1972) found that dependence symptoms correlated with whether or not the man had drunk at the time of his arrest, the number of drunken arrests, the number of times he had been in prison and with unemployment, and with 'often' having amnesia. In another predominantly lower-class sample, Vaillant et al. (1982) found that deviant behaviour and dependent drinking went together. In our company directors, an upper-class sample, severity of alcohol dependence correlated with adverse consequences in the domains of general health, marriage and home life, work, and public order. Slightly higher correlations were found in our manual workers from distilleries.

The surveys of Cahalan and Room (1974) likewise found that dependent drinking tended to occur more frequently than would be expected by chance with social and interpersonal problems. There are, of course, bound to be other factors, such as personality and social position, which influence whether someone who is alcohol dependent runs into social and interpersonal problems. The link is clear, namely, if you have dependence symptoms, you are likely to run into some other problems that may be ascribed to your drinking. What is less clear, as with predicting natural history, is whether the relation depends on consumption, that is, whether if you are simply drinking enough to be dependent on alcohol then you will run into other problems.

Predicting Response to Treatment

Orford and Edwards (1977) reported a comparison of brief treatment with extended treatment in male, married problem drinkers. At one year, the outcome was the same irrespective of style of treatment. However, they were able to obtain complete information on 65 out of 100 patients at two years and classified outcome using three categories - good, equivocal and bad (Orford, Oppenheimer and Edwards, 1976). Table 3.4 shows the number of patients in each group, excluding those with equivocal outcomes, categorised according to style of treatment and to severity of alcohol dependence. It can be seen that there is a tendency for severely dependent individuals to do better with intensive, rather than brief, treatment. To my knowledge, this result has not been replicated elsewhere.

Table 3.4: Outcome After Two Years of Alcohol Dependent Patients by Severity of Dependence and Type of Treatment Received

Proportions of cases with good outcome

		Treatment	
		Brief	Extended
Dependence	Mild	6/12	11/13
	Severe	9/13	0/7

Proportions of cases with bad outcome

		Treatment	
		Brief	Extended
Dependence	Mild	3/12	4/13
	Severe	1/13	4/7

Source: From Orford et al. (1976).

The complicated relationship between degree of dependence and outcome in the Rand study has been mentioned by Hodgson and Stockwell in Chapter 1. The present state of the evidence suggests that people who have dependence symptoms are less likely to achieve problem-free drinking during the four years after they have been in treatment than are individuals who were not dependent on alcohol. However, I would agree with Madden (1979) when he says that clinicians have too readily grasped at severity of dependence as the key to the complex task of deciding which patients can safely resume drinking. Perhaps a better predictor is simply, as patients come into treatment, to ask them the questions at face value, as Heather, Rollnick and Winton (1983) did: e.g. 'Do you believe you could have one drink (or six drinks) and not go on a drinking spree? Have you done this in the past year?' etc. Answers to questions such as these did better, in their small study, than score on the SADQ in predicting harm-free drinking in treated patients.

UTILITY OF THE ALCOHOL DEPENDENCE SYNDROME IN COMMUNICATING WITH COLLEAGUES OR PATIENTS

When communicating with patients, it is desirable if simple concepts can be conveyed. There are some patients in whom it is useful for them to know that they have 'got' a condition and that they must therefore abstain from alcohol. My experience is that for other patients this mystifies rather than clarifies. They want a conceptual framework showing why some individuals find it difficult to alter their drinking habits. I find that both colleagues and patients often prefer a diagrammatic explanation, something perhaps on the lines of the simplistic model in Figure 3.2.

It was Orford and Edwards (1977) who mused about 'that moment of decision which leads people to seek to change their drinking habits'. In our scientific work we tend to lean over backwards to avoid terms like decision, choice, intention, but we should not be afraid, in my view, to be 'soft determinists' (Matza, 1964).

In response to some informal social control (e.g. criticism by family) or a threat (threatened loss of job) or some newly acquired attitude (e.g. it is a bad thing to be overweight), the drinker may decide to change his habits. There will often be ambivalence about this decision; they enjoyed aspects of their drinking; or they may even, if they are among those with cognitive impairment and/or brain atrophy (Ron, 1983), have difficulty seeing new ways of looking at their problem. There are a variety of impediments to sticking to new decisions once they have been formed - withdrawal discomfort, cues, the reinstatement phenomenon. These are impediments that are construed under the rubric of the alcohol dependence syndrome. But why single out some of the predictors and leave out others, such as the role of brain damage, the influence of social milieu? We need a model that allows for interweaving among many dimensions. Each drinker should be assessed on each dimension. One patient may do badly because of learnt cues and reinstatement phenomena, another because of lack of rewards and informal controls. Why single out only certain predictors and give them a mystifying label, dependence?

CONCLUSIONS

To summarise, the alcohol dependence syndrome does have a core that hangs together empirically though, as its authors originally behove us to do, it probably still needs refining. It has some value as a predictor. But let us continue in the spirit of Edwards and Gross who suggest it as a provisional model and avoid premature closure of our thinking.

Acknowledgements
Figure 3.1 is reproduced by permission of Dr L. Ojesjo, and the editor of the British Journal of Addiction.

The survey quoted here among distillery workers and company directors was conducted with Dr N. Kreitman, Dr M. Plant and Mr J. Duffy.

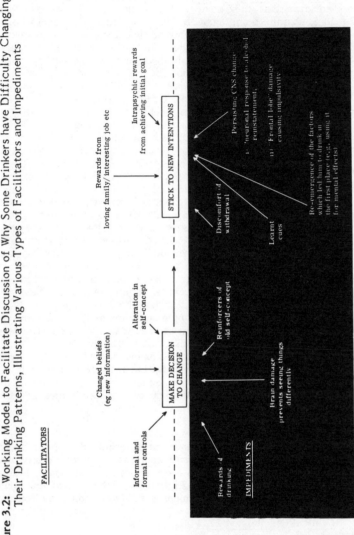

Figure 3.2: Working Model to Facilitate Discussion of Why Some Drinkers have Difficulty Changing Their Drinking Patterns, Illustrating Various Types of Facilitators and Impediments

FACILITATORS

Informal and formal controls

Changed beliefs (eg new information)

Alteration in self-concept

Rewards from loving family/ interesting job etc

Intrapsychic rewards from achieving initial goal

MAKE DECISION TO CHANGE

STICK TO NEW INTENTIONS

Rewards of drinking

IMPEDIMENTS

Brain damage prevents seeing things differently

Reinforcers of old self-concept

Discomfort of withdrawal

Learnt cues

Persisting CNS change ("neuronal response to alcohol reinstatement")

"Frontal lobe" damage causing impulsivity

Re-emergence of the factors which led him to drink in the first place (e.g. using it for mental effects)

REFERENCES

American Psychiatric Association (1980) Diagnostic and Statistical Manual (DSM III), Washington, DC: Task Force in Nomenclature and Statistics

Cahalan, D. and Room, R. (1974) Problem Drinking Among American Men, New Haven: Rutgers University Press

Chick, J. (1980a) 'Alcohol dependence: methodological issues in its measurement, reliability of the criteria', British Journal of Addiction, 75, 175-86

____ (1980b) 'Is there a unidimensional alcohol dependence syndrome?', British Journal of Addiction, 75, 265-80

____ and Duffy, J. (1979) 'Application to the alcohol dependence syndrome of a method for determining the sequential development of the symptoms', Psychological Medicine, 9, 313-20

____ Kreitman, N. and Duffy, J. (1981) 'Mean cell volume and gamma glutamyl transpeptidase as markers of drinking in working men', Lancet, i, 1249-51

Clark, W.B. and Cahalan, D. (1976) 'Changes in problem drinking over a four-year span', Addictive Behaviours, 1, 251-9

Cochrane, A.L. (1965) 'Science and syndromes', Postgraduate Medical Journal, 41, 440-2

Donovan, D.M. and Marlatt, G.A. (1980) 'Assessment of expectations and behaviours associated with alcohol consumption', Journal of Studies on Alcohol, 41, 1153-85

Edwards, G., Gattoni, F. and Hensman, C. (1972) 'Correlates of alcohol dependence scores in a prison population', Quarterly Journal of Studies on Alcohol, 33, 417-29

____ and Gross, M.M. (1976) 'Alcohol dependence: provisional description of the clinical syndrome', British Medical Journal, 1, 1058-61

Elwood, P.C. Jacobs, A., Pitman, R.G. and Entwhistle, C.C. (1964) 'Epidemiology of the Paterson-Kelly Syndrome'. Lancet, ii, 716-20

Foucault, M. (1970) The Order of Things: An Archaeology of the Human Sciences, London: Tavistock Publications

Funderburk, F. and Allen, R. (1977) 'Alcoholics' disposition to drink', Quarterly Journal of Studies on Alcohol, 38, 410-25

Goldstein, D. (1979) 'Some promising fields of inquiry into biomedical alcohol research', Journal of Studies on Alcohol, Supplement No. 8, 204-15

Heather, N., Rollnick, S. and Winton, M. (1983) 'A comparison of objective and subjective measures of alcohol dependence as predictors of relapse following treatment', British Journal of Clinical Psychology, 22, 11-17

Hodgson, R.J., Rankin, H.J. and Stockwell, T.R. (1979) 'Alcohol dependence and the priming effect' Behaviour Research and Therapy, 17, 379-387

Jellinek, E. (1960) The Disease Concept of Alcoholism, Hillhouse Press, New Haven

Madden, J.S. (1979) 'Commentary on Shaw', British Journal of

Addiction, 74, 349-52

Matza, D. (1964) Delinquency and Drift, New York: Wiley

Ojesjo, L. (1981) 'Long-term outcome in alcohol abuse and alcoholism among males in the Lundby general population, Sweden', British Journal of Addiction, 76, 391-400

Orford, J., Oppenheimer, E. and Edwards, G. (1976) 'Abstinence or control: the outcome for excessive drinkers two years after consultation', Behaviour Research and Therapy, 14, 409-18

____ and Edwards, G. (1977) Alcoholism, London: Oxford University Press

Ron, M.A. (1983) 'The Alcoholic Brain: CT scan and psychological findings', Psychological Medicine, Supplement No. 3

Stockwell, T.R., Hodgson, R.J., Edwards, G., Taylor, C. and Rankin, H.J. (1979) 'The development of a questionnaire to measure severity of alcohol dependence', British Journal of Addiction, 74, 79-87

____ and Rankin, H.J. (1982a) 'Tension reduction and the effects of prolonged alcohol consumption', British Journal of Addiction, 77, 65-74

____ and Taylor, C. (1982b) 'Alcohol dependence, beliefs and the priming effect', Behaviour Research and Therapy, 20, 513-22

____ Murphy, D. and Hodgson, R.J. (1983) 'The Severity of Alcohol Dependence Questionnaire: its use, reliability and validity', British Journal of Addiction, 78, 145-56

Tang, M. and Falk, J.L. (1983) 'Production of physical dependence on ethanol by a short drinking episode each day', Pharmacology, Biochemistry and Behaviour, 19, 53-5

Vaillant, G.E., Gale, L. and Milofsky, E.S. (1982) 'Natural history of male alcoholism: II. The relationship between different diagnostic dimensions', Journal of Studies on Alcohol, 43, 216-32

Waters, W.E. (1973) 'The epidemiological enigma of migraine', International Journal of Epidemiology, 2, 189-94

Chapter 4

WHY ALCOHOL DEPENDENCE - AND WHY NOW?

Douglas Cameron

There can be few acts of human behaviour that are so emotive, so coloured by value judgement, and so tinged with pseudo-scientific beliefs as those which involve drug taking. Over the centuries people's need to alter their perception of the world using psychoactive substances has been variously encouraged, condoned, manipulated and condemned. Society's attitudes to alcohol use remain as inconsistent and ambivalent now as ever. Quite clearly the current debate over the validity and significance of the alcohol dependence syndrome is but one thread of the tangled skein of man-in-relation-to-alcohol. But it is a thread that is generating much interest at present, so is worth examining.

People whose drinking behaviour is unacceptable have no doubt been with us for as long as alcohol has been with us. Definitions of acceptable drinking behaviour, and therefore of deviant drinking behaviour, are predominantly, if not entirely culturally determined; and cultures have attached to those designated as deviant a variety of labels. Over the past couple of hundred years in Britain, the most popular labels have been Habitual Drunkard, Chronic Inebriate, Dypsomaniac, Alcoholic and Problem Drinker. Why it happens that every few decades one label is discarded in favour of a new one is a matter of some interest, and it is of note that we are yet again at such a transition point. 'Alcoholism' is being discarded. It is by no means dead, but it would appear to have outlived its usefulness, whatever that was. And as it dies, an attempt is being made to elevate the alcohol dependence syndrome to the same status - i.e. to the status of an explanatory concept.

Dependence is an altogether more elusive, shifting, flexible structure than is alcoholism; indeed the main protagonists of the alcohol dependence syndrome have published three rather different definitions of it (Edwards and Gross, 1976; Edwards, Gross, Keller, Moser and Room, 1977; Edwards, 1977). But regardless of how they try to define it, of one thing they are absolutely sure and that is that it exists. Griffith Edwards in the WHO offset publication Alcohol Related Disabilities (Edwards et al., 1977), states that 'the reality and significance of this syndrome seemed to be well supported by a review of the present evidence' (p.6), and that 'dependence is a psychobiological reality, not an arbitrary social label' (p.9). It needs to be said that in that publication, Edwards cites no data for this view. Simply, he states, dependence is.

Dependence, having been made a fact, is then defined as a clustering of phenomena - such things as salience, compulsion to drink, reinstatement after abstinence and so forth. It depends upon which publication you read as to what phenomena are included, but it is a ragbag of things which are purported to happen to drinkers. It is further stated that to be considered dependent, it is not necessary to show all the phenomena listed. But you do need some of them, that 'some' not being specified. In other words, the protagonists of this 'syndrome' will not be drawn on the question, 'How tight is the cluster?'

The process through which the alcohol dependence syndrome has gone seems to me to be akin to saying that 'urbafanity' consists of Birmingham, Glasgow, Leicester and Manchester. Because those cities exist 'urbafanity' exists and because it does, it doesn't need Glasgow to be present to have 'urbafanity'. That argument is, of course, circular and meaningless, but could be seen as the first stage towards discovering the links between the cities mentioned.

What events, what phenomena is dependence purporting to explain? And more crucially, are there any parts of that dependence ragbag which a general model of drinking cannot adequately and comprehensively encompass? In other words, is it necessary to create a new dypsomania, or have we a theoretical structure which would enable us to discontinue that particular process?

The reality is of course that there are all sorts of ways of making sense of a person's drinking, from the microsomal to the mystical, but to be of any value the structure must be both explanatory and predictive. So in the next section, I wish to examine a simple determinants and consequences model of drinking to see how well that can meet these two criteria.

DETERMINANTS AND CONSEQUENCES OF DRINKING

The model to be explored may be represented visually as in Figure 4.1, in which the curve illustrated as a triangle, but in fact of unknown shape, represents the drinking population in any geographic area. The curve can be moved from left to right by internal and external determinants of drinking along a drinking consequences dimension - from totally harmful to totally beneficial. It should be noted that, while it is likely that this dimension is correlated with quantities consumed, it is not a quantity dimension. It is shown as a straight line, but again its actual shape is unknown. In fact it is likely to be a number of dimensions of short-term and long-term consequences with differing correlations.

But for the sake of this argument the simple model of a triangular curve on a unidimensional axis is adequate. On this axis,

Figure 4.1:

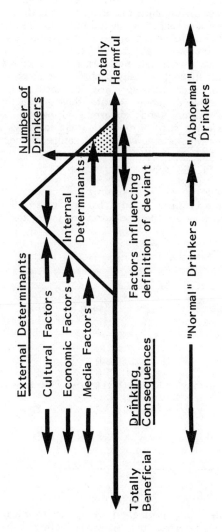

there is also a vertical moveable line - a 'cursor' which divides socially defined normal and abnormal drinkers. It can move independently of the movements of the triangle, thus changing the proportion of drinkers defined as deviant. Its extreme positions can be found. For instance, in fundamentalist Muslim countries such as Iran, where drinking of any sort is purported to be unacceptable, the cursor converges with the left-hand angle of the triangle - that is, all drinkers are deviant - whereas in old Tibet which recognised problems of alcohol use as normal, the cursor converged with the right-hand angle of the triangle - many problems of alcohol use but no deviance. Most societies, however, are not absolutist and the cursor 'cuts' the curve at some point, thus producing some dichotomy between normal and abnormal drinkers. What is important about proposing such a model is that it shows how all drinkers, including so-called problem drinkers, can be conceptualised within one model and that they are subject to the same determinants of drinking behaviour.

Determinants of Drinking

I wish now to examine in more detail a framework to explore the determinants behind my, or anyone else's drinking (see Table 4.1).

Table 4.1: Personal Determinants of Drinking

	Start	Stop
Single session		
Internal	A	C
External	B	D
Session frequency	Increase	Decrease
Internal	E	G
External	F	H

The framework consists simply of eight cells; for instance, cell A contains a list of those internal cues, triggers, feelings which make it more likely that I will make a decision to start off a single drinking session, and similarly, for example, cell H contains a list of those things in the world about me which may well influence me to reduce the frequency with which I have drinking sessions. The experimental subject whose determinants I wish to discuss is me, but while I am listing some of the determinants which strike me as being important to myself I think it would be appropriate if you would reflect on the determinants of your own drinking.

A few of the 'fillers' in each cell are listed below:

A. Thirst. Anxiety about certain situations - getting up on a dance floor. A need to procrastinate, particularly about asserting myself. A perceived need to be sociable.

B. Pub open. Friends or my wife suggesting going down for a drink. Special occasions, weddings, New Directions conference! Dinner parties, any parties. There is a very large number of these.

C. Feeling bloated. The dizziness caused by Positional Alcohol Nystagmus. I had a nerve damaged in the dentist's once, and a small bit of my chin goes numb sometimes when I've had quite a lot to drink. Clumsiness. Knowledge that I'm driving my car. Tiredness. Perceived disapproval of those around me.

D. Pub closing time. (I appear to do quite a lot of pub-drinking!) End of a bottle of wine at home. Other plans - 'We'll go for a pint and then we'll go and watch the football'. No money. Wife saying come to bed!

E. A perceived need to socialise. Unresolved emotional conflicts within me. The wish to procrastinate, again.

F. Holidays. Available cash. Weekends. Not being on call. Increased requests of those around me, the Christmas party season. The very occasional appealing advertisement.

G. A recent bad drinking experience, usually a hangover. 'That January 3rd feeling', a wish to become unfuddled to become intellectually sharper and crisper again. The failure of procrastinations, a need to get on with other things.

H. End of holidays or festive season. Sub-cultural changes, spending time with people who drink less than I usually do. Alternative activities. No companion with whom to drink.

I need to stress that this is a framework for exploring individual differences. For instance, as I have just stated, I have rules for myself about drinking alone. I don't do it. Hence in cell H, no companion for me equals no drinking. But that rule might well not apply to you. It's only the framework that is generalisable. I am trying, however, to create a dynamic image of all these cells perpetually changing, having varying absolute strengths, and strengths varying relative to one another. Depending upon what individuals are, believe, have learned and experienced, there will be various weightings of the various cells, and the system is perpetually changing in a very flexible way to allow drinking decisions to be made and not made at any particular point in time. What I want to do now is to make an attempt to fit the individual phenomena of the dependence ragbag into this framework (see Table 4.2).

Using this model, theories about some of the dependence phenomena can be meticulously explored. For instance, impaired control can be examined. All one needs to assume is that for some people a falling or no-longer rising blood alcohol concentration increases the strength of Cell A in relation to Cell C. It also

Table 4.2: A Determinants of Drinking Explanation
of Dependence Symptoms

'Dependence symptoms'	Increase of Strength of cell relative to cell	
Narrowing of drinking repertoire	E or F	G or H
Salience	E or F	G or H
Compulsion to drink		
(i) Intensity of felt need	A	C
(ii) Impaired control	A or B	C or D
Increased tolerance	A or B	C or D
Withdrawal	*	*
Relief drinking	A	G or H
Reinstatement after abstinence**	A or B	G or H

Notes

*   Withdrawal phenomena (including hangover) are a consequence of drinking so not directly influenced by these determinants.   Clearly they can 'loop back' and have determinant value. For me, a hangover is G determinant, but for those who believe in the 'hair of the dog' it is an A determinant.

**   It is reasonable to assume that while abstinent the strength of the single session determinants (A,B,C,D) to each other is likely to be relatively stable, and thus once drinking is resumed old patterns of alcohol use will re-emerge. Abstinence per se suggests superordinance of G or H, and nothing else. Once A or B have 'overpowered' G or H, what Alan Marlatt terms the 'Abstinence Violation Effect' could ensue (Marlatt, 1978).

explains how external contingencies, such as those so adequately described and reviewed by Nancy Mello (1972), can obliterate the phenomenon of loss of control. Simply, if you increase the absolute or relative strength of bribing, or what have you, of Cell D and H, or decrease however you like the absolute or relative strength of Cells B and F, then the balance of drinking decisions can be changed and loss of control could be obliterated from a drinking repertoire. Similarly, it is possible to conceptualise using this very simple framework any other of the dependence phenomena.

Consequences of Drinking

In terms of consequences, it is not necessary to look beyond direct alcohol effects for explanation. If one accepts that drinking is functional, then of course the behaviour has consequences, some of which are initially intended and others of which emerge during a drinking session. Further, some of the adverse consequences of drinking (hangovers, for instance) could be unplanned events, errors of over-dosage. Again, one does not need to create an umbrella concept to explain continued drinking despite recurrent adverse consequences. 'A good idea at the time...' may be a quite adequate explanation particularly for drinkers in whom the good feelings induced by alcohol on certain sessions occur inversely correlated to interest in the future.

So if a model as simple and general as this can describe and perhaps even give us some etiological clues about, inter alia, the phenomena that make up the dependence ragbag, without recourse to any categorical or syndromal view, then the question one needs to ask is: 'Why is the concept of the alcohol dependence syndrome becoming so popular?' It certainly is not because it is based upon an irrefutable scientific data-base (see Hodgson and Stockwell, Chapter 1). Thus, I believe that one needs to look elsewhere for the answer to that question and I am going to argue that it is a Zeitgeist, a belief which fits with our current views of the nature of persons who present with problems of alcohol use. For that reason, in the next section I am going to engage in a simple mathematical exploration of our current beliefs about those people to try to 'pick out of the air' from whence came the alcohol dependence syndrome.

A DIMENSIONAL EXPLORATION OF MODELS OF ABNORMAL DRINKERS

As I hinted at the beginning of this chapter, at different times different ways have been used to understand and deal with persons designated as deviant drinkers. They have been punished, preached at, medicalised and so forth. Teasing out from each other the various ways of looking at problem drinkers is not easy since now, as ever, we do not operate a pure model but in a mixture of perspectives. At times we are preoccupied with the sickness aspects of a person's problems, at other times interested in a person's psychopathological processes, and at yet others determined to modify his or her drinking habits.

Thus, the exercise undertaken by Siegler, Osmond and their

colleagues, firstly on madness (Siegler and Osmond, 1966), thence extending into other areas including 'Alcoholism' (Siegler, Osmond and Newell, 1968), will be used as the starting point for this section. These authors published a series of papers in which they attempted to unravel the various discrete philosophical models underpinning our beliefs about mental disturbance. Using much the same basic framework as do they, but abbreviated and somewhat changed, I have elicited what I believe to be six discrete models of problem drinkers. While I am indebted to these authors for the concepts and the framework, I have not adhered strictly to their view, since for reasons beyond the scope of this paper I am particularly unhappy with their 'Models of Alcoholism' paper. The framework and 'my' six models are shown as Table 4.3.

Having elicited these six discrete models, I wish to examine them upon four dimensions:

(1) An abnormality of drinking dimension.
(2) A personal abnormality dimension.
(3) A personal culpability dimension.
(4) An expertise dimension. (Do our 'clients' or we 'helpers' know best about the nature of problem drinking?)

Each dimension has been expressed as a five-point scale with at either end the absolute position, in the middle the balanced, equivocal position, and at the $\frac{1}{4}$ and $\frac{3}{4}$ points the 'more' and 'less' positions. When the models are individually fitted onto these dimensions the result is the highly complex Figure 4.2.

If one starts at the left-hand side, the sickness model is absolutist on all four dimensions - the client's drinking is totally deviant; the client himself is diseased and thus totally abnormal; he is a hapless victim of his disease process so not responsible; and we the (medical) experts know about his status whereas he, the sufferer, does not. At the right-hand side, the conspiracy (normal) model is similarly absolutist - believing that both the client and his drinking are absolutely normal; that he is totally responsible for his drinking behaviour; and that he knows that he is normal, a view at variance with those who would wish to modify his conduct for their own (sinister) reasons.

All the other models occupy to varying degrees less absolutist positions. For instance, according to the wicked model, the client's drinking is equivocal, neither normal nor abnormal, in fact irrelevant to the more important dimensions of his being abnormal (a criminal) but totally responsible for his conduct. Further, we (of law abiding status) know how to deal with criminals and have the right to do it (punish them). Each of the other three models is similar in its profile, as can be seen in Figure 4.2.

Having elicited these profiles, it is possible on the basis of only two assumptions to derive a consensual view. These are firstly, that all models are of equal validity - that demonic possession is no less acceptable as an explanation than is an (as yet undiscovered) biochemical or metabolic abnormality - and secondly, that simple

Table 4.3: Six Models of Abnormal Drinkers

	Disease	Psychological disturbance	Bad habit	Wickedness (weakness, indulgence)	Spiritual problem	Normal (scapegoat)
Nature of Disorder	Disease	Psychological disturbance	Bad habit	Wickedness (weakness, indulgence)	Spiritual problem	Normal (scapegoat)
Cause	Unknown ? genetic	Scars of childhood	Faulty learning	Unknown but the person's fault	1. Demonic possession 2. Alienation from spirit	Nothing wrong, so no cause
Behaviour to be changed	Excess consumer Disease process	Excess consumer Underlying conflicts	Excess consumer	Excess consumer	Excess consumer	None
Method of changing	1. Medical care 2. Self help (AA)	Psychotherapy	Behaviour therapy (relearning)	Punishment	Spiritual counselling and love	No change required
Personnel	1. Doctors etc. 2. AA Recovering Alcoholics	Trained psychotherapists or analysts	Psychologists	Courts, police, prison	Priests, gurus	Delabellers, drinker's companions, publicans, etc.
Success, drinking non-problematic since:	1. Cured 2. Abstinent 'Arrested' since no cure	Psychologically 'mature'	Good habits	Reformed	'State of Grace'	People leave him/her alone
Cause of failure	1. Denial, lack of co-operation 2. Denial, not at rock bottom	Lack of insight	Unco-operative	Incorrigible	'Infertile ground'	Society won't leave him/her alone for its reasons
Duties of client	1. Come for sickness to be treated 2. Co-operate with AA	Co-operate with therapist	Co-operate with psychologist	None	To seek spiritual realisation	None
Duties of society	1. To provide medical care 2. To accept AA and encourage it	To provide psychotherapy	To provide facilities for relearning	None	To make available spiritual guidance and resources	Not to scapegoat

summation of the models upon these dimensions is valid.

If one makes these two assumptions, adds up the total scores on each dimension and divides each by six, one ends up with the profile shown in Figure 4.3.

Figure 4.3 suggests that the consensual view is that the client's drinking is more towards abnormal than normal, that he himself is marginally more abnormal than normal, but that none the less he is more responsible than not responsible for his behaviour. Further we 'experts' know more about his 'problem drinking' than he does.

This view has been derived totally empirically from simple averaging of the six 'pure' models and is, of course, the profile of alcohol dependence, which carries with it beliefs about the client's drinking being not exclusively but somewhat abnormal, about the clients having predispositions to become dependent, and about the substance (alcohol) being addictive in its own right.

I do not think it is too farfetched to argue that the protagonists of the alcohol dependence syndrome have distilled out intuitively from our current beliefs what to them must appear a 'nugget of gold', a real phenomenon, but what in fact is no more than a single frame of a long-running motion picture.

If one returns to the 'pure' models, it is interesting to note that the newest, the normal (scapegoat) model, is that of the conspiracy theorists (e.g. Szasz, 1974) which really came into being only in the 1960s. The addition of this new model onto the existing five has had the effect of pulling the consensual view of the problem drinker away from the left-hand side of the four dimensions towards a more central position, i.e. away from 'alcoholism' the disease towards the 'alcohol dependence syndrome', a psychobiological reality.

It will remain a reality for just as long as it converges with the generally held philosophical beliefs about the nature of normal and abnormal drinkers and drinking. If and when that day passes, it will become yet another of yesterday's simpleminded conceptualisations. But at the present time it is new, increasingly determining the position of the deviant/non-deviant cursor (of Figure 4.1) and increasingly being seen as the proper subject of research. Woe betide those of us who in the latter half of this century march to a different drum!

Acknowledgements
I wish to acknowledge the help of Bob McGowan of the Department of Philosophy at the University of Leicester and of Marilyn Christie in the writing of this chapter.

Figure 4.2:

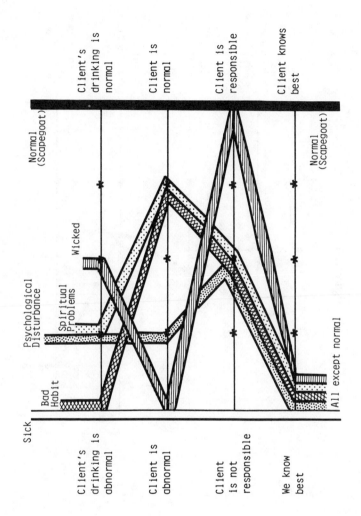

Figure 4.3:

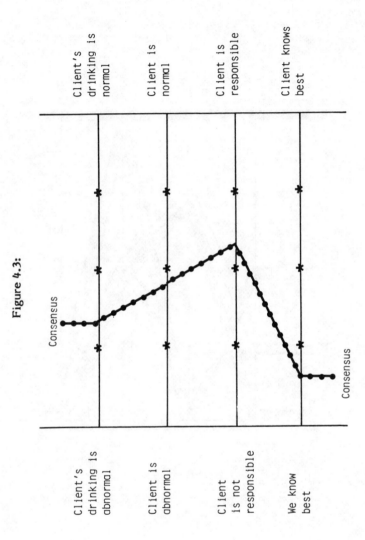

Client's drinking is normal

Client is normal

Client is responsible

Client knows best

Consensus

Consensus

Client's drinking is abnormal

Client is abnormal

Client is not responsible

We know best

REFERENCES

Edwards, G. (1977) 'The Alcohol Dependence Syndrome: usefulness of an idea' in G. Edwards and M. Grant (eds), Alcoholism: New Knowledge and New Responses, London: Croom Helm
_____ and Gross, M.M. (1976) 'Alcohol dependence: provisional description of a clinical syndrome', British Medical Journal, 1, 1058-61
_____ Keller, M., Moser, J. and Room, R. (1977) Alcohol Related Disabilities, WHO Offset Publication No. 32, Geneva: World Health Organisation
Marlatt, G.A. (1978) 'Craving for alcohol, loss of control and relapse: a cognitive-behavioural analysis' in P.E. Nathan, G.A. Marlatt and T. Loberg (eds), Alcoholism: New Directions in Behavioural Research and Treatment, New York: Plenum
Mello, N.K. (1972) 'Behavioural studies of alcoholism' in B. Kissin and H. Begleiter (eds), The Biology of Alcoholism Vol. II, New York: Plenum
Siegler, M. and Osmond, H. (1966) 'Models of madness', British Journal of Psychiatry, 122, 1193-203
_____ Osmond, H. and Newell, S. (1968) 'Models of alcoholism', Quarterly Journal of Studies on Alcohol, 29 571-91
Szasz, T.S. (1974) Ceremonial Chemistry: The Ritual Persecution of Drugs, Addicts and Pushers, London: Routledge & Kegan Paul

Chapter 5

THE LIMITATIONS OF THE ALCOHOL DEPENDENCE SYNDROME IN MULTIDISCIPLINARY SERVICE DEVELOPMENT

Anthony Thorley

A fertile diagnosis is one in which medical attention, curative or palliative, must follow. A sterile diagnosis is one in which a patient's general life predicament is assessed in medical terms and there is no treatment, curative or palliative. Alcoholism is a sterile medical diagnosis because the major methods of helping the alcoholic are not medical. Alcohol dependence as a simple common sense assessment is a good evaluation of one per cent of the average alcohol dependent's problem.

Alan Freed (1976)

Dependence is a highly important clinical reality, and understanding of all its implications is one essential part of the therapist's competence if he is to deal with drinking problems. But nothing which is being said should be misinterpreted as implying that dependence is everything. Dependence only exists in a personal and social context and it would be an absurd abstraction ever to see things otherwise. Furthermore, and as has already been stressed, many patients with drinking problems are not suffering from the dependence syndrome.

Griffith Edwards (1982)

The two statements quoted above seem to reflect quite different views as to the utility of a concept of dependence and its distillate, the alcohol dependence syndrome, in a clinical and casework setting. Is a better understanding of dependence, and a more refined application of this in the dependence syndrome, an essential basis of better and more effective understanding and treatment responses to alcohol problems? Or is the dependence syndrome a rather academic and sterile concept, of interest to experimental, research and clinical psychologists, but of little interest or even relevance to those involved at the coalface of services for problem drinkers? This account will attempt to pursue these questions in the light of current practice and the author's experience in multidisciplinary teaching.

To some extent, any conceptual model or framework in clinical or casework practice is a reflection of pre-existing models interacting with new external and societal demands. The explanatory and facilitatory model of alcohol dependence and the alcohol dependence syndrome is no exception, and stands squarely in the sociopolitical evolution of multidisciplinary services for problem drinkers.

THE USEFULNESS OF THE SYNDROME FOR TREATMENT AND REHABILITATION SERVICES

Following publication of the various accounts of the alcohol dependence syndrome as a refinement of alcohol dependence, there has been considerable academic comment and a lively debate has ensued (Edwards and Gross, 1976; WHO, 1977; Edwards, 1977; Royal College of Psychiatrists, 1979; Hodgson, Stockwell, Rankin and Edwards, 1978; Shaw, Cartwright, Spratley and Harwin, 1978; Shaw, 1979; Madden, 1979b, 1980; Chick and Duffy, 1979; Chick, 1980a, b; Rankin, Hodgson and Stockwell, 1980; Hodgson, 1980; Edwards, 1980, 1982; Rankin, Stockwell and Hodgson, 1982; Raistrick, Dunbar and Davidson, 1983; Stockwell, Murphy and Hodgson, 1983) and continues in the pages of this book. It is not the intention here to dwell upon the scientific evidence and academic validation of the syndrome except in so far as clinical utility is affected. The syndrome certainly derives in part from good scientific evidence, and there is no doubt in my mind that it can be demonstrated as a clinical reality (e.g. Stockwell et al., 1983).

One central feature, however, does require prior consideration when we examine the usefulness of the syndrome for those who work clinically with problem drinkers. That is whether the syndrome, as a cluster or constellation of related clinical elements, truly exists in a matter of degree or whether the whole syndrome is a more absolute occurrence and a core entity among alcohol related disabilities. Edwards (1977) appears to present an ambiguous picture. Thus, when it is convenient for the syndrome to be a matter of clusters and degrees, so it appears. When it requires the character of a central core, a reductionist stance, the psychobiological bedrock of physical dependence and withdrawal phenomena is presented.

Shaw (1979) has exposed this ambiguity in recent accounts of the syndrome, but it is clear that it is an unresolved problem since first mention of the syndrome in the mid-1960s (Edwards, 1967, 1982). A question of diagnosis or appropriate labelling arises here. Does an individual who is somewhat dependent on alcohol, but in no way physically dependent, get diagnosed as having an alcohol dependence syndrome or not? The Severity of Alcohol Dependence Questionnaire developed by Stockwell, Hodgson, Edwards, Taylor and Rankin (1979) to assess the severity of the syndrome appears to rest almost wholly on physical dependence, and therefore suggests that only those individuals with some evidence of physical dependence have the syndrome. A wider view of dependence, as related to elements of the syndrome other than those based on withdrawal phenomena, has been developed into an instrument by Chick (1980a) and more recently by Raistrick and his colleagues (1983), but the use of these important adjustments is not widely reported to date.

It may therefore be concluded from the evidence currently available that the alcohol dependence syndrome principally measures or describes physical dependence (see Edwards, 1982, p. 36). This conclusion is supported by evidence presented by Rankin et al. (1980) as to the behavioural measurement of dependence. Subjects were divided into moderate or severe dependence according to drinking pattern and presence of some degree of physical dependence, and were observed drinking a specified amount of alcohol in an open-ended situation. It was found that the severely dependent drank the alcohol significantly faster than their less dependent counterparts, showing that degree of physical dependence has predictive value in drinking behaviour. The cut-off point appears to be the commencement of physical dependence in a general dependence continuum; the matter of degree refers only to degree of physical dependence. The clinical value of this limitation within physical dependence will be examined in due course.

In 1980, Hodgson responded to the 'all or none' criticism of the syndrome. He makes it clear that he considers that dependence is a matter of degree, not 'all or none' but 'some or none', but that disabilities from non-dependent drinking are possible and important. He goes on:

> It also follows that there is a grey area on the drinking continuum where regular free and easy social drinking becomes dependent drinking. On the lower slopes of the dependence continuum the drinker begins to have difficulty resisting drink on those occasions when he knows that he should, and short-term gratification begins to take precedence over long-term goals (Hodgson, 1980, p. 259).

Hodgson does nothing here to clarify whether the alcohol dependence syndrome can exist before physical dependence has appeared. Indeed, he appears to confuse the issue further by mixing terms such as drinking continuum and dependence continuum. No one would doubt the importance of a general dimension or continuum of dependence existing in several modalities and probably in a matter of degree (Russell, 1976). The question we have addressed here is where on the continuum of dependence the syndrome itself stops and starts, if indeed it does start! The weight of the evidence so far reviewed suggests that in practical terms the syndrome is confined to physical dependence but expressed in a matter of degree. This may represent the syndrome in rather caricature terms, but clearly it does have its limitations in the clinical casework arena.

THE ALCOHOL DEPENDENCE SYNDROME AS AN INTERDISCIPLINARY MODEL

Can the alcohol dependence syndrome emerge as a framework for explanation and clinical or casework action, common and useful to the wide variety of professional disciplines necessarily involved in treatment and rehabilitation services? Edwards (1977) rightly states that:

> Successful communication between referring agents and between different members of any treatment team can substantially contribute to the efficacy with which the needs of patients will be met - if terms are being used ambiguously and with the nature of their meaning so arcane that definition becomes the property only of the super-specialist, patients are likely to suffer in many ways... Terms such as 'alcoholism' and 'alcoholic' are by now so lacking in precision as only to be passports to confusion. The idea of the dependence syndrome might usefully remedy this confusion (p.145).

Here, and in later writing, Edwards (1982, p.42) seems to suggest that the variety and breadth of the syndrome will allow non-medical members of the team easier access to an idea, a facilitation for working with alcohol problems. This may be a reasonable hope, but what of the reality?

Shaw (1979) makes no specific responses to this important suggestion, but earlier, together with his colleagues (Shaw et al., 1978) he has shown how different professions have considerable dificulties in coping with the management of alcohol problems. Further evidence of the paucity of basic skills and disparity of knowledge among primary care workers (general practitioners, community and district nurses and area team social workers) has been clearly provided by Fisher (1980). This is evidence that treating problem drinkers does not come easily, even to those professions where basic or generic skills are assumed (DHSS, 1978), and may reflect the common observation that medical concepts of alcoholism as a disease are acceptable to non-medical professions in part because they feel no responsibility for taking up this client group whilst ever it is clearly part of a medical remit. Many GPs still consider that helping the 'alcoholic' is best done by a psychiatrist or a specialist based in the hospital service. If 'alcoholism is a disease' has problems in ease of multidisciplinary use, can we expect the alcohol dependence syndrome, implicitly a disease model, to fare better?

Although at times social work appears close to taking some of the worst aspects of medical and disease models into its general thinking (e.g. ideas of diagnosis, labelling and treatment), it does try to distance itself from an implicit disease-model approach, and is sometimes frankly critical of medical approaches to some psychiatric disorders. Similarly, psychologists, particularly in psychiatry, are often critical of an explicit disease model and may favour approaches based more on learning and educational ideas for dysfunctional behaviour (Heather, 1976). There is no specific evidence yet available as to how the alcohol dependence syndrome will be utilised by other disciplines, but an exercise discussing the merits and demerits of the syndrome at a recent basic summer school of the Alcohol Education Centre, comprising in the main non-medical professional workers, met with very little interest (AEC, 1980). Further experience running an AEC advanced summer school dealing simply with assessment of problem drinkers, gained by the author and Howard Rankin, again suggested strongly that, at least in that mixed social work and medical setting, concepts of dependence and more specifically identification of the alcohol dependence syndrome were not to the fore in assessment and treatment priorities (Rankin, 1982). This is slight evidence indeed, but it supports an impression that many non-medical workers do find the terms and ideas of the syndrome arcane, distant and more an academic matter than a reflection of the practicalities of dealing with clients. The syndrome like its forebear alcoholism, does, it appears, as Hodgson (1980) has anticipated with concern, run the risk of mystification and damaging caricature.

The major impediment for a concept which is academicised and mystified is that unless it immediately strikes a chord for other workers and has a natural place in their practical working models and conceptual ground-base, it is likely to have a slow acceptance or to become frankly redundant. If working with alcohol problems is so obviously a multidisciplinary exercise, and if other disciplines, for example social work, have been slow to admit responsibility partly because of a predominant medical approach, the need for a real multidisciplinary model becomes a priority in the political process of facilitating non-medical professions into playing their part in developing services. It is not my impression that disciplines using a social work model find that the syndrome or the concept of alcohol dependence offers them very much to connect with. Many clients with drinking problems present to social workers and probation officers, but dependence, and certainly physical dependence, is not often present; yet the problems for the client or his family are profound. Preliminary attempts to measure serious drinking problems presenting in Scottish social work offices in terms of the SADQ have shown very little success (Allan, 1979; McGarva, 1979). If one holds with a chronological, symptomatically developmental perspective of drinking and alcohol problems, it is clear that social workers often come up against 'early cases', as well as persons who may never become dependent. For these cases the alcohol dependence syndrome has little relevance. As yet, the question remains unanswered as to whether generic social workers could valuably utilise the dependence syndrome when working with clients who are physically dependent.

If social workers have difficulties with the syndrome, psychologists may find it more appealing, in that degree of dependence and the postulated learning mechanisms of dependence related to physiological withdrawal symptoms suggest a more objective approach which is consistent with elements of learning theory and many psychologists' thinking. Psychologists have introduced insights and practical techniques to the treatment of problem drinking from their experience in obsessional and phobic disorders, and have played a key part in the development of harmfree drinking as a viable alternative to abstinence (Heather and Robertson, 1981). If the alcohol dependence syndrome is supported by evidence that degree of physical dependence carries important implications, especially for recovery rates (Rankin et al., 1980; Polich, Armor and Braiker, 1980), these findings are likely to make the syndrome an attractive and viable construction for psychologists to work with in the future. Perhaps the major challenge the syndrome presents to psychologists is to clarify and develop the measurement and relevance to alcohol problems of the range and types of dependence which are not based on physiological withdrawal symptoms (e.g. Russell, 1976).

It is my impression that doctors and medical students find the apparent clarity at the core of the syndrome to be of clinical value. 'I never did really know what an alcoholic is' is a common sentiment unlikely to be so easily applied to the syndrome or a rating of degree of dependence. The reductionism implicit in the syndrome - the tidying up of the confused thinking behind 'alcoholism' - makes it instantly appealing to medical men and women brought up on a diet of core syndromes and the ten causes of so and so! Doctors and medical students who take up the essence of the alcohol dependence syndrome will at least be more sophisticated and informed in their approach to the physically dependent patient, and will not expect withdrawal symptoms to necessarily include epileptic seizures, hallucinations or a full-blown delirium tremens. Such discrimination would, for many practitioners, be an important step forward (Hore, Ritson and Thomson, 1982).

However, the caveat for the medical profession must be that there is a great deal more to alcohol problems than dependence or the dependence syndrome. Alcohol-related disabilities, medical and even non-medical, have been outlined (WHO, 1977; Royal College of Psychiatrists, 1979) but as yet inadequately related to alcohol dependence. Many patients present their alcohol problems obliquely or through a leading edge of social or emotional problems even when dependence is present, but many doctors are ill-equipped in knowledge or attitudes to pick up these non-medical presentations (Fisher, 1980; Thorley, 1980). This issue of 'the rest of the problem' is reflected throughout most of the papers on alcohol dependence and the syndrome; no author has a clear way of solving it although attempts have been made to help the doctor with 'early recognition' and appropriate responses (Murray and Bernhadt, 1980; Thorley, 1980). It is clear that many cases and problems are not going to be spotted using the terminology and concept of the dependence syndrome. Madden (1980) has raised part of this issue in a recent essay: 'How are we to view and describe minor forms of substance abuse?', but at present he can only observe that the question remains unanswered.

The place of the professional role of the nurse, with or without psychiatric training, is of increasing importance in identifying and treating patients with alcohol problems (DHSS, 1979; Plant, 1980; Dobson, 1980). Nurses tend not to develop their own conceptual models central to treatment, whilst they do clarify a nursing role in practical matters but work within the context of models developed by doctors. Nurses who are working in settings to identify early cases (e.g. primary medical care, accident and emergency departments), or who are working in an advanced clinical role as therapists and counsellors (Dobson, 1980), are going to utilise social-work ideas and a broader perspective of alcohol problems than those implied by, or centred on, alcohol dependence. It may be discovered, therefore, that for nurses, even more so than with doctors, the dependence syndrome has only a partial contribution to make.

How then do we best summarise the utility of alcohol dependence and the alcohol dependence syndrome for different disciplines and professional groups? It may yet be too early to make a firm judgement, the evidence is meagre, and more is surmise and impression than established fact. But an interim view may be that, at best, it provides a potential of improved communication regarding physical dependence between workers. At worst, its medical base and language of symptoms is in danger of mystification and identification with expertise so like its forebear 'alcoholism' may cause it to be avoided by non-medical workers for whom its centrality of dependence is strangely irrelevant as they attempt to cope with the wider range of alcohol problems and patients or clients who only uncommonly present dependence as their leading complaint.

THE SYNDROME AS A BASIS OF UNDERSTANDING FOR CLIENTS AND PATIENTS

Edwards (1977) suggests that 'as there is no functionally useful concept of alcoholism latent within our society which can be called on as a coinage of understanding' between clinician and patient, the idea of a dependence syndrome may functionally serve this purpose. It is less clear whether Edwards considers that the syndrome can work as effective currency between a worker and client in a non-medical setting, but his earlier remarks as to its hoped-for interdisciplinary validity would imply some value in that setting also (Edwards, 1982).

It is impossible to anticipate the likely value of the syndrome without briefly considering the implicit understanding between doctor and patient (and hence client and worker) with regard to alcoholism-as-a-disease. In a medical setting, some patients are relieved to admit their alcoholism and to embrace a framework of diseases which allows them to structure and order the perplexing chaos of their drinking experience. For some, to realise or to affirm being an alcoholic is a therapeutic relief. Others, and I suspect the majority, less able or prepared to embrace a non-accountable sick role, are keen to avoid the diagnosis with its negative connotations and implications of necessary abstinence. These individuals feel the stigma of alcoholism, do not perhaps see themselves as ill 'in that kind of way', and contemplate the impossible goal of abstinence with renewed hopelessness. As Freed (1976) has remarked, alcoholism can be a sterile diagnosis and for many over the last 50 years I suspect it has been. The question to be answered is, is the alcohol dependence syndrome any less sterile?

The answer would seem to lie very much with the patient and the language of doctor-patient negotiations. It is widely recognised that doctors in part teach their patients what to say, and alcohol dependence is no exception to this. For instance, it is my impression that patients who regularly attend Alcoholics Anonymous meetings, or who mix in a drinking or agency subculture of those who do, will express strongly held ideas about loss of control and will value abstinence more than those patients who do not. Thus, it might be that patients 'trained' in AA thinking will perhaps find the alcohol dependence framework of explanation more useful than others. Many patients, and even more clients attending non-medical agencies, are not particularly inconvenienced by or aware of their dependence. More significantly, they do not express their difficulties or life predicament, as Freed (1976) calls it, in terms of dependence or complaints of physical dependence. What I am calling into question is how natural it is for even physically dependent patients to express themselves in terms of dependence, unless they are well imbued with AA thinking or the traditional subculture of medical treatment of alcoholism. The alcohol dependence syndrome is based upon clinical impression, but how representative is that clinical impression of alcohol problems as they present in their richness and variety?

Two clinical examples come to mind. One is the intelligent working-class patient who is naive to ideas about dependence. He is drinking about 20 pints of beer every 24 hours. He wakes each morning with tremor and some nausea, but it has not dawned on him to take a drink first thing to change this. An early morning cup of tea improves his electrolytic and fluid balance and alleviates his discomfort, but it is not until a first lunch-time pint of beer with his mates at work that he has had his first alcohol of the day. No doubt some significant relief is felt at this stage but the learning connection between the drink and the relief is apparently not made. Patients like this often exhibit no inherent or learned craving. His complaint did not centre on his dependence, but on the significance of an episode of mid-afternoon intoxication which placed his job as a hospital porter in jeopardy.

The other clinical example is the businessman (more occasionally the labourer) who is drinking a bottle and a half of spirits a day but functioning remarkably satisfactorily. Most significantly, his high tolerance and continuous day-long drinking ensure that he barely appears intoxicated at any time of the day.

Although he is physically dependent, in the early morning he shows no withdrawal symptoms because his blood alcohol concentration is still sufficiently high from the previous night's drinking. His first drink will be in the office or in the boardroom and, again, before withdrawal manifests itself. This patient may be physically dependent and may show avoidance drinking in accord with the syndrome, but he hardly realises it, so accustomed is he to drinking all through the day. Nor does he experience significant craving, and he may therefore never come to the notice of treatment agencies.

It is to be noted that, as well as presenting physical dependence in a paradoxical or oblique way, neither patient in these examples shows significant craving. Of course they could have, but although craving appears central to the core elements of the dependence syndrome and plays a prominent part in the experimental validation of the syndrome by Hodgson and his colleagues (e.g. Hodgson, Rankin and Stockwell, 1979), in my clinical impression it is very variable in quality and intensity and often not prominent, or absent, in cases with demonstrable physical dependence. Hodgson may have satisfactorily correlated physical elements associated with a status of presumed craving (e.g. hand tremor, speed of drinking etc.) with degree of physical dependence, but the subjective experience of craving or reported desire to have a drink related poorly with the objective measurements (Hodgson et al., 1979; Rankin, Hodgson and Stockwell, 1979). There are probably many reasons for this, but the lack of reliability placed upon subjective craving in the experimental situation does weaken its relevance in the clinical situation.

This is not the place to dissect out and unstitch each element of the dependence syndrome. It has been presented by its protagonists as provisional, and is indubitably based on clinical impression and the experience of a large number of patients. The representativeness of those patients in terms of all clients and patients with alcohol problems may be an issue more in doubt. Suffice it to say that, even for the physically dependent person, it is the variety of presentation and interpretation of each or any of the elements of the syndrome which remains an overriding clinical impression. Cultural and class differences inevitably stretch the correlation of the syndrome elements even further. For instance, in the North East of England where, for men, 93 per cent of all alcohol consumption is beer (Wilson, 1980), drunk in a fairly ritualised and predictable way, a narrow drinking repertoire is the cultural norm not the exception. Here 'late cases' or those far down the degree of physical dependence continuum seem to widen out their repertoire, certainly in terms of beverages, and not to narrow it.

Impairment of control, compulsion and craving, and reinstatement after abstinence are all so variable in their clinical presentation and relate so strongly, in my impression, to cognitive elements that, notwithstanding some relationship to degree of physical dependence, this relationship as described in the terms of the syndrome may be over-emphasised when compared to the reality of the clinical setting. It is well known to clinicians that the reinstatement phenomenon, underpinned somewhat less than fairly by the 'one drink, one drunk' view, is often anticipated by patients who restart drinking after abstinence, but these patients often do not drink to the point of rapidly returning to their previous level of physical dependence (McKee, 1980). That is not to deny the phenomenon of relatively rapid reinstatement of degree of physical dependence if a person continues heavy drinking, but many persons (whether clients or patients) do not choose to do so, and may even be less likely to if they have been treated in such a way as to alter their view of 'loss of control' and 'reinstatement' (Heather and Robertson, 1981; McKee, 1980).

Perhaps there is a basic point to make here. Patients who come eventually to believe that their drinking problem centres on their own inability to control their consumption or behaviour, and have that cognitive set, will probably drink and lose control more often than those who view their behaviour and drinking from a less fatalistic or determinist stance. The use of concepts of dependence and implicit ideas of impairment of control may or may not have validity in terms of explaining a cluster of life problems, as Shaw (1979) has illustrated in a particular clinical example, and it may therefore be entirely valid, as Cameron (1981) has argued, to take dependence right out of the clinical situation (see also Chapter 4).

Clinical examples must be considered with caution, unless it can be shown that these kind of exceptions are more common than the rule. In this account, clinical examples have been instanced where physical dependence does exist, may not be recognised, or may not be recognised as being related to other life problems. The syndrome does seem to be in difficulties where it is applied to those who are physically dependent yet continue to hold their job down - a figure which may be in excess of 50 per cent of cases. It is also in difficulties when women are considered. Women's problems related to drinking behaviour are in a different mould as compared with men (Camberwell Council on Alcoholism, 1980). The relationship between degrees of physical dependence and problems and other factors, such as those measured by Rankin and his colleagues (1980), does seem to be different between the sexes. If the male/female sex ratio of physical dependence is six to one, the alcohol dependence syndrome may need fundamental rethinking for 14 per cent of all cases presenting!

To summarise, there is no doubt that the syndrome may have value when talking with some patients, especially in a medical setting, but it has difficulties as a concept in dealing with cases who are physically dependent and do not recognise it, cases who are not physically dependent and have gross problems related to drinking behaviour, cases who are physically dependent but do not recognise their problems as being related, and cases who have problems which are only slightly related to any form of drinking behaviour. It might be argued that the population most likely to embrace the syndrome model are those alcoholics who attend AA meetings but here, fixed belief in alcoholism as a disease predominates, and as Max Glatt has recently observed: 'I do not believe that alcoholics attending AA meetings in the future are likely to stand up and say: "My name is so-and-so and I have the alcohol dependence syndrome"'! (Glatt, 1980).

THE SYNDROME AS A BASIS FOR DRINKING GOALS AND TREATMENT STRATEGIES

If the syndrome as a model of understanding between client and worker or doctor and patient has limitations, particularly in a social work setting, it may nevertheless have value as a basis for negotiating treatment goals for drinking. Edwards (1977) has suggested that severity or degree of dependence is a basic assessment to make when considering the distinction between treatment of drinking behaviour with an abstinence goal as against a controlled or harm-free drinking goal. Thus, when the syndrome is only 'minimally developed' (occasional recent experience of mild but definite withdrawal symptoms), the patient has some chance of returning to social drinking. However, 'if the syndrome is severe as judged by the whole picture, then it is reasonable to tell the patient that his chances of returning to social drinking are slender, unless he is receiving treatment especially designed for "unlearning" the dependence' (Edwards, 1977, p. 147). Hodgson (1980), recently reviewing the matter, concludes that as 'the available evidence suggests that severity of dependence appears to have some predictive significance it should not, in my opinion, be ignored'. Here is a piece of advice with clear clinical relevance.

Severity of dependence, as measured in terms of elements surrounding physical dependence and withdrawal symptoms, may account for a major part of the variance and suggest a core construct. What exactly is severity or degree of dependence? Russell (1976) has suggested that the basic model of dependence is like a climber hanging for his life on a rope. The tighter the rope, we may infer, the stronger or more 'severe' the dependence. Strength is a description which calls to mind power: the force necessary to alter the dependence or break it. Severity may or may not imply power or strength; it certainly implies a judgement with regard to some degree of impediment, handicap or problem associated with the dependence. Thus, there is an assumption, perhaps unintended, that patients who are 'severely' dependent are more strongly dependent and have more severe problems. Russell (1976) has suggested that the strength of dependence is essentially represented by the ability of the individual to refrain from the act (drinking) and that this strength may not be wholly derived from physiological dependence but from dependence in other modalities. Thus severity of problems may only poorly relate to degree of physical dependence or dependence as a whole. The alcohol dependence syndrome, when centred round the core construct of physical dependence, may have limitations in assessing the wider relevance of dependence in all modalities.

The debate about harm-free drinking goals as a clinical option raises the important question of what drinking strategy patients are best advised to try in response to their drinking problems.

Sometimes there are clear medical or social grounds for definitely maintaining abstinence (Thorley, 1980), but indications for alternative goals are much more difficult to ascertain. 'Mild cases', early cases, people who do not see themselves as having a disease, have all been made the basis for suggestions reinforced by the concept of the syndrome as 'minimally developed', i.e. those with only a moderate degree of physical dependence. It is surely correct not to ignore these distinctions, as Hodgson (1980) has rightly advised, but should they dominate clinical attitudes and decision-making about non-abstinent goals, so as to become concretised as new clinical law?

Although it may be entirely unintended, the assumptions of the clinician rating his patient's dependence and proceeding with the appropriate treatment regimen do seem to overlook the most powerful and significant factor in the system - the patient or client himself. The negotiation over an appropriate drinking goal may have medically or dependence-based guidelines, but must take account of what the patient or client actually wants for himself or herself. To date, informed advice and advocacy about abstinence from clinicians has not been matched by informed advice regarding non-abstinent goals, and hence abstinence has been the preferred overall regime. Most patients cannot manage a prolonged abstinence goal, and may want to try a goal of harm-free drinking. In the absence of strong contraindications perhaps, when the patient or client particularly wants it, it is advice and information about harm-free goals we should offer (Thorley, 1980). In my opinion this does not especially involve special techniques to 'unlearn' dependence as opposed to an opening-up of prejudiced clinical attitudes.

However, degree of dependence, however ascertained, may be an important factor in a more paradoxical way. Following an initial period of abstinence and in the absence of other contraindications, it may be that more strongly dependent clients should be advised to try a harm-free drinking regime, particularly if experience shows they cannot abstain (Thorley, 1980), and less dependent patients advised to try abstinence, which they can manage more easily because they are less dependent! If mildly dependent patients fail to remain abstinent, perhaps they too should be advised to try a harm-free drinking goal, which again they might more easily achieve. Drinking goals and success rates may not be so clear cut as 'moderate' equals social drinking and 'severe' equals abstinence. Studies are beginning to appear which suggest that harm-free drinking goals negotiated with physically dependent patients after an initial period of abstinence actually lead to more patient compliance and finally more abstinence! (Caddy, Addington and Perkins, 1978).

It is certainly my own clinical experience that, after an initial period of abstinence, the majority of patients who have been physically dependent respond better in terms of compliance and commitment to a harm-free drinking goal than to an abstinence goal. Alcohol education with regard to risks of varieties of drinking behaviour so as to allow safe drinking without guilt, close support and long-term follow-up seem to be essential components of such an approach. Some of the complexities in the overall management of drinking goals have been discussed elsewhere (Thorley, 1980).

One of the difficulties about the dependence syndrome and related drinking behaviour is that it implies a response to the patient's problems which separates the drinking from the wider antecedent or consequent problems. This is probably not intended by the syndrome's protagonists, and yet a basic issue is at stake. Part of the aridity of clinical responses to alcoholism as a disease has been that they have been too much centred on drinking and abstinence. This was one of the observations that Howard Rankin and I made in our advanced summer school assessment (Rankin, 1982). 'Stop drinking and your problems will stop too' is obviously naive, but a commonly held clinical opinion. Alcohol dependence in degree or strength is in some danger of similarly developing too strong an emphasis between degree of dependence and drinking goal to the exclusion of wider etiological issues. Shaw (1979) in his critique of the syndrome has drawn attention to the omission of a wider etiological view in favour of dependence - centredness. Madden (1979) in reply to Shaw states that his argument

> overlooks the point that alcohol dependence (whatever its aetiology in a given subject) becomes an ongoing and self-perpetuating entity that overshadows its causes and continues when they are no longer operative. Management of the alcoholic requires first and foremost a ruthless and determined assault on the excessive drinking. The results achieved in the course of attendance at AA show that not too much more may be required. (p. 350)

Madden's commitment to the alcohol dependence syndrome is not doubted, but here he appears to state clearly a view that places alcohol dependence and inexorable process to the fore and minimises wider factors. Although the immense value of AA recovery is certain, it applies only to a minority of 'alcoholics', and our thinking must turn from the success of AA to its (and our) failure to be relevant for the vast majority of people with severe drinking problems. Hodgson (1980), perhaps sensing that Madden's extremism was no answer to Shaw's case, which he feels is overstated, admits that in order to understand and help a person who is drinking excessively, it is essential to carry out a broad-based psychosocial assessment

> to identify the minefields that can lead to heavy drinking, the coping strategies that are lacking, negative and irrational thoughts which need to be uprooted and a wide range of personal, social, marital and vocational problems which must be solved. From this kind of thorough assessment, treatment hypotheses will be suggested and it could be argued

that estimating the degree of dependence adds nothing at all. (p. 261)

Such a broad assessment, obligatory when working with drinking problems, gives some idea of the potential complexity of the total system that the patient or client is in. Attempting to estimate the role or degree of dependence is in my opinion also obligatory as it is part of the system, but how much it becomes the central currency of understanding, exchange and dialogue between client and worker depends much more on the particular patient, his circumstances and his existing valuation and cognitive investment in dependence as an idea. He will personally require some organised belief system or framework to hang his meanings on and so order his chaotic world. Perhaps he will bring such a system - for example ideas of having a disease - to the consultation; perhaps he will require one working out with him. Whatever the case, it is the constructions and meanings of the problem, the drinking behaviour and maybe the relatedness between the two which are the most important factors among the wide complexities of dealing with alcohol problems. His problems are his basis for motivation; they may or may not be about drinking. Viewed in this way, it is not my experience that many patients naturally present their problems, their model or conceptual framework, in terms of a dependence continuum or a cluster of events around such an idea. That is not to say that such ordering around a dependence concept is not possible, or not valid for some when it is present, but that it may not be the best strategy with a good many patients and certainly may be less appropriate when talking with clients.

It is in fact the client's or patient's reordering of the meaning of drinking and its relatedness to problems which is at the centre of counselling, a technique of major importance in the alcohol problem field. Counselling encourages self-determination and personal control and responsibility and may not be a very natural interaction for those trained in a 'doctor-patient relationship', centred on diagnosis, prescription and regimen.

THE SYNDROME AS A BASIS FOR PREVENTION

There is little doubt that most alcohol workers now see prevention and alcohol education as a central part of clinical and casework activity. Indeed, all treatment and rehabilitation practice needs to be carried out within a preventive framework. How well does alcohol dependence and the alcohol dependence syndrome fit in with such a preventive framework? Is dependence a useful currency for picking up or averting 'early cases'?

Edwards (1982) has stated that:

> it would be useful health education if the public in general were aware that alcohol had dependence potential. The public need to know more of the dangers and the danger signals, what dependence can mean for themselves or someone in their family, for

someone at work or someone they meet in the pub. Understanding of alcohol dependence should, without overdramatisation, become a part of ordinary awareness. (p. 43)

As well as secondary prevention, this approach implies a primary preventive thrust and there is little doubt that, as part of a package of general health education about alcohol and its harmful effects, dependence, including physical dependence, should be more widely discussed, clarified and demystified. There is no doubt about the value of this in treatment of problem drinkers, in the secondary prevention of the confirmed case. However, unless dependence material is handled very sensitively, a state like the dependence syndrome can appear to the general public, or the 'early case', as nothing but a comforting yardstick for missing or avoiding their own problems. Thus the man in the street can say 'Oh, I am not as bad as that! I can still take or leave my drinks. I've not got that. I am not dependent', when in fact the person concerned has a major intoxication-related problem or is damaging his health and family by regular excessive consumption. Thus, primary prevention media campaigns about alcohol education have learned that emphasis on dependence is emphasis on 'alcoholism', and whilst certainly causing needy clients to come forward for help, it confirms to many other individuals with alcohol problems that they are not at risk (see Chapter 16).

Somehow, the presumed chronological and developmental ordering of alcohol dependence should lend itself easily to preventive strategies. Yet the early dependence features are so variable and heterogeneous, the course so fluctuating and peppered with spontaneous remission that there are no factors firmly predictive of the later stages. So dependence and the dependence syndrome do not form a satisfactory basis for prevention work but only a component of a wider prevention strategy.

THE SYNDROME AS A DISEASE

Finally, what is not in doubt is that Edwards has squarely nailed the syndrome's colours to the disease mast on at least two counts. (1) The scientific evidence suggests pathological mechanisms and processes. (2) The cultural and political background, especially internationally, favours a disease model (Edwards, 1977, p. 137, 1982, p. 4).

The significance here of disease is its implication for practice and meaning between patient or client and practitioner. In countries developing services it may be valid and useful to centre the political thrust and development around a medical, disease-orientated concept and existing organised services. Most countries (Finland's social-work orientated view is an exception) appear to have to pass through a medical model before developing a multidisciplinary model. In countries like the UK and USA, where medical power is dominant and increasingly called into question, services are already multidisciplinary, and invite a model which has more currency and meaning. The problem for both practitioners and patients is that a disease model, however much it is separated from a narrow traditional view, implicitly carries that view (Clare, 1979). The issue of disease models and concepts is not whether they are narrow or eclectic in their ideal application, but how they are perceived and how they are applied practically. In practice, diseases are implicitly, to most observers or sufferers, organic, biological, individually centred, or altered-state orientated. Although the etiology may be broad, or the system between causes and complaints most complex, the problem or condition is always viewed in intrinsic reductionist terms.

So for some patients the intrinsic features of their condition will make it easier for them to present, to be motivated and to recover. This has been the advantage of alcoholism for the last 50 years. For many more, the intrinsic disease features, hinting at cause and personal non-accountability, produce confusion and fail to provide an adequate framework of meaning. These persons either do not come forward, or fail to adjust or recover if they do. This may have been a major dynamic in the failure of alcoholism services to be satisfactory for the majority of persons with alcohol problems. It seems that in developed countries where sophisticated treatment and rehabilitation services exist, alcohol dependence and the alcohol dependence syndrome seen as a disease will have the same shortcomings and disadvantages. Increasingly, developing a multidisciplinary, psychosocial model orientated to early cases and prevention will cause some workers to find the alcohol dependence syndrome conceptually inadequate or limited in application, and thus the onus falls upon them to develop alternative models with wider application and conceptual relevance to developing services. Such models are likely to eschew symptoms, disease and reductionism and embrace problems, people and causal systems (Gawlinski and Robertshaw, 1980; Thorley, 1980, 1981, 1982, 1983, 1985a, b). One alternative model will now be briefly considered.

PLACING ALCOHOL DEPENDENCE IN A MODEL OF PROBLEM DRINKING

We have seen from the preceding discussion that there are serious practical limitations in conceptualising alcohol dependence in the context of work with patients and clients, and indeed many patients and clients will find such concepts quite alien. Alcohol dependence seen as degrees of physical dependence makes for only a narrow range of negotiation and exchange by the client and worker. Is it therefore possible to find a more fundamental and basic view of dependence which can be more easily, or indeed universally, translated into clinical and casework action? There are probably no clear answers to this question but a start has been made by Russell (1971, 1976) and elaborated further by myself (Thorley 1980, 1981, 1982, 1985a, b).

As early as 1971 Russell had been critical of the kind of definition of dependence exemplified by Paton (1969): 'Drug dependence arises when, as a result of giving a drug, forces -

physiological, biochemical, social or environmental - are set up which predispose to continued drug use', and the prominence given to pharmacological evidence and withdrawal symptoms. Russell was concerned about the powerful dependence that man can show on behaviours alone or on drugs or alcohol in the absence of physical withdrawal. Russell (1971, 1976) thus argues that it is not frequent or continued use which denotes dependence but rather the difficulty in refraining from further drug or alcohol use. He suggests a definition that brings together all the elements of so-called 'psychological' dependence and allows for the co-existence of physical dependence:

> The notion of dependence on a drug, object, role, activity or any other stimulus source requires the crucial feature of a negative affect experienced in its absence. The degree of dependence can be equated with the amount of this negative affect which may range from mild discomfort to extreme distress, or it may be equated with the amount of difficulty or effort required to do without the drug, object, etc. (1976, p. 184)

It is easy to see how this would apply to alcohol and so do some justice to the complexity of alcohol dependence: a specific beverage (e.g. whisky), a specific glass, a specific role of 'alcoholic' or 'manliness', a specific activity like going to a pub, in a specific cultural setting, all become modalities of dependence. Here, argues Russell, are powerful bonds related to drinking, bonds that are difficult to break, and it is correct to be reminded of the dependence implicit in Bowlby's (1977) concepts of attachment and loss. Similarly, positive compulsive elements, whether in the obsessive-compulsive category or seen as appetitive behaviours (Orford, 1978), and physical dependence withdrawal symptoms, whether clinically apparent or more covertly pharmacological, may only serve to amplify the negative affect and experience of loss at the core of Russell's view. Dependence seen in this way is basically psychological, not physical, and is also normal but on a continuum of degree or strength and measured by inability to refrain. In 1971 Russell made it clear that the degree of dependence required before it becomes a dependence disorder or is termed addiction is somewhat arbitrary. Here again, we are in the deep waters of assessing 'degrees' or 'severity', but at least the range of dependence to be considered is broader than an alcohol dependence syndrome loaded towards a physiological dependence (Edwards, 1977).

First, there are the various modalities derived from Russell's model: dependence on alcohol, objects, roles, activities etc., all of which can be examined in a wider assessment of dependence and its import to the patient. Then, on entirely empirical and practical grounds, for drugs as well as alcohol, I have further subdivided dependence in order to encourage workers to analyse the dependence system in a way which is still grounded in Russell's phenomenon of negative effect.

Thus, dependence is basically psychological and best considered as a state of sadness, loss, anxiety and, more rarely, craving when an individual has to cease some valued activity. It is made up of at least four related but mutually exclusive elements: (1) <u>primary gain</u>: the reward of the pleasurable intoxicant or anxiolytic effects of alcohol; (2) <u>habit</u>: the repeated ritualised drinking leading to a reinforced <u>drinking</u> pattern; (3) <u>social/subcultural</u>: drinking in a particular social role (e.g. to be manly) or social group (e.g. to be one of the boys!); (4) <u>physiological</u>: evidenced by tolerance and a withdrawal syndrome, clinically or subclinically manifest, relieved and reinforced by further drinking and thus amplifying the basic psychological dependence. Any one of these elements may be 'stronger' than another, and should be taken into account in any assessment of the dependence system. Strong or weak overall dependence does not necessarily bring problems, but where it does, the clinical or casework task is not to eliminate dependence, which is impossible, but to dismantle its problematic elements and constructively direct them into other less problematic activities (Thorley, 1980). A mass of clinical and casework techniques already exist to facilitate such a reorganisation of dependence. Such a dependence model, which is empirical and emphasises psychological rather than physiological factors, has been found by this author to have been easily understood and seen as practically useful in various multidisciplinary teaching and training settings.

How then does such a concept of dependence fit into a wider multidisciplinary view of problem drinking? Basically, it does so by relating various modalities of problems to various basic elements of drinking behaviour, in a non-diagnostic but problem- and task-orientated perspective. Thus, I have defined a problem drinker as 'any person who experiences psychological (personal), physical (medical), social or legal problems related to intoxication and/or regular excessive consumption and/or dependence associated with his or her own drinking of alcohol' (Thorley, 1983, 1985a).

Strictly speaking, each element of drinking behaviour can be represented as non-problematic or normal: intoxication without hazards; regular consumption without being excessive and hence problematic; and dependence without related problems. However, the definition described above implies alcohol related consequences and problems, and each drinking element can be operationalised for research purposes and a more objective clinical use. Thus intoxication refers to significant mental and physical inco-ordination due to alcohol and a blood alcohol concentration in excess of 40mg%. Regular excessive consumption refers to drinking on four or more days a week in excess of a daily critical limit of ethanol associated with excess morbidity and social problems: ten units a day for men and six units a day for women. Dependence is defined in a multimodal way as above.

This problem- and task-orientated model of problem drinking informs a preventive, rehabilitative and treatment approach for a wide range of disciplines. The pattern of problematic drinking may fall into any of the three interrelated (but not mutually exclusive) elements and, conveniently, each element produces its own characteristic problems which fall into medical, social and legal categories. Thus the model requires a careful assessment of the system of antecedent and consequent factors, both positive and negative, in medical, social and legal modalities (Thorley 1980, 1982, 1983, 1985a) (see Figure 5.1).

Figure 5.1: An Explanatory System for Problem Drinking

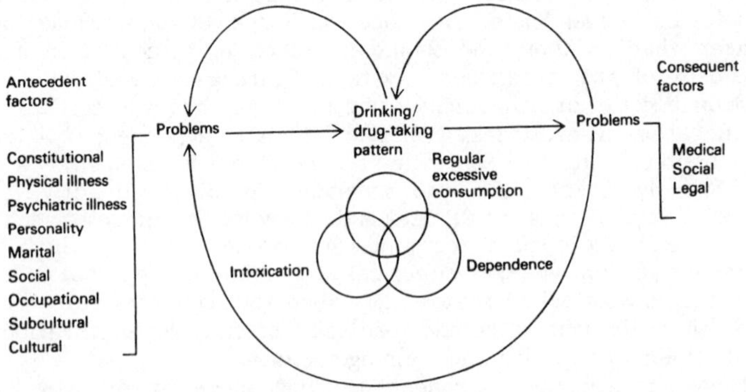

It is clear that alcohol problems are not seen here implicitly as diseases, although physical pathology may be present, but as patterns of behaviour leading to a variety of problems of personal and social functioning. Often, the three basic elements overlap to give a composite, but in planning prevention, rehabilitation and treatment it is most instructive to identify the contribution of each element to the whole. So here, dependence is placed in a wider context of alcohol-related problems. The model avoids fitting people into a diagnosis of alcoholism or alcohol dependence, neither does it take a syndromal view with its implicit symptomatology and outcome, but concentrates on the variety of an individual's problems and the implications of a variety of relevant responses. It is more a psychosocial system than a medical model.

The variety and reliability of such a model has yet to be tested under rigorous conditions. However, it is easy to see how it could be developed in a multiaxial classification with both clinical and research applications. Experience already shows it to be particularly valuable in multidisciplinary teaching, whether teaching social workers about physical damage, doctors about social process, or teaching both about principles of education and early intervention. While in no way entirely avoiding the medical model, it is sufficiently demedicalised and neutral to have a potentially wider appeal amongst professions than a narrower dependence-orientated view. It attempts to relate alcohol disabilities (problems) more specifically to drinking patterns which include dependence, along with intoxication and regular excessive consumption. It may therefore answer some of the problems raised by the alcohol dependence syndrome in a multidisciplinary setting, but will doubtless generate questions and limitations of its own. Further work to test this model is actively under consideration.

REFERENCES

Alcohol Education Centre (1980) Evaluation of 12th Summer School on Alcoholism, York 1980, unpublished internal report
Allan, H. (1979) The Assessment of Alcohol Related Problems in Social Work Case Loads, unpublished dissertation: Alcohol Studies Centre, Paisley College of Technology
Bowlby, J. (1977) 'The making and breaking of affectional bonds. I. Aetiology and psychopathology in the light of attachment theory', British Journal of Psychiatry, 130, 201-10
Caddy, G.R., Addington, H.J. and Perkins, D. (1978) 'Individualised behaviour therapy for alcoholics: a third-year independent double-blind follow-up', Behaviour Research and Therapy, 16, 345-62
Cameron, D. (1981) 'Is dependence a necessary explanatory concept?', New Directions in the Study of Alcohol Group, Members' Booklet No. 1
Camberwell Council on Alcoholism (1980) Women and Alcohol, London: Tavistock
Chick, J. (1980a) 'Alcohol dependence: methodological issues in its measurement, reliability of the criteria', British Journal of Addiction, 75, 175-86
____ (1980b) 'Is there a unidimensional alcohol dependence syndrome?', British Journal of Addiction, 75, 265-80
____ and Duffy, J.C. (1979) 'Application to the alcohol dependence syndrome of a method of determining the sequential development of symptoms', Psychological Medicine, 9, 313-19
Clare, A. (1979) 'The disease concept in pschiatry' in P. Hill, R. Murray and A. Thorley (eds), Essentials of Postgraduate Psychiatry, London: Academic Press
DHSS (1978) The Pattern and Range of Services for Problem Drinkers, Report by Advisory Committee on Alcoholism, London: HMSO
____ (1979) Education and Training, Report by Advisory Committee on Alcoholism, London: HMSO
Dobson, M.C. (1980) 'Nursing assessment in the intervention and management of the problem drinker', paper presented at International Conference of Psychiatric Nursing, Maudsley Hospital

Edwards, G. (1967) 'The meaning and treatment of alcohol dependence', Hospital Medicine, December, 272-80
___ (1977) 'The Alcohol Dependence Syndrome: usefulness of an idea' in G. Edwards and M. Grant (eds), Alcoholism: New Knowledge and New Responses, London: Croom Helm
___ (1980) 'Alcoholism treatment: between guesswork and certainty' in G. Edwards and M. Grant (eds), Alcoholism Treatment in Transition, London: Croom Helm
___ (1982) The Treatment of Drinking Problems: A Guide for the Helping Professions, London: Grant McIntyre Medical and Scientific
___ and Gross, M.H. (1976) 'Alcohol dependence: provisional description of a clinical syndrome', British Medical Journal, 1, 1058-61
Fisher, W. (1980) The Primary Care Team and Alcohol Related Problems, unpublished diploma dissertation: Alcohol Studies Centre, Paisley College of Technology
Freed, A. (1976) Alcoholism: The Interaction of Alcoholics in a Therapeutic Community, unpublished MS.
Gawlinski, G. and Robertshaw, S. (1980) 'Differential approaches to the problem drinker within a framework of personal growth' in J.S. Madden, R. Walker and W.H. Kenyon (eds), Aspects of Alcohol and Drug Dependence, Tunbridge Wells: Pitman Medical
Glatt, M.M. (1980) Personal communication
Heather, N. (1976) Radical Perspectives in Psychology, London: Methuen
___ and Robertson, I. (1981) Controlled Drinking, London: Methuen
Hodgson, R.J. (1980) 'The Alcohol Dependence Syndrome: a step in the wrong direction?', British Journal of Addiction, 75, 255-64
___ Stockwell, T., Rankin, H.J. and Edwards, G. (1978) 'Alcohol dependence: the concept, its utility and measurement', British Journal of Addiction, 73, 339-42
___ Rankin, H.J. and Stockwell, T. (1979) 'Alcohol dependence and the priming effect', Behaviour Research and Therapy, 17, 379-87
Hore, B.D., Ritson, E.B. and Thomson, A.D. (1982) Alcohol and Health: A Handbook for Medical Students, London: Medical Council on Alcoholism
Madden, J.S. (1979) 'Commentary on Shaw', British Journal of Addiction, 74, 349-52
___ (1980) 'Controversy and development' in J.S. Madden, R. Walker and W.H. Kenyon (eds), Aspects of Alcohol and Drug Dependence, Tunbridge Wells: Pitman Medical
McGarva, S. (1979) The Measurement of Alcohol Problems in Social Work Case Loads, unpublished dissertation, Paisley College Alcohol Studies Centre
McKee, A.D. (1980) A Study of Alcoholic Relapse, unpublished diploma dissertation, Paisley College Alcohol Studies Centre
Murray, R.M. and Bernhadt, M. (1980) 'Early detection of alcoholism', Medicine, 35, 1811-15
Orford, J. (1978) 'Hypersexuality: implications for a theory of

dependence', British Journal of Addiction, 73, 299-310

Paton, W.D.M. (1969) 'Definitions and approaches', in H. Steinberg (ed.), Scientific Basis of Drug Dependence, London: Churchill

Plant, M.L. (1980) 'Nurse education: present problems and future needs' in J.S. Madden, R. Walker and W.H. Kenyon (eds), Aspects of Alcohol and Drug Dependence, Tunbridge Wells: Pitman Medical

Polich, J.M., Armor, D.J. and Braiker, H.B. (1980) The Course of Alcoholism: Four Years after Treatment, Santa Monica: Rand Corporation

Raistrick, D., Dunbar, G. and Davidson, R. (1983) 'Development of a questionnaire to measure alcohol dependence', British Journal of Addiction, 78, 89-96

Rankin, H.J. (1982) 'Teaching assessment', British Journal of Addiction, 77, 225-7

___ Hodgson, R. and Stockwell, T. (1979) 'The concept of craving and its measurement', Behaviour Research and Therapy, 17, 389-96

___ and Stockwell, T. (1980) 'The behavioural measurement of dependence', British Journal of Addiction, 75, 43-8

___ Stockwell, T. and Hodgson, R. (1982) 'Cues for drinking and degrees of alcohol dependence', British Journal of Addiction, 77, 287-96

Royal College of Psychiatrists (1979) Alcohol and Alcoholism, London: Tavistock

Russell, M.A.H. (1971) 'Cigarette smoking: natural history of a dependence disorder', British Journal of Medical Psychology, 44, 1-16

___ (1976) 'What is dependence?' in G. Edwards, M.A.H. Russell, D. Hawks and M. MacCafferty (eds), Drugs and Drug Dependence, London: Lexington Books

Shaw, S. (1979) 'A critique of the concept of the Alcohol Dependence Syndrome', British Journal of Addiction, 74, 339-48

___ Cartwright, A., Spratley, T. and Harwin, J. (1978) Responding to Drinking Problems, London: Croom Helm

Stockwell, T., Hodgson, R., Edwards, G., Taylor, C. and Rankin, H.J. (1979) 'The development of a questionnaire to measure severity of alcohol dependence', British Journal of Addiction, 74, 79-87

___ Murphy, D. and Hodgson, R. (1983) 'The Severity of Alcohol Dependence Questionnaire: its use, reliability and validity', British Journal of Addiction, 78, 145-56

Thorley, A. (1980) 'Medical responses to problem drinking', Medicine, 35, 1816-22

___ (1981) 'Beyond the medical model: developing a pragmatic task-orientated model of alcohol problems for multidisciplinary services', paper presented at Fifth International Conference on Alcohol Related Problems, Liverpool

___ (1982) 'The effects of alcohol' in M. Plant (ed.), Drinking and Problem Drinking, London: Junction Books

___ (1983) 'Problem drinkers and drugtakers' in F.N. Watts and D.H. Bennett (eds), Theory and Practice of Psychiatric

Rehabilitation, London: John Wiley

_____ (1985a) 'Psychiatric aspects of problem drinking', Medicine International, March

_____ (1985b) 'Drug problems' in P. Hill, R. Murray and A. Thorley (eds), Essentials of Postgraduate Psychiatry, London: Academic Press

WHO (1977) Alcohol Related Disabilities, Geneva: WHO Offset Publication, No. 32

Wilson, P. (1980) Drinking in England and Wales, London: OPCS, HMSO

PART TWO

DOES TREATMENT WORK?

INTRODUCTION

Ian Robertson

The issue of whether treatment is the most appropriate way of dealing with problem drinkers is as controversial now as it was a hundred years ago, not least among problem drinkers themselves. After all, if problem drinkers were fully in favour of treatment there would hardly exist the clamour for compulsory intervention which is growing today. Nevertheless, large numbers of desperate people present themselves every day for help, and the question posed in this part of the book is whether we as therapists and professionals can, with a clear conscience, offer them more than they could do themselves.

The question posed begs a myriad of other questions, not least of which is how we conceive of the problem to be treated. If 'alcoholism' is an illness caused by biochemical imbalances in the brain, then treatment is a straightforward pharmacological exercise. But, of course, it is in vain that we await such a panacea. Even Alcoholics Anonymous did not sit around waiting for the scientific breakthrough; they developed a religio-moral/social-psychological/behavioural programme for the treatment of the problem which has only the most superficial links with a disease model of alcoholism.

If, on the other hand, problem drinking is seen as a moral failing, then moralistic exhortation follows as the logical treatment and substantial vestiges of such an approach in medical consultations have been documented by Davies (1979, and Chapter 10 below). Viewing problem drinking as a bad habit, habit-changing, behavioural interventions take their place as the treatment of choice and Alcoholics Anonymous are the most widespread practitioners of behavioural treatment for alcoholism in the world, setting as they do short-term goals for their members, and offering as they do highly structured programmes for achieving these goals.

Until we have a working consensus about the nature of problem drinking, it is unlikely that we will ever be able to offer a conclusive answer to the question, Does treatment work? This is because we do not agree what we are treating, as the papers in Part One of this book clearly demonstrate. Why, then, ask the question? First, in the act of asking it we have elicited some very interesting answers

97

which, even if they do not provide unequivocal solutions, set out a promising agenda for future discussion and research in this area. Secondly, a number of commentators, notable among them Saunders (see Chapter 6), have interpreted some recent studies as saying that treatment most definitely does not work. However premature such a conclusion may be, given the uncertainty as to what it is that is being treated, their having answered the question in this way requires us to examine it again. Thirdly, we must face up to the fact that, as Saunders cogently demonstrates, treatment has had no measurable impact upon the prevalence of drinking problems; if treatment works, why is this so? Finally, and perhaps most importantly, the question must be asked because the implications of concluding that treatment does not work are profound. At best, treatment personnel must then cope with a sense of professional futility, and at worst, with unemployment. What effects would this conclusion about treatment have on public attitudes to problem drinkers? How would their families react if told that nothing could be done? Would the problem drinkers more readily face up to their own responsibilities if thrown entirely upon their own resources, or would they more readily commit suicide? These crucial questions inevitably follow, however unwelcome, from asking whether treatment works. Most of the contributors in the six chapters of this section tackle the central question by asking, What is meant by 'treatment' and what is meant by 'work'? We will consider some of the issues raised by each of these queries in turn.

Treatment conceived of as detoxification is not discussed here, though there is little doubt that at times medical treatment for the short-term effects of alcohol on the body is both necessary and, in some senses of the word, that it works. The role of purely medical interventions in producing long-term abstention or moderate drinking is far less obvious, with the use of antabuse and abstem-type drugs standing out as possibly the only contenders for a place in this therapeutic basket - hence, perhaps, the present assembly of authors from the disciplines of psychology, sociology, social work and management consultancy.

A number of themes emerge from some or all of Chapters 6-11 which help clarify discussion of what is meant by treatment. The first concerns the extent to which the client is expected to be active or passive in the treatment endeavour. Cartwright (Chapter 7) and Yates (Chapter 9), in particular, question the way in which treatment is often prescribed as if it were some form of pharmacological agent administered to a patient whose expectations and views were irrelevant to its action. When one attempts to view treatment from the client's point of view, many therapists and therapies are shown to be wanting in that they simply do not take into account the beliefs and aspirations of the recipients of that treatment.

A second theme arising below concerns the relationship between treatment and spontaneous remission. Both Rollnick (Chapter 8) and Cartwright (Chapter 7) suggest a common conceptual base underlying the processes involved in therapeutic change on the one hand, and in spontaneous remission on the other. Saunders (Chapter 6) also allows that 'rehabilitation' might work to the extent that it harnesses natural recovery forces in the client's life. A potentially extremely fruitful area of research is suggested by such a synthesis.

A third issue arising below concerns matching clients to treatment. This relates closely to the question of client activity/passivity and Rollnick suggests that a systematic analysis of client expectations would allow a more adequate treatment response tailored to the individual. Cartwright provides some interesting preliminary data suggesting that different types of client experience different aspects of a therapeutic regime as helpful. Whether a policy of 'horses for courses' is practicable in most treatment agencies is left to the reader to decide.

Fourthly, the question arises as to who should treat. Is a corps of highly trained professionals carrying out sophisticated therapies what is needed, or is it a collection of committed and empathic counsellors with a minimum of technical expertise that is required? Perhaps it is managerial acumen in service providers which is most sorely lacking, as Gawlinski and Otto (Chapter 11) would suggest.

Fifthly, the issue of treatment goals may be relevant to the discussion of what treatment is. Until recently, abstinence was the only acknowledged goal of treatment, yet we know now that many problem drinkers benefit from non-abstinence goals. This imbalance should be borne in mind when assessing the treatment efficacy literature.

Finally, the reader is asked to decide to what extent each writer considers treatment technology a dead issue. Is it the case that everything works as well, or as badly, as everything else? Is therapeutic effectiveness really simply a question of therapist characteristics? Rollnick and Cartwright argue from opposite positions here, though there are some interesting hints of common ground between them. It is a useful exercise to try to place the other writers on this dimension, though Gawlinski and Otto (Chapter 11) regard it almost as an irrelevance against the background of practical complexities in maintaining a service. Their contribution is surely a most necessary antidote to the tendency, especially apparent among clinical psychologists, to set up sophisticated treatment research programmes which they then abandon once the data are collected. The psychologists do not often wait around to see whether the prestige programme crumbles once the limelight and funds are withdrawn.

The diversity of meanings of treatment described above demonstrates just how difficult it is to answer the question, 'Does treatment work?' What treatment? With whom? Under what circumstances? The area is further complicated, however, when one considers the diversity of ways in which treatment might be considered to 'work'. One can look, as Saunders does, at the prevalence figures for alcohol problems in a given country and see whether an increase in treatment services results in a reduced prevalence of the problem. At the other end of the spectrum, one can ask the individual whether he or she has been helped by treatment. Both of these approaches have their methodological difficulties; extrapolation from national figures to individual outcome in this manner has many pitfalls, while anecdotal reports are notoriously unreliable.

The controlled treatment trial is probably the most frequently used way of trying to overcome the types of problem inherent in the evaluation methods mentioned above. Cartwright criticises the philosophical basis of such trials when applied to interventions based upon human relationships, however; he maintains that the human variables which these trials attempt to equalise are the very factors which produce therapeutic change. It is left to the reader to decide whether this is in fact a fundamental philosophical problem of the controlled trial, or merely a case of researchers failing to control the most relevant variables.

Another issue in treatment evaluation concerns absolute versus relative effectiveness. Given that most treated problem drinkers drink some alcohol within a year of completing treatment (e.g. Orford and Edwards, 1977), the outcome category 'successful abstinence' is not likely to be a useful one. The extent of abstinence and moderate drinking as outcome measures is likely to give richer and more representative descriptions of post-treatment behaviour. Where post-treatment data are supplied without any comparative control data, little can be concluded about treatment efficacy, though conclusions continue to be drawn in this way (see, e.g., Pendery, Maltzman and West, 1982). Although the controlled trial is a powerful way of providing such comparisons, it is often difficult to implement and other methods are available (see Orford, 1980).

One must also consider whether an improvement in drinking need always be the primary aim of treatment. Yates (Chapter 9) argues that an unacknowledged use of treatment made by some clients is simply that of recuperating between bouts, and he suggests that making this explicit to staff and clients, where appropriate, might reduce confusion and demoralisation among all involved. For such individuals, treatment 'working' might mean no more than the prevention of severe physical deterioration.

The notion of treatment effectiveness should be broadened such that it focuses less strongly on drinking itself and more on the adjustment of the client. While this point has been made many times before (e.g. Gerard and Saenger, 1966), the reader must decide how seriously this is taken by the authors writing below. And finally, let us not forget that the touchstone of treatment effectiveness may not lie ultimately in the results of controlled trials conducted under extraordinary experimental conditions. While these are important, they are only valuable insofar as they lead to routine services which are capable of sustained therapeutic effectiveness in the everyday clinic or counselling centre. Gawlinski and Otto's chapter again makes a salutary point here.

Does treatment work? Not surprisingly, no clear answer has emerged to this bald question, though all of the authors agree that, in some senses of the phrase, therapeutic endeavours with the problem drinker can work. The strength of these contributions is that they begin to spell out the conditions under which effective treatment might be achieved, and the reader must decide whether treatment is a cost-effective enterprise given these conditions. An agenda has been set for researchers and clinicians which will result, it is to be hoped, in a clearer specification over the next decade of these parameters.

REFERENCES

Davies, P. (1979) 'Motivation, responsibility and sickness in the psychiatric treatment of alcoholism', British Journal of Psychiatry, 134, 449-58

Gerard, D.L. and Saenger, G. (1966) Out-patient Treatment of Alcoholism: A Study of Outcome and its Determinants, Toronto: University of Toronto Press

Orford, J. (1980) 'Understanding treatment: controlled trials and other strategies' in G. Edwards and M. Grant (eds), Alcoholism Treatment in Transition, London: Croom Helm

___ and Edwards, G. (1977) Alcoholism, Oxford: Oxford University Press

Pendery, M., Maltzman, V. and West, L. (1982) 'Controlled drinking by alcoholics, new findings and a re-evaluation of a major affirmate study', Science, 217, 69-174

Chapter 6

TREATMENT DOES NOT WORK: SOME CRITERIA OF FAILURE

Bill Saunders

INTRODUCTION

Any consideration as to whether a product works involves the setting up of standards against which it may be assessed. Naturally, different criteria may produce different estimates of effectiveness, and thus any evaluation of a product requires that the standards against which it is tested are deemed as fair by both supporters and critics alike. It is contended in this chapter that the treatment of alcohol-related problems, as currently perceived and practised, fails to measure up to the various criteria against which it may reasonably be evaluated, and therefore can be considered as 'not working'.

However, before becoming embroiled in this examination of the effectiveness of treatment for alcohol problems, it is necessary to set some parameters as to what constitutes treatment. This is not an easy task to fulfil, and since this chapter is contentious it is essential to establish a framework of treatment with which most treatment providers will agree. It seems appropriate, therefore, to borrow from the work of one treatment provider who does believe that treatment works. In a recent paper, Thorley (1983) has argued that treatment is an activity which is characterised by its individual focus, and by the use of specific modalities of intervention aimed at removing or reducing identified symptoms or problem behaviours. Treatment is perceived as being 'done to' passive recipients and is usually a short-term response. Thorley usefully distinguishes between treatment and rehabilitation, with the latter being a far broader concept in which individuals are helped to 'establish a state ... in which they are capable of coping with situations encountered, thus enabling them to take advantage of the opportunities that are available to other people in the same age group'. In this model of rehabilitation, the individual's responsibility for his/her own behaviour is stressed, as is the emphasis on the active acquisition of new skills.

It would, I suspect, be tempting for the pro-treatment lobby to suggest that rehabilitation is what they really do, and treatment as defined is some anachronistic hangover from the early days of the disease _Zeitgeist_. Before such claims are made, however, it is important to note Thorley's own contention that in the current response to alcohol problems rehabilitation approaches are uncommon, and he argues for a shift to rehabilitation in the future.

It is also relevant to note that there is nothing in the two most recent and major evaluations of counselling procedures for alcohol problems (viz Orford and Edwards, 1977; Polich, Armor and Braiker, 1980) to suggest that what was being offered as intervention was anything other than counselling that falls well within Thorley's parameters of treatment. Although both studies have been criticised on various grounds (e.g. see Emrick and Stilson, 1977; Tuchfeld, 1977), none of these objections indicate that the intervention being evaluated was unrepresentative of, or not in accord with, current thinking or practice about help for people with alcohol problems. It is contended, therefore, that most persons coming into contact with a helping agency do receive aid which comes within the criteria of treatment outlined above.

THE IMPACT OF TREATMENT ON THE PREVALENCE OF ALCOHOL PROBLEMS

A comparatively straightforward test of the success of an endeavour is to determine whether the service as delivered actually achieves the expectations or goals of those who initially planned it. The development of treatment services for people with alcohol problems in Britain is of recent occurrence and owes its origins to a sub-committee of a WHO Expert Committee on Mental Health (WHO, 1951). This sub-committee was set up in 1951 to consider appropriate responses to the problems posed by alcohol. The committee, having reviewed the various options of prevention, education and treatment, concluded that an urgent and extensive treatment endeavour was necessary so that the number of persons with alcohol problems could be reduced. The committee also decided that this treatment response needed to occur before any preventive exercises were mounted. The expectation and intent were clear -the provision of an extensive range of treatment agencies would reduce the number of persons experiencing problems relating to their consumption of alcohol.

It is unfortunate, but only too evident, that this prime objective has not been achieved (e.g. see Department of Health and Social Security, 1981). In spite of the adoption by successive Ministers of Health of this treatment-oriented policy and the acceptance of subsequent recommendations from WHO Expert Committees, the establishment of a network of regional Alcohol Treatment Units and voluntary agencies has not reduced the number of people with alcohol problems. As we are all only too aware, over the past two decades all the indices of alcohol-related harm have increased dramatically. The realisation that treatment was not containing, let alone reducing alcohol problems caused the WHO to reverse its recommendations. In the most recent technical report on alcohol problems (WHO, 1980), it was duly recorded that:

In recent years, the treatment of people identified as

'alcoholics' has been the main focus of attempts to combat alcohol problems...however there has been a progressive disenchantment with this approach. Partly this is due to an increasing recognition of the fact that alcohol dependence is only one component in a broad range of disorders, but the primary reason is the disturbing lack of evidence of the efficacy of elaborate and expensive therapeutic regimes. (pp. 45- 6)

This Expert Committee emphasised that a change of perspective from treatment to prevention was vital and noted that even in wealthy and well-equipped countries (and this includes Britain) treatment should not be the main response. They also damningly noted that: 'Indeed it could be argued that countries which have as yet invested little in the treatment of alcohol-related problems have a valuable opportunity to respond in more appropriate ways than countries whose massive investment in treatment makes any shift in priorities extremely contentious' (p.54). As is indicated in the WHO Report, a re-examination of the value of treatment can be contentious, especially to those who invest their time and endeavour in the provision of services. None of us like to believe that the emperor we serve has no clothes.

TREATMENT OUTCOME RESEARCH
A second test of the effectiveness of treatment is to review the existing treatment-evaluation research and determine whether such research contains answers to some basic questions. Of course, what questions you ask vary according to your perspective, and to some extent, according to your naivety. Clinical work repeatedly brings one into contact with some embarassingly forthright queries. These usually come from the spouses of patients and may include questions like the following: 'Will he get better? Will she get better? What are his chances of being cured, or where can she get the best treatment from?'

The answers to such questions are, I suspect, more likely to reflect the clinical need to encourage hope and optimism rather than a true regard of research and clinical findings. It is pertinent to note that researchers and clinicians will eschew such questions, noting that they are improper, lack an understanding of the real nature of the problem, or require considerable fine tuning before accurate answers could be given. Such equivocation is due to two reasons, and one is to do with treatment and the other with research. To deal with treatment first, it is relevant to consider a comment from Orford (1978) who noted that: 'If we are honest with ourselves, we have to admit that we are impotent to prevent alcoholism occurring and have recorded little success in treating it.' (p.5)

This statement seems to be esentially correct; for whilst it is beyond the scope of this chapter to review exhaustively the alcohol-problem treatment literature, the overwhelming impression to be gained from any perusal of the literature is indeed one of 'failure to record much success'. Although a variety of reviews do exist it is pertinent to cite the work of three authors and re-state with some added riders the conclusions drawn by each. The selection of the following quotations from these works has been careful and is deemed to reflect the central thrust of the reviewer's conclusions.

Emrick (1974, 1975) reviewed some 380 treatment studies published prior to 1974. He discarded all but 72 of these on the grounds of flawed or inadequate research design, and out of these, only five indicated that any one treatment approach was superior to its control method. A close examination of these studies showed that the reported superiority was in all probability due to the comparison treatment being offered as a second-best or mock treatment which may have actually harmed participants' prospects of recovery. Emrick also analysed the outcomes of those studies which allowed a comparison to be made of treatment against no or only minimal treatment. He duly concluded that: 'In a practical sense alcoholics are as likely to stop drinking completely for six months or longer . . when they have no or minimal treatment as when they have more than minimal treatment.' (p.98) Emrick then continued on the following page to note that 'clearly the sizeable expenditure of human and financial resources for alcoholism has not been in vain.' (p.99)

This contradictory statement appears to be based on the finding that the 'total improved' rate (an accumulative index including non-abstinent but functioning-well patients) was associated with amount of treatment received. Here Emrick seems to have fallen into the pernicious trap of interpreting a finding of association as one of cause and effect. It is just as (or perhaps more) likely that persons who are determined to stop drinking as they enter treatment remain in that treatment, whereas the less convinced drift away after initial contact. Thus, any association between amount of treatment and good outcome could well be spurious. It is relevant to add that in Orford and Edwards' study of 100 male out-patient attenders (Orford and Edwards, 1977) no significant effects were found between overall outcome and amount of treatment, and similarly Armor, Polich and Stambul (1978) warn against accepting this type of association as indicative of some type of treatment/outcome interaction. There is thus little in Emrick's review which promotes the view that treatment is a potent force in recovery.

The second review, that by Clare (1977), is of interest because he was able to include the results of the two major treatment studies reported in the 1970s (i.e. Orford and Edwards, 1977 and Armor et al., 1978) and draw up a set of conclusions about the nature of treatment for alcohol problems. Of his six conclusions, four speak directly to the 'does treatment work' question. Clare's first conclusion was that only a small proportion of 'alcoholics' achieve abstinence after receiving treatment, no matter how intensive or prolonged that intervention. Indeed, the second Rand Report shows just how small that proportion is. In this four-year follow-up study, Polich et al., (1980) found that 7 per cent of patients reported being abstinent throughout the four-year period, and only a further 14 per cent reported being abstinent throughout the 12 months prior to their fourth-year interview. Thus, the main objective of the overwhelming majority of treatment programmes - that of permanent abstinence - is not being achieved by the overwhelming majority of participants in these programmes.

This is emphatic evidence of treatment failure, yet many treatment providers will claim that compensatory or secondary goals are being met. If this is true, then the many sessions of education and interminable group discussions about the need to stop should be abandoned, and the resources thus liberated given over to the promotion of activities that further enhance the realisation of these secondary goals. However, it is doubtful if many such secondary benefits are being achieved. Any examination of the post-treatment social or psychological functioning of patients indicates that they remain a seriously disadvantaged group (e.g. see Polich et al., 1980). This practice, whereby in the light of negative evaluation the avowed objectives of treatment are altered but the treatment remains the same, is neither helpful to patients nor staff, and tends to engender pessimism in both.

It is also necessary to consider the reported rates of abstention against one of Clare's further conclusions that 'spontaneous' (i.e. without formal treatment) remission is not uncommon, and may well account for a substantial proportion of any successful outcome. Gauging this rate of natural recovery is difficult and estimates vary widely. Clare quotes a figure of 50 per cent, but fails to note over what time period such natural recovery may accrue. In fact 50 per cent is probably an inaccurately high figure, as the rates of spontaneously occurring abstinence obtained in two long-term follow-up studies of problem drinkers by Ojesjo (1981) and by Vaillant (1982b) were, at 15 years, 30 per cent and 35 per cent respectively. It is pertinent to record, however, that in Vaillant's study, which allowed a comparison with treatment-outcome rates, the author was forced to conclude that the results of treatment 'were no better than the natural history of the disease'.

Clare also concluded that different methods or settings of treatment could not be shown to produce different recovery rates. This conclusion of uniformity, that no matter what treatment is given in which locality it does not alter outcome rates, is a real indictment of treatment, and again suggests that recovery or improvement may have little to do with treatment. Indeed, Armor et al. (1978) duly noted, 'It is hard not to conclude that remission and eventual recovery depend to a major extent on the characteristics and behaviour of the individual client rather than on treatment characteristics.'

Clare's final conclusion concerns intensive or less intensive treatment regimens, and he decided that the evidence overwhelmingly supported the notion that circumscribed and modest treatment interventions are as efficacious as more protracted and extensive clinical endeavours. It is interesting that this finding, based at the time of Clare's review on abstinence programmes, has subsequently been reflected in the reduced-alcohol-taking literature. Some findings have shown that a self-help manual with no therapist contact is as good as technologically sophisticated controlled-drinking training which includes in vivo practice (Miller and Taylor, 1980). This lack of support for the assumption that intensive treatment equals better treatment may be, and has been, variously interpreted, but taken in conjunction with Clare's other findings again suggests that the occurrence of treatment is not a major factor in the remission process.

The final, and undoubtedly most authoritative treatment review is that of Miller and Hester (1980). This review is so extensive, and testimony to so much painstaking endeavour, that it is almost churlish to add caveats to its conclusions. However, before doing just that, it is relevant to cite part of the authors' summing up:

> First of all, it is clear that certain treatments are not supported by research to date, which has suggested that they are ineffective, uneconomical or unjustifiably hazardous for problem drinkers ... The majority of treatment procedures for problem drinkers warrant a 'Scotch Verdict' of unproved at the present time. Ironically the most widely accepted and commonly used treatment techniques currently fall into this category of 'unproved'. (p.108)

Again, these reviewers concluded that there was nothing to be gained from intensive treatments, and the overall conclusion from their survey of over 500 treatment studies is that treatment, as currently practised and delivered, cannot be accorded a major role in the giving up of excessive drinking. In making this statement, I am aware that it runs counter to a number of claims made by Miller and his colleagues in subsequent papers, and this is especially true of one very positive and succinct review published by Miller (1980). However, a dispassionate reading of this paper strongly suggests that Miller's favourable opinion of treatment in general may have been influenced by his own specific research into controlled drinking programmes.

In a most interesting series of publications (e.g. see Buck and Miller, 1981; Miller and Munoz, 1982; and Miller, 1982), Miller has compared various approaches, and has established that the original, technologically sophisticated controlled drinking programmes (e.g. Sobell and Sobell, 1973) are no more effective than short-term practical-advice sessions backed up with written material. Miller's reported success rates of 70 per cent or better are impressive, and he has further refined his work to involve testing a form of bibliotherapy (i.e. using a self-help manual) against other treatment procedures. These included testing bibliotherapy against an untreated waiting-list control group and a self-monitoring procedure (Miller and Taylor, 1980). In these trials the bibliotherapy proved to be significantly superior to the no-treatment or self-monitoring procedures and effective for the majority of clients.

However, before this series of experiments is cited as evidence of treatment actually working, it must be noted that all the clients in these experiments were self-referred and the majority were socially stable and employed. These patient characteristics are well known as good prognostic indicators (see, e.g., Costello, 1980), but a more important consideration is the fact that the consumption data reported by this group of patients prior to treatment were on average no more than 50 units per week. This level of consumption is surprisingly modest and should be compared to data obtained in British hospital samples (Plant and Plant, 1979; Allsop, MacIntyre, Saunders and Kershaw, 1983) which indicate that the patients attending various treatment agencies report drinking a mean of between 120 and 175 units of alcohol per week. Indeed, consumption of 50 units per week is within the safe levels laid down by the Royal College of Psychiatrists and, although Miller deserves congratulations for being able to lure such clients into some form of counselling, it is difficult to believe that his results are generalisable to what might be called more 'normal' treatment seeking populations. In many ways these are analogue studies, and before these encouraging results can be admitted to the treatment evaluation literature, their replication using more representative clinical samples is required.

Before leaving the treatment evaluation literature, it is necessary to return to a comment made earlier about research and treatment evaluation. A number of writers have quite correctly criticised the quality of much of the evaluation research, and commented on flawed research design and inadequate statistical analyses. Recently, however, a number of criticisms have appeared which suggest that the methodology appropriate to clinical medicine, most especially the controlled trial, is an inappropriate design for evaluating alcohol problems treatment (e.g. see Chapter 7). It has been argued that the use of research designs and sampling which obscure the individuality of the patient (i.e. by ascribing homogeneity to a heterogeneous group) has also obscured subtle patient-treatment interactions. Whilst having some sympathy for this argument, it is not one which should unduly detract from the overwhelming accumulation of evidence which shows that the experience of treatment adds little to any recovery from alcohol problems. If treatment really was the powerful force some people contend it to be, then this impact would be open to detection even by the putatively limited power of our current research methodology. It seems a dubious practice to lay the blame for the lack of demonstrated effects of treatment on inadequate research, when the alternative interpretation of inadequate treatment is equally available. When there is also evidence from other unrelated areas that treatment may be only a weak contributor to remission, the demand for continuously refined and exact research methodology hints at some lack of objectivity or personal over-investment in the delivery of treatment.

'THE CLIENT SPEAKS': CONSUMERS' VIEWS OF TREATMENT

Having contended that treatment neither reaches the standards set for it initially, nor can be demonstrated by evaluation to be effective, a third source or system of assessment is to question the users of the service about their views of it. In fact, there is little research of 'the client speaks'-type available. There are, however, two studies of treatment in which the patients were asked about their views on what contributed to successful, or at least improved, outcome. In their study of treatment and advice, Orford and Edwards (1977) asked patients to report on the factors they considered to be important in their improvement. Orford and Edwards duly noted:

> In rank order, and in both treatment and advice groups, the four items which are accorded the highest rating do not include in-patient care, out-patient care, AA, or other helping agency contact. What might be deemed the elements of the overt package of help are being seen as less helpful than the three items relating to changes in external reality, intra-psychic change and change in marital relationship. (p.50)

With similar intent, Ross (1980) interviewed a small sample of recovered problem drinkers who during their recovery had made almost exclusive use of the services of one agency - an Alcoholism Treatment Unit, a Council on Alcoholism, a Salvation Army Hostel or AA. In addition, 7 out of the 39 respondents had recovered without receiving any formal treatment. Ross' original intention was to demonstrate that clients attending different agencies would highlight different aspects of the overall treatment they had received as being helpful. It was considered that this would be suggestive of some intuitive matching by clients of their needs to treatment. However, in the event, Ross found that aspects of treatment were seldom reported as an important factor in recovery and that across the different groups surveyed, clients reported a surprising commonality of reasons. These were classified as psychological or social factors, accounted for over 88 per cent of all reasons given, and the single most pertinent factor concerned the vivid recall, or apprehension, of some disastrous personal crisis whilst drinking. Ross duly concluded: 'Treatment has only a very modest role in the maintenance of recovery or remission from alcohol problems.'

In some more detailed research of this nature, Davies (1981) has shown that although the majority of patients are satisfied with what therapists have to offer, those who are dissatisfied are not reluctant to challenge therapists or express their dissatisfaction. In particular, Davies found that patients actively go about seeking practical advice, explanations and guidelines, the absence of which is the source of most dissatisfaction. But in interpreting all of these findings, Kendell's (1979) comment should be borne in mind: 'The most innocent and dangerous of all medical assumptions is that when patients improve it is because of the treatment they have received.'

WHAT MAKES PEOPLE GIVE UP ADDICTION?

Consideration of Kendell's comment opens up the fourth and final part of this analysis of the effectiveness of treatment - that of attempting to find out how people naturally give up addictive behaviour, and then considering whether treatment, as currently practised and delivered, reflects this process. In this examination, three studies are relevant. The first by Tuchfeld (1976) is an intriguing and thought-provoking study in which 51 recovered problem drinkers were carefully interviewed. All of these respondents had achieved their remission without receiving formal treatment. In his report Tuchfeld proposed a tentative model of the process of the giving up of addiction behaviour.

In this essentially two-stage model, Tuchfeld suggests that for the regular heavy drinker adverse consequences gradually accrue so that drinking becomes an increasingly 'costly' behaviour. This increasing toll of drinking eventually impinges upon the drinker who makes a commitment to change. This recognition of costs may be attained gradually or may intrude upon the individual in a sudden, dramatic way. Tuchfeld suggests that the commitment to change leads to successful resolution only if it is supported by the existence or development of maintenance factors. These factors include changes in objective social conditions (such as better housing and employment status) and in the informal social controls of the individual such as peer or family support. These changes are closely interrelated with a gradual change in the overall lifestyle of the individual and the development of new social and psychological reinforcers.

In his final report, Tuchfeld outlined in considerable detail the individual drinking careers of his respondents and the highlighting of one case as an example of the remission process is merited. Case number 101 is the history of a 49-year-old, black, working-class woman who, following the death of her husband, developed a severe drinking problem. Although moderate-to-heavy drinking had been a feature of their marriage, the death of her spouse was associated with a marked increase in her alcohol consumption. The respondent reported regularly drinking in excess of a bottle of spirits a day and sometimes as much as a half-gallon of corn whisky. She experienced a myriad of social and physical harms related to her drinking, and these included vomiting blood, hospitalisation for bleeding ulcers, severe shakes and DTs. This excessive alcohol consumption continued until the following events occurred. The respondent reported that:

> I was sitting in this room - it was 1963 - and my
> mother was in the back stringing beans and I had been
> on a drunk for about 4 weeks just steady ... and I was
> sitting here by myself and I had the T.V. on ... and
> Oral Roberts came on the T.V. and was talking about
> people ... breaking the chain of alcohol ... and I said

'now he's talking jazz you know' ... I had an argument
with everything he said ... my oldest son and his friend
was back there and my mother had a stroke. I ran in
the back, she had fell up against the wall ... her eyes
were open ... her hair was hanging down. I got to
thinking (later) and I wrote Oral Roberts a letter. I had
one dollar and I sent it to him and told him just what
was what ... How I was like I couldn't stop. That I had
children to raise, all the rest. From that day to this
one I haven't drunk anything any stronger than Coca
Cola! (p.F6)

Tuchfeld's report is replete with similar examples, and they
bear out Vaillant's recent comment that: 'Alcoholics appear from
nowhere, bewilder us for a while and then mysteriously vanish.'
Vaillant (1982a)

This natural and 'mysterious' disappearance is a process which
has been little researched, though some investigators have
tentatively addressed the phenomenon. Mulford (1972) has suggested
that the occurrence of adverse events is a vital component in
recovery, and has proposed that as problem drinkers get worse then
so they sow the seeds for their own recovery. This idea has been in
part supported by Chick (1982), who in a provocative and succinct
paper has suggested that treatment may actually harm patients
because it shelters them from the consequences of their own
behaviour. Many questions about the impact of adverse events upon
addiction behaviour need to be asked, and the psychological
processes that underlie this transition from inimical 'dependence' to
remission warrant urgent investigation.

In some ways the second stage of Tuchfeld's model holds less
mystery. In both his study and that of Saunders and Kershaw (1979) a
number of factors that maintain a resolution have been isolated. In
their study of some 60 ex-problem drinkers located in a community
survey, Saunders and Kershaw found that the most common, self-
reported reasons for recovery were items such as physical ill-health,
marriage (or re-marriage), job change and overall life circumstance
change. Tuchfeld's respondents reported likewise, and it is pertinent
to note that in the former study the majority of respondents who
had received some form of treatment did not report the actual
experience of counselling as being of much importance. Several
repeated treatment failures noted that it was only when a new
relationship or new job occurred that the break with heavy alcohol
use became possible. Thus remission is attributable to the social
milieu of the individual rather than the impact of treatment.

The implications of these retrospective studies have been
supported by the work of Moos and his colleagues, who in a series of
publications (e.g. Cronkite and Moos, 1980; Moos, Finney and Chan,
1981, Billings and Moos, 1983) have contrasted the relative
contributions of treatment and external psychosocial factors in the
recovery process. In a recent prospective study, Billings and Moos
(1983) evaluated the impact of post-treatment factors upon the

eventual outcome of 124 alcoholic patients who attended for treatment. On two-year follow-up, 55 of the 113 successfully contacted patients were classified as 'recovered' and 58 'relapsed'. The investigators determined that three factors differentiated between the two outcome groups. The three factors related to family functioning, coping skills and overall level of life stress. When compared to 'relapsers', the 'survivors' were found to have significantly higher levels of familial cohesion, expressiveness and shared recreational activities. The successful clients were also more likely to report the use of active problem-solving skills rather than the use of avoidance coping strategies, such as ignoring problems, blaming others or suppressing problems by taking tranquillizers. The relapsed group also reported significantly higher levels of adverse life events, and fewer - about half as many - positive life events. Importantly, Billings and Moos found that these post-treatment factors were not the consequence of abstinence but were actually contributing toward abstention. They note:

> While we believe that there are reciprocal or bidirectional relationships between alcoholics' environments and their functioning, we wished to determine whether the post-treatment factors under investigation had some 'causal' impact on the recovery that was independent of the alcoholic's prior level of functioning. In a series of longitudinal analyses, we found that stressors (such as negative life events) and social resources (as indexed by work and family support) were significantly related to alcoholic's follow-up functioning even after controlling for prior levels of functioning ... The results support a framework in which post-treatment factors play an active role in the recovery process rather than simply being reflections of alcoholics' level of adaptation. (p.213)

Indeed, in terms of outcome at two-years follow-up, post-treatment factors accounted for more of the explained variance than did treatment or pre-treatment characteristics. Not surprisingly, Billings and Moos urge clinicians to be more flexible and to consider a wider range of personal and environmental factors in their treatment responses. Interestingly, this work is itself supported by research in the other addictions. One major British study of heroin users also places the 'engine room' of remission firmly within the social milieu of the individual (Wille, 1980). In the most recent report of this study in which the careers of 127 heroin addicts who were attending Drug Dependence Clinics in London in the late 1960s were carefully followed for a ten-year period, the interplay between treatment and environmental influences is clearly illustrated.

Wille found that over the period of the follow-up, 40 (31 per cent) of the sample became abstinent. The routes to recovery reported by these ex-heroin users closely parallel those reported in the alcohol studies cited above. One case study, that of Bob O., bears elegant testimony to this. The subject started using heroin at 16, and by 18 was being prescribed 120 mg heroin and 120 mg methedrine on a reducing script. This failed because Bob O. 'wasn't ready to come down' and his life became increasingly chaotic. Job loss, an overdose, trouble with the police and physical ill-health were experienced. Wille notes that 'he was worried by his physical deterioration, his abscesses and overdoses, the death of his best friend from a barbiturate overdose, the decline of his old drug scene and his mother's illness and her complaints about his way of life'. (p.107)

Bob O. then ceased his misuse of sleeping pills and started working regularly, and a gradual reduction of his heroin prescription was begun - this time with his agreement. The subject noted: 'Because I met Ann and I wanted to get married and pack it all in, because I always made a thing in my own head that I would never get engaged or married until I was off drugs; because I knew if I was to get engaged while I was on drugs that I'd still be using today' (pp.107-8).

Wille further reports that: 'After ten years of heroin use, Bob O. became abstinent ... married his girlfriend ... completed a government retraining course as a carpenter and started a successful career. He has his own house and car, and ... has been abstinent for four years'. (p.108)

It is contended that the role of treatment in this remission is very much akin to that of treatment in recovery from alcohol problems. In the case of Bob O., treatment was at best a weak influence, and his decision-making and overall recovery were due to an interaction of chance factors and life events which prompted a commitment to change, plus the opportunities to establish a new, significant relationship and gain employment, social stability and self-respect. Our treatment of alcohol problems with its essentially sick, essentially passive, essentially medical perspective can neither induce nor compel commitment to change, nor ensure the availability of friendships, jobs, houses and enhanced quality of life. Thus treatment is condemned to remain ineffective.

Only one study has directly attempted to manipulate just these external factors and, perhaps not surprisingly, has been found to be very successful (Azrin, 1976; Azrin, Sisson, Meyers and Godfrey, 1982; and see Chapter 8). However, providing problem drinkers with new homes, friendships, motor vehicles and surrogate families is a far cry from the normal provision of treatment services. Within Thorley's (1983) framework such endeavour is emphatically one of rehabilitation. However, in a society bereft of employment, housing and opportunities for self-enhancement, the demand to provide such services to problem drinkers is likely to earn little support.

CONCLUSIONS

In conclusion, therefore, it is contended that in the four areas of assessment undertaken above, treatment must be viewed as not working. It has failed to contain, let alone reduce, the number of problem drinkers, and by so doing has failed to achieve the goals initially set. Research into the overall effectiveness of treatment consistently shows remission rates to be uniform, that no matter the treatment the results remain the same. The majority of participants in treatment fail to achieve the goal(s) set for them by that treatment, and those that achieve some type of recovery constantly fail to cite the treatment received as being of importance in their remission. Finally, close study of untreated remission indicates that recovery is orchestrated by a subtle interaction of personal experience, personal decisions and the opportunity to alter one's lifestyle. Treatment as currently practised and delivered does not address such issues, and as a consequence fails.

I am aware that some colleagues in the field will label this statement as nihilistic, but such a charge is vigorously denied in advance and countered by noting that this perspective is both realistic and essential. In essence our treatment emperor is naked, and pretending that all is well only delays the advent of new and better responses. There is an urgent need for our current haberdashers to set out on the task of refurbishment, a task that will not be achieved by the ever more delicate fine tuning of ineffective and outmoded methods. For those who have already acknowledged the lessons of the recent past and are embarked on the task of radically revising our response to people with alcohol problems, the words of Chick (1982) should be heeded and heeded well: 'The gauntlet has been thrown down: the onus of proof is now on therapists who try to provide more than just succour to show that they are necessary agents in the recovery of their patients.'

Acknowledgements

This chapter has benefited greatly from the helpful comments and advice of Steven Allsop, plus the usual high order of secretarial skill of Georgina Barr.

REFERENCES

Allsop, S., MacIntyre, D., Saunders, W. and Kershaw, P. (1983) A Study of the Effect of an Assessment and Minimal Counselling Session for Persons with Alcohol Problems admitted to a General Medical Ward. A two-year Follow-up Study, Report to the Scottish Home and Health Department, Alcohol Studies Centre, Paisley College of Technology

Armor, D., Polich, J. and Stambul, H. (1978) Alcoholism and Treatment, New York: John Wiley & Sons

Azrin, N. (1976) 'Improvements in the community-reinforcement approach to alcoholism', Behaviour Research and Therapy, 14, 339-48.

_____ Sissons, R., Meyers, R. and Godfrey, M. (1982) 'Alcoholism treatment by Disulfiram and community reinforcement therapy', Journal of Behaviour Therapy and Experimental

Psychiatry, 13, 105-12

Billings, A. and Moos, R. (1983) 'Psychosocial processes of recovery among alcoholics and their families: implications for clinicians and program evaluators', Addictive Behaviours, 8, 205-18

Buck, J. and Miller, W. (1981) 'Why does bibliotherapy work? A controlled study' in W. Miller (ed.), Effectiveness of Bibliotherapy: Empirical Research, Proceedings of Association for Advancement of Behaviour Therapy, Toronto

Chick, J. (1982) 'Do alcoholics recover?' British Medical Journal, 285, 3-4

Clare, A. (1977) 'How good is treatment?' in G. Edwards and M. Grant (eds), Alcoholism: New Knowledge and New Responses, London: Croom Helm

Costello, R. (1980) 'Alcoholism treatment effectiveness: slicing the outcome variance pie' in G. Edwards and M. Grant (eds), Alcoholism Treatment in Transition, London: Croom Helm

Cronkite, R. and Moos, R. (1980) 'The determinants of post-treatment functioning of alcoholic patients: a conceptual framework', Journal of Consulting and Clinical Psychology, 48, 305-16

Davies, P. (1981) 'Expectations and therapeutic practices in outpatient clinics for alcohol problems', British Journal of Addiction, 76, 159-74

Department of Health and Social Security (1981) Drinking Sensibly, London: HMSO

Emrick, C. (1974) 'A review of psychologically orientated treatment of alcoholism. I. The use and inter-relationship of outcome criteria and drinking behaviour following treatment', Quarterly Journal of Studies on Alcohol, 35, 523-49

_____ (1975) 'A review of psychologically orientated treatment of alcoholism. II. The relative effectiveness of different treatment approaches and the effectiveness of treatment versus no treatment', Journal of Studies on Alcohol, 36, 88-108

_____ and Stilson, D. (1977) 'The Rand Report: some comments and a response', Journal of Studies on Alcohol, 38, 152-93

Kendell, R. (1979) 'Alcoholism: a medical or political problem?', British Medical Journal, 1, 367-71

Miller, R. (1980) 'Treating problem drinkers: what works?', The Behaviour Therapist, 5, 15-18

Miller, W. (1982) 'Teaching responsible drinking skills' in P. Miller and T. Nirenberg (eds), Prevention of Alcohol Abuse: Current Issues and Future Directions, New York: Plenum Press

_____ and Hester, R. (1980) 'Treating the problem drinker: modern approaches' in W. Miller (ed.), The Addictive Behaviours, New York: Pergamon Press

_____ and Taylor, C. (1980) 'Relative effectiveness of bibliotherapy, individual and group self-control training in the treatment of problem drinkers', Addictive Behaviours, 5, 13-24

_____ and Munoz, R. (1982) How to Control Your Drinking, 2nd edition, Alburquerque: University of New Mexico Press

Moos, R., Finney, J. and Chan, D. (1981) 'The process of recovery from alcoholism: I. Comparing alcoholic patients and matched community controls', Journal of Studies on Alcohol, 42, 383-402

Mulford, H. (1972) 'Becoming an ex-problem drinker', paper presented at the 30th International Congress on Alcoholism and Drug Dependence, Amsterdam

Ojesjo, L. (1981) 'Long-term outcome in alcohol abuse and alcoholism among males in the Lundby general population, Sweden', British Journal of Addiction, 76, 391-400

Orford, J. (1978) 'The future of alcoholism', Psychological Medicine, 8, 5-8

_____ and Edwards, G. (1977) Alcoholism, Oxford: Oxford University Press

Plant, M.A. and Plant, M.L. (1979) 'Self-reported alcohol consumption and other characteristics of 100 patients attending a Scottish Alcohol Treatment Unit', British Journal on Alcohol and Alcoholism, 14, 197-207

Polich, J., Armor, D. and Braiker, H. (1980) The Course of Alcoholism: Four Years after Treatment, Santa Monica: Rand Corporation

Ross, T. (1980) A Study of Self-Reported Important Factors maintaining Recovery or Remission from Problem Drinking, unpublished ms, Alcohol Studies Centre, Paisley College of Technology

Royal College of Psychiatrists (1978) Alcohol and Alcoholism, London: Tavistock Publications

Saunders, W. and Kershaw, P. (1979) 'Spontaneous remission from alcoholism: results from a community survey', British Journal of Addiction, 74, 251-65

Sobell, M. and Sobell, L. (1973) 'Individualized behaviour therapy for alcoholics', Behaviour Therapy, 4, 49-72

Thorley, A. (1983) 'Rehabilitation of problem drinkers and drug takers' in F. Watts and D. Bennett (eds), Psychiatric Rehabilitation in Theory and Practice, London: John Wiley

Tuchfeld, B. (1976) Changes in Patterns of Alcohol Use without the Aid of Formal Treatment, North Carolina: Center for Health Studies, Research Triangle Institute

_____ (1977) 'Comments on Alcoholism: a controlled trial of "treatment" and "advice"', Journal of Studies on Alcohol, 38, 1804

Vaillant, G. (1982a) 'On defining alcoholism', British Journal of Addiction, 77, 2, 143-4

_____ (1982b) The Natural History of Alcoholism, New York: Yale University Press

Wille, R. (1980) 'Processes of recovery among heroin users' in G. Edwards and A. Arif (eds), Drug Problems in the Sociocultural Perspective, Geneva: WHO Public Health Paper No. 73

WHO (1951) Report of the First Session of the Alcoholism Sub-Committee, Geneva: WHO Technical Report Series No. 42

_____ (1980) Problems related to Alcohol Consumption: A Report of an Expert Committee, Geneva: WHO Technical Report Series 650

Chapter 7

IS TREATMENT AN EFFECTIVE WAY OF HELPING CLIENTS RESOLVE DIFFICULTIES ASSOCIATED WITH ALCOHOL?

Alan Cartwright

Those who answer this question after reviewing studies evaluating alcoholism treatments are invariably pessimistic about the effectiveness of these therapeutic interventions. Yet this opinion conflicts with the experience of many clients and therapists, who see benefit arising from the treatment situation. Debates between the research workers and clinicians invariably bring about stereotyped responses. Research workers may adopt the stance that whilst treatment may work, this has not yet been proved. Alternatively, they may respond that, whilst some alcohol abusers do actually improve, this improvement cannot be attributed to the treatment itself, but is due to a process of 'spontaneous remission', which brings those who have already begun the path of recovery into treatment situations. This argument is based upon the observation that alcohol abusers in control groups do as well as those in treatment groups, implying that treated alcohol abusers would have been equally likely to improve if they had not received any treatment. Such responses tend to be treated with incredulity, anger or despair by the clinician who can point to the simplicity and mundane nature of the research approach, but still feels somewhat impotent in the face of the research worker's claim to 'scientific objectivity'.

In this chapter it is argued that the nihilistic attitude to treatment which often results from an uncritical acceptance of the research studies is unjustified. To a large extent, they have been based upon an inappropriate 'scientific' model of treatment drawn from organic medicine. Consequently, they have been conducted in a manner which has failed to identify the relevant therapeutic processes and effects (see Glaser, 1980 for one interpretation of these results). In this chapter an alternative model for understanding treatment is proposed. This suggests that an often necessary but not always sufficient requirement for treatment effectiveness is a therapeutic relationship marked by a quality called 'therapeutic commitment'. An aspect of 'therapeutic commitment' is that the treatment offered is based upon the presented needs of the client. It is argued that for drinking clients these needs may be quite diverse and that one cannot apply a single treatment approach to all.

Implicit in this model is the view that alcohol abusers can differ quite markedly from one another. They have different needs and may require different types of response to create the type of 'therapeutic experience' which will be most helpful. Further, the type of response that might meet the needs of one person may be quite ineffective when applied to another with ostensibly similar needs. Thus, this chapter argues that the effective therapeutic relationship is based upon the therapist's capacity to understand and respond to clients within their physiological, psychological and social context, whilst also creating the type of therapeutic environment in which the client feels secure.

Before proceeding, a comment needs to be made about the terminological confusion that reigns in this area. Often, the words we use to describe our activities tell us more about the ways we see ourselves than about our behaviour. The very concept of treatment is drawn from the model which is being rejected in this chapter, yet it is often used for the simple reason that colloquially it makes sense. On other occasions, the term 'intervention' is used to describe similar activities, whilst the terms 'alcohol abuser' and 'client' are used to describe the people to whom the therapeutic response is directed.

THE METHODOLOGY OF THE CONTROLLED TRIAL

Most treatment-evaluation studies seek to demonstrate a relationship between changes in the alcohol abuser's condition and exposure to specified treatment. To this end, a methodological tradition, based upon the random assignment of alcohol abusers to 'control' and 'treatment' conditions, has evolved. Random assignment ensures that only those factors relevant to the experiment are systematically allocated. For instance, if a group of alcohol abusers diagnosed as 'alcoholics' were to be included in a treatment experiment, then each would be given an equal chance of being in either 'treatment' or 'control' groups. By this procedure, other characteristics, for instance 'personality factors', are randomly assigned to each group and will not effect the results. The experimental design seeks to achieve a condition in which the results can be interpreted as being due to the effect of a specific treatment on the subject's alcoholism. Concurrently, the 'treatment techniques' are reduced to simpler forms in the hope of identifying an 'active' component. The most obvious examples of this are the study by Edwards, Orford, Egert, Guthrie, Hawker, Hensman, Mitcheson, Oppenheimer and Taylor (1977), which compared a brief counselling procedure with the whole spectrum of treatment offered by the Maudsley Hospital, and the study of focused versus broad-spectrum behaviour therapy by Miller, Taylor and West (1980).

This approach is similar to that used in clinical drug research, where research workers seek to identify the effects of a single active chemical from a compound by the experimental exclusion of all factors except the condition to be treated and the chemical. In the past in these trials, the relationship between the tester and the subject has sometimes influenced the measured effect of the drug, and therefore a sophisticated research design has been evolved to prevent these distortions occurring.

Whilst alcohol treatment studies have not yet gone to the extreme of using these sophisticated methodologies, they have ignored the possibility that the relationship between the person providing the treatment and the alcohol abuser may be an important and genuine therapeutic factor. Indeed, in a seminal review of alcoholism treatment studies (Emrick, 1975), none of the studies described considered this relationship as a possible influence on the outcome of treatment. Instead, they used a model which sought to identify the active technique (i.e. the chemical), whilst excluding the distorting relationship effect (i.e. the placebo). This model would only be appropriate if we assumed that the processes by which alcoholism treatment works were analogous to the chemical effects of a drug on the body. Is the present fashion for using predictive models drawn from the physical sciences, rather than interpretive models drawn from the humanities, to help understand human behaviour which leads to the assumption that such an analogy must be valid.

The limitations of these methodologies were considered in an earlier paper (Cartwright, 1981), where it was argued that there was little justification for considering alcohol abusers as being different from other groups of people with problems, nor for ignoring the role that therapist/client relationships may play in their treatment. Without published studies to support this contention, the argument was advanced by showing that the predictors of successful outcome among treated alcohol abusers were similar to those found when helping other groups of people with problems. The predictors identified were the severity of the problem, the prevalence of crises prior to entering treatment and general levels of social and personal functioning. On this basis, it was suggested that the quality of the relationship between patient and therapist would be as influential in the treatment of alcohol abusers as in other areas of psychotherapy.

Whilst most alcoholism-treatment studies ignore these relationship factors, there are some exceptions. Several studies report that more successful treatment groups were involved in 'treatment milieus' which stressed a more positive relationship between staff and alcohol abusers. In Cartwright's review, it was suggested that the key element in this positive relationship was 'the therapist's communicated commitment to the therapy interaction and involvement in the problems of a specific patient in that interaction' (Kiesler, Mathine and Klein, 1967). This concept was referred to as 'therapeutic commitment'.

Examination of the general psychotherapy literature made it possible to describe some of the characteristics of therapists which might be associated with the development of therapeutic commitment. These included therapists' willingness to work with drinking clients, their expectations of finding this work satisfying, their feelings concerning the adequacy of their skills and knowledge, the extent to which they felt they had the right to be undertaking this work, and their general feelings of worth in regard to the specific task of helping drinkers. Other studies had shown that these features were most likely to develop when therapists were clinically well-trained, experienced, of high self-esteem, and working in conditions where they felt themselves to be supported (Shaw, Cartwright, Spratley and Harwin, 1978; Cartwright, 1980, 1982). The presence of these features seemed to appear in conjunction with the therapist's capacity to develop an empathetic relationship with the client, and together they could facilitate clients' experience of talking to someone who was committed to their well-being. In this context the term empathy was used to describe the therapist's ability to understand the client's experience from the client's perspective, and to communicate that understanding.

THE ROLE OF EMPATHY AND COMMITMENT IN COUNSELLING PROBLEM DRINKERS

Though empathy is a central feature in many different therapeutic systems, there are three main ideas about its influence. First, empathy is seen as the basic medium by which one can understand another person's inner world (e.g. Kohut, 1959). Secondly, when accurately communicated, it may bring into focus thoughts, feelings or behaviours of which the other person is only vaguely aware, and may then have the effect of deepening the 'depth of self-exploration' (e.g. in Truax and Carkhuff (1973), and indirectly in the discussion of interpretation in Malan (1979)). Thirdly, the effect of being in an empathetic relationship is sometimes considered to directly bring about changes in the way persons experience and understand themselves (e.g. Kohut, 1971). Central to the second and third viewpoints is the suggestion that a link exists between therapeutic empathy and the types of change in self-experience which often accompany a successful recovery. Consequently, one might predict that the presence of therapeutic empathy would facilitate recovery among alcohol abusers.

Two studies allow one to test the hypothesis that the presence of empathy in the relationship between clients and therapists will predict a more successful outcome for alcoholic clients. The first (Miller et al., 1980) could almost have been designed to test the hypothesis that the random allocation of alcohol abusers across treatment conditions masks the effects of the therapeutic relationship on the eventual outcome.

Miller et al. were primarily concerned to assess the impact of focused versus broad-spectrum behaviour therapy on alcohol abusers. Clients were randomly assigned to four therapy conditions, ranging from one in which only written material was provided, to an intensive condition in which therapists were free to explore any relevant aspects of the client's life. Three of the groups involved client/therapist interaction and these were rated for empathy by three separate raters. At follow-up it was discovered that those in each treatment group did equally well. However, when the correlation between therapist empathy and outcome was calculated, it was found that therapist empathy explained a statistically significant 67 per cent of the variance in drinking behaviour. The most empathetic therapists were successful with 100 per cent of their cases, whilst the least empathetic was successful only with 25 per cent. Sixty per cent of the alcohol abusers who were given the minimal treatment condition of bibliotherapy improved. Of the four most empathetic therapists, two exceeded this rate of improvement by 15 per cent and two by 40 per cent. Of the least empathetic therapists, one equalled this controlled condition, one bettered it by 15 per cent and three did substantially worse. Two years after this brief intervention, therapist empathy was still strongly associated with outcome, whereas there was no difference according to technique (Miller and Baca, 1983). The implication of this study is that empathetic therapists will achieve results better than control conditions, whilst the alcohol abusers of therapists lacking in empathy will not do as well as they would if they had not seen the therapist at all!

A second study that considered the relationship between therapists' 'interpersonal functioning' and their success in influencing alcohol abusers, drinking behaviour was presented by Valle (1981). He randomly assigned alcohol abusers to eight alcoholism counsellors, all of whom were recovered alcoholics. Counsellors' levels of interpersonal functioning were assessed on the basis of their responses to written material in accordance with the methods developed by Carkhuff and others (Carkhuff and Berenson, 1977). On this basis, nine levels of interpersonal functioning were formulated, ranging from the lowest, 'indicating that the response was not helpful at all in that the counsellor did not respond to the affect or the content of the patient', to the highest, 'an accurate response to the personalised problems involved and accurate identification of the steps to implement the goal'.

Valle concluded after a two-year follow-up that 'higher levels of interpersonal functioning were associated with fewer relapses of alcohol abusers, fewer relapsed days, and less use of alcohol during the two years after treatment'. Higher levels of functioning were not related to the length of treatment.

Valle's scale suggests that accurately focused problem-solving techniques may build upon empathy in facilitating therapeutic commitment. The initial levels of low functioning are essentially failures of accurate empathy, that is, the therapist is not really relating to the patient. However, after the mid-way point on the scale, accurate empathy, as defined by an understanding of the client's thoughts and feelings, is assumed and scores are given for increasingly accurate formulation of personal problems, goals and steps to implement these goals. Thus Valle's scale of 'interpersonal functioning' takes us beyond basic empathy into the sort of individually-focused behaviour which was associated with 'therapeutic commitment'. Whilst Miller et al. do not make clear what modifications they made to the accurate empathy rating scales when making their ratings, we can be fairly certain that within a behaviour therapy context similar factors were involved.

Interpreted within the context of the earlier review paper (Cartwright, 1981), these studies provide convincing evidence for a strong link between characteristics of the therapeutic encounter and the eventual drinking status of alcoholic clients. They suggest that the status of the therapists (volunteers or professionals), their general orientation (recovered alcoholics or behaviour therapists) and the intensity of therapeutic input all play a lesser role than the therapeutic style adopted. In suggesting that general therapeutic style has greater influence on client behaviour than these more specific characteristics, these studies of alcoholism treatment are entirely consistent with those concerned with the treatment of other client groups.

From this general literature one might adopt the viewpoint that the core of therapeutic skill (i.e. those behaviours associated with the client experiencing the therapist as committed) may well be the ability to establish and maintain a client-orientated, problem-focused contract. Because these qualities often appear more influential than the more specific aspects of intervention, it is sometimes argued that the latter are unimportant features of the helping relationship. Whilst such an argument would appear to be supported by much of the existing evidence, it could be postulated that it is based upon a misunderstanding of the nature of the processes which occur when a person begins to change. Essentially, the purpose of adopting a treatment technique is to facilitate certain types of therapeutic experience for the patient. These experiences are the intervening variables between the treatment technique and the process of change. There seems to be no reason why only formally-adopted techniques will bring about such relevant experiences. It could be the case that the adoption of a client-orientated, focused approach may lead to relevant types of treatment experiences occurring, irrespective of the conscious perspective being adopted by the therapist. In the broadest sense, this has certainly been the case with regard to the role of the basic relationship. Thus behaviourists may have thought they were helping the client by a specific technique, such as systematic desensitisation, while psychoanalysts may have attributed their success to analysis of resistances. In fact, the important event for the client may be the participation in an intimate and encouraging relationship. This would occur because the client's interpretation of that experience would include drawing the personally most relevant conclusions and taking the appropriate course of action. Provided the therapists maintain a therapeutically committed stance and do not impose their personal viewpoint in an unempathetic fashion, the alcohol abusers of behaviour therapists may achieve psychoanalytic insights and those of psychoanalysts, behaviour change!

The implications of this perspective may become clearer if one returns to the basic assumptions implicit in many research approaches to treating alcoholic clients. In the introductory paragraphs of this chapter, it was suggested that these assumptions implied the view that the treater could be separated from the treatment, and the alcoholic from his alcoholism. The studies by Miller and Valle each question the first of these assumptions by showing the quality of that relationship to be an essential ingredient in the treatment process. A therapeutically committed relationship is the base from which treatment can move into the areas considered relevant by the client, rather than those considered relevant from a narrow theoretical perspective.

TREATMENT AND SPONTANEOUS REMISSION
In much of the alcoholism literature there is an implicit assumption that the processes which occur when treatment is effective are somehow different from those which take place when change occurs without treatment. This view is implicit in the use of the term 'spontaneous remission', which is only meaningful if a radically different process of change occurs under treatment and non-treatment conditions. Such a view is obviously justified when considering organic medicine. In this context, the term treatment often implies surgical or pharmacological interventions which are unlikely to be present in any form when an illness remits 'spontaneously'. However, in the field of more general human problems it could be argued that such a clear distinction between treatment and non-treatment processes is unjustified. One might argue that there is a range of processes by which alcohol abusers come to define, understand and solve problems, and that these are likely to be qualitatively the same whether they occur within a treatment or non-treatment context.

The above hypothesis allows us to reconceptualise the nature of the treatment endeavour. If we work on the assumption that the majority of alcohol abusers solve most of their problems either alone or with the support of their immediate peer groups, we can see that the most likely difference between those who solve their difficulties without professional help and those who seek such help is likely to be in either the complexity of the problem or the availability of relevant resources. In this context, resources refer to psychological resources, such as knowledge, interpersonal skills and capacity for self-understanding, as well as social resources such as money, accommodation and support from others.

From such a perspective the role of the treatment agency would not be to provide something 'different', but to compensate for the resources the client lacks. Thus, one would assume that processes of change occurring in spontaneous remission would be similar to those found in formal treatment situations.

The argument evolved so far has two major themes. The first suggests that the level of therapeutic commitment developed between the client and the treatment agency will play a very important role in determining the success of the treatment endeavour. The second suggests that there is a range of processes by which alcohol abusers come to solve problems, and that these will be the same whether they occur in a treatment or community situation. The function of treatment is to facilitate those processes which have not evolved in the natural setting. Taken together, these arguments suggest that treatment approaches based upon single models of alcoholism are likely to be relatively ineffective unless they can facilitate a variety of processes of change. Thus, they question a fundamental tenet around which most alcohol research studies have been designed - namely, that the most important determinant of a person's treatment requirements is his or her 'alcoholism'.

CLIENTS' PERCEPTIONS OF TREATMENT: SOME ILLUSTRATIVE FINDINGS

An opportunity to explore some of these issues occurred when a research student interviewed a sample of alcohol abusers about their experiences with alcohol since leaving Mount Zeehan Alcoholism Treatment Unit in Canterbury. During this interview a self-completion instrument called the Therapeutic Effects Questionnaire (TEQ) was completed, which asked about the client's experiences during treatment.

The sample consisted of alcohol abusers who had started treatment and who had completed the routine set of questionnaires used in the Unit. For the present analysis, 30 alcohol abusers designated as 'successes' were selected. These included nine totally abstinent alcohol abusers, ten light drinkers (never having drunk more than ten units in a day since entering the Unit) and eleven drinkers who had drunk heavily on no more than 28 days. None of the latter group had drunk heavily in the month preceding the interview. The average length of time between entering the treatment facility and being interviewed was greater than ten months for each group.

Each of the alcohol abusers in this study had attended the day programme at Mount Zeehan. Attendance would normally involve taking part in an educational programme which consists of ten group sessions within the space of one week. In each of these, audio-tapes containing factual information about alcohol and alcohol problems are played and then discussed. They would also have attended an Alcohol Awareness Programme involving 20 group sessions over a two-week period. The aim of these groups is to enable clients to examine the part alcohol has played in their lives and to facilitate an exploration of different attitudes and alternative behaviours. Finally, there is the opportunity to attend support groups which are open discussion groups meeting twice daily.

Once the formal programmes are completed, clients attend the Unit according to their own needs. Support groups meet twice daily, and there are a limited number of individually planned follow-up programmes which may include psychotherapy, social skills or marital therapy. Most new referrals come from medical sources and the Kent Council on Alcoholism, whilst re-referrals are usually made by the clients. Clients who relapse will normally be seen within 24 hours, the sole rule being that they must attend the Unit free of alcohol and unprescribed drugs. When planning the treatment we kept in mind our clinical experience which suggested that alcohol abusers often require quite different things from treatment. We sought to provide a structure which enabled each person to evaluate his or her situation in his or her own terms, and to make a personal decision about his or her own life. The major responsibility for implementing this treatment programme falls upon the nursing staff, who follow a three-year training programme which leads to internal recognition as 'Nurse Therapist'.

The TEQ was developed specifically to collect information about the alcohol abuser's experiences since first attending the Unit. It is based upon the 'Q Sort' used by Yalom (1975), with alterations made to the phrasing of some items to suit the questionnaire format. Yalom's orignial list was subdivided into twelve groups of five items which he felt constituted 'curative factors'. The groups were altruism, group cohesiveness, universality, interpersonal learning 'input', interpersonal learning 'output', guidance, cathexis, identification, family re-enactment, self-understanding, instillation of hope, and existential factors. Some additional items were included to broaden this list. The major additions were six items concerned with the feeling of being understood and accepted and able to trust another person. These were classified under the heading of 'personal commitment'. Two other items concerned with changed perspectives on life were added, under the heading of 'existentiality', as they seemed to fit into the existential dimensions discussed by Yalom in later work (Yalom, 1980).

Although Yalom's labels may be unfamiliar, his scales cover a range of widely understood therapeutic processes. The 'input' dimension of interpersonal learning concerns 'feedback' from the group to the respondent about the impression they make upon other members. The 'output' element of interpersonal learning is primarily concerned with enhanced coping skills. 'Identification' refers to 'modelling' processes, whilst 'family re-enactment' refers to transference experiences. The self-understanding scale (to which a number of items were added) refers to an understanding of present behaviour as well as links between the present and past.

In total there are 76 items on the TEQ. For each item the respondent was asked to indicate whether this statement was true for them, and if so to indicate on a seven-point scale how helpful they felt that experience had been. To discover whether a common set of therapeutic experiences was shared, 27 items, each said to describe their experiences by 85 per cent of the respondents, were selected. These were examined and the items most highly correlated with one another and considered to be most 'helpful' were selected. They represent the first component in explaining variations in 'helpfulness'.

These items are listed in Table 7.1 in order of 'helpfulness'. The 'least helpful' item in this table scores 0.3 standard deviations above the mean 'helpfulness' score for all items in the TEQ, whilst the 'most helpful' item scores 2.3 standard deviations above the mean. Examination of Table 7.1 provides a clear picture of the therapeutic experiences shared by the majority of the alcohol abusers and considered by them to have been 'most helpful'.

Table 7.1: Items Considered True by at Least 85% of the Sample and Ranked in Order of Their Helpfulness

---

Felt there was a member of staff whom I could depend upon and trust

Felt there was at least one member of staff who understood and accepted me

Felt there was a least one person who understood and accepted me

Felt there was someone whom I could depend upon and trust

Received suggestions and advice from staff about the things I could do in the future

Learnt a lot of facts related to my difficulties

Been able to see my life from a different perspective

Felt understood by another person

Learnt that I am not the only person with my type of problem

Been able to view myself and others in a new light

Been able to get things off my chest

Received definite suggestions about the ways to handle my problems

Been encouraged by the knowledge that others had been helped

Been encouraged by improvements in other people

Learnt that I must take ultimate responsibility for my new life no matter how much guidance and support I get from others

Revealed embarrassing things about myself and yet still felt accepted

Belonged to a group of people who understood and accepted me

Every indication is given that experiences associated with trust, dependability, understanding, acceptance and encouragement (nine items) were considered to be the most 'helpful' therapeutic experiences. In terms of the earlier discussion, they clearly relate to the concepts of therapeutic commitment and empathy.

Three items are concerned with receiving advice and information (guidance), whilst four refer to changes in 'existentiality'. Two involve the idea of cathexis.

The most highly ranked items were consistently rated as most helpful by all respondents for whom they were true. Lower ratings tended to occur because some rated the items highly whilst others did not feel them to be so important. Examination of these trends suggested that the respondents tended to fall into two broad groups - those who felt that 'supportive' experiences were most helpful and those with a preference for 'expressive' experiences.

The most general feature of the 'supportive group' was the importance of guidance and direction in their responses. They tended to be concerned with gaining control and tended to rate items concerned with cathexis and self-understanding as relatively unhelpful. The expressive group did not reject the supportive elements but tended to rate aspects of self-understanding as only slightly below commitment in helpfulness. This pattern tends to suggest the value of a supportive/expressive model of therapeutic experience like that described by Luborsky (1978) for substance abusers.

There were indications that these preferences in some way followed social groupings. The supportive-type model was associated with older, male and married alcohol abusers, whilst preference for expressive experiences was shown by the younger, female and single. There was no evidence that severity of dependence as rated by the SADQ (Stockwell, Hodgson, Edwards, Taylor and Rankin, 1979) was associated with such preferences.

There were, however, considerable differences within these groups and the range of therapeutic experiences associated with the concepts of 'support' and 'expression'. This point is illustrated below where it is shown that certain aspects of self-understanding (those concerned with psychodynamic phenomena) appear to be particularly relevant to alcohol abusers with symptoms of severe mood disturbance.

It is rarely disputed that many alcohol abusers who come to psychiatric facilities show marked disturbances of mood. Though it tends to be assumed that these difficulties are related to withdrawal symptoms and immediate life crises, there is also substantial evidence from the most recent reviews (e.g. Heather and Robertson, 1981) that many who do reduce their alcohol consumption find that such difficulties persist. Thus the assumption sometimes made that, if treatment focuses upon clients' drinking, physical health and social situation, then their psychological state will improve would seem to be only true for a proportion of alcohol abusers. It was to discover the impact of basic alcoholism treatment on various measures of 'mental health' that the data described in this chapter were originally collected.

As part of the routine assessment procedure, each client completes the 30-item version of the General Health Questionnaire (Goldberg, 1973). This instrument, which asks about recent occurrences of the type of symptoms associated with diagnosis of psychiatric illness, is sensitive to change. A cut-off point of 5 will correctly identify approximately 80 per cent of those who would normally receive such a diagnosis. High scores are normally taken to indicate the existence of chronic difficulties rather than the 'normal' mood disturbances associated with life crisis.

On first attending the Unit the sample had a mean score of 14.69 items (std. dev. 9.3), whilst at the time of their follow-up interview they had a mean score of 5.84 items (std. dev. 7.23). The mean difference was 8.8 and the value of the paired t-statistic was 4.01 ($p<0.001$). To discover if these changes were in any way associated with therapeutic experiences, changes in the GHQ scores were correlated with items in the TEQ. Those scores rated as 'not true' were given a zero score for helpfulness. A scale was then constructed from the first principal component which emerged from the correlated items. The nine items on this scale are presented in Table 7.2. They seem to fall into two major groups. Four refer to understanding and trust and these also appear in Table 7.1. The first three, however, refer to the self-understanding dimension which was not represented in Table 7.1. From a psychodynamic perspective, they represent understandings about defences and transference phenomena which one might expect to be found most helpful by the person with severe psychological difficulties.

Table 7.2: Scale of Items Associated With Changes in GHQ Scores

---

Understood how and why I prevent myself from overcoming my problems

Learnt that I can have feelings about a person which have little to do with that person and more to do with my experiences with people in the past

Understood the ways in which I unconsciously avoid unpleasant thoughts and feelings

Seen others benefit from revealing embarrassing things and take other risks and consequently been able to do the same

Felt understood by another person

Felt more able to trust other people

Felt there was someone whom I could depend upon and trust

Belonged to a group of people who understood and accepted me

Scale Alpha = 0.96

This point can be best understood from Table 7.3. The overall correlation between scores on the predictive scale and changes in GHQ scores of -0.59 is statistically significant. However, significant correlations also exist between the initial-level score and the amount of change. That is to say, those who had the highest scores also tended to reduce their scores most. Furthermore, those with the initially highest scores also scored most highly on the predictive scale. Thus, though the partial correlation (the relationship between the predictive scale and the change score with account taken of differences in initial level) is significant, some suspicion must exist that the result is in some way misleading.

Table 7.3: Correlations Between Changes in GHQ Score and the Predictive Scale

	Correlated Items				
	Change/ predict	Change/ initial	Initial/ predict	Partial	Sig
All cases	-0.59	-0.84	+0.49	-0.41	0.05
High GHQ	-0.70	-0.48	+0.1	-0.75	0.01
Low GHQ	-0.34	-0.72	+0.44	-0.02	ns.

Confidence in the result is gained once one assumes that this predictive scale is mainly relevant to those who initially had the highest scores on the GHQ, because these experiences are relevant to their particular needs. The sample was thus divided into two groups of high and low scorers on the initial GHQ scale and the two groups analysed separately. The high GHQ scorers rated the items on the predictive scale as significantly more helpful than those with lower initial scores, but both groups agreed that such experiences had occurred for them.

When the partial correlations are calculated for the two groups, one can see that for those in the high group 56 per cent of the variance in the change score was explained by the therapeutic experience, whilst for the low initial scorers this did not play a major part. For the low scorers, the reduction in alcohol consumption in association with the core therapeutic experience seems to have been sufficient to bring about an improvement, but for the high scorers additional types of therapeutic experience were necessary. Thus, an expressive quality to the therapeutic experience was associated with changes in GHQ scores, but this does not necessarily imply that expressive experiences are always necessary to bring about change in psychological functioning. On another scale used in this study, a quite different pattern appears.

The Time Competence Scale is a scale provided with the Personal Orientation Inventory (POI) (Shostrom, 1974). The POI sought to measure the concept of self-actualisation. The Time Competence Scale (TCS) is one of two summary scales and is concerned with future and past orientations. The person with poor time competence is one who is preoccupied with the past and the future; it thus measures the existential rather than the symptomatic aspects of anxiety and guilt. Alcohol abusers in this sample were particularly 'time incompetent' with their average score being more than two standard deviations below the standard score provided. At follow-up there was a slight but non-significant improvement. There were, however, greater differences between alcohol abusers, suggesting that some had changed and not others.

Table 7.4: Items Associated With Changes in Time Competence for Members of the Sample Married Throughout the Last Six Months

---

Items Considered Helpful:

    Been able to work out my difficulties with one particular person

    Learned a lot of facts related to my difficulties

    Been inspired by seeing others get better

Items Considered Not Helpful:

    Been able to get things off my chest

    Been able to say what was bothering me rather than holding back

---

Analysis of these change scores, using methods similar to those described above, showed two distinct patterns. For single members of the sample there was a statistically significant partial correlation of 0.57 ($p<0.05$) between scores on the predictive scale and changes in time competence, whereas for married members of the sample this relationship was virtually zero. However, a completely separate predictive scale emerged for the married group. This is shown in Table 7.4.

The partial correlation between this scale and the change scores is 0.77 ($p<0.01$) for the married members of the sample, but for the single members it is zero. It is noticeable that this dimension is obviously 'supportive', with those who either did not utilise cathectic experiences or did not find them helpful being the most likely to improve their TC scores.

Whilst changes in GHQ and TC scores were associated with specific therapeutic experiences, changes in other psychological scales were not. For instance, the POI contains two self-esteem scales on which changes were not correlated with specific therapeutic experiences. On one scale measuring positive aspects of self-evaluation (the self-regard scale), changes were associated with the length of time since the person last drank heavily. On another, measuring the capacity to accept one's limitations (the self-acceptance scale), only those who remained totally abstinent changed. Generally speaking, those who had successfully limited their drinking changed least but this group tended to score more highly on all the scales initially.

These findings illustrate a number of points made in the early part of this chapter. First, the experiences which the more successful alcohol abusers consistently rated as 'most helpful' were those associated with therapeutic commitment and experience empathy. Secondly, in conjunction with that dimension, they tended to report different types of experiences as being 'helpful'. This was best illustrated in relationship to changes in time competence where single but not married members of the sample changed if they were able to find an 'expressive' experience helpful. For married members, such change would only occur in relationship to a supportive experience. Marital status was not associated with changes in mood disturbance, these occurring in relationship to the expressive experience for each group. Other aspects of change were not directly related to therapeutic experiences, but were related to the person's success in handling drinking.

THE MAIN FEATURES OF THE ALTERNATIVE MODEL

The alternative model for understanding the responses we might make to alcohol abusers is clearly a variant of the 'non-specific' or 'common factors' approach to explaining outcome from psycho-therapy with other client groups. This model suggests that the most important element in effecting therapeutic change is the alcohol abuser's experience of being in a 'therapeutically committed' relationship. At the core of this experience are feelings associated with trust, acceptance, understanding and encouragement.

As has been described earlier, the therapist who is most likely to create the environment where these experiences might occur is a person who feels secure in their therapeutic role and in their personal position with the alcohol abuser. When such conditions occur, then the therapist is much more likely to be able to develop an empathetic relationship, such a quality being central to the development of the client's experience of being in a therapeutically committed relationship. Because alcohol abusers are so often at the centre of relationships marked by mistrust, misunderstanding and conflict, these qualities may be even more important with this client group than with others.

It is from this point that the hermeneutic aspects of the model come into play, and one can clearly see the differences between the present model and that drawn from organic medicine. In the original model, intervention is conceptualised as 'treatment', often in a fashion directly analogous to 'dose'. Thus treatment is evaluated in terms of the effects of different treatments (i.e. drugs) and different intensities of the same treatments (i.e. smaller and larger doses). In terms of the present model, intervention is conceptualised in terms of 'process'. At the heart of the treatment process lies the client's experience of the therapist and the development of their relationship. For one client, there may be an immediate impact and rapid change, whilst for another, apparently similar, the same process may take years with many relapses.

This greater stress on subjective aspects is also apparent when we consider the two approaches to 'theories' of alcoholism. From the scientific/medical perspective, there is a perpetual search for the correct or 'true' explanation of alcoholism, whereas from the perspective of the model proposed here such an endeavour is interesting but not essential. Within the confines of the therapeutic encounter, the 'true' model of alcoholism must be the one that the client finds most relevant and helpful, even if it does not fit the 'facts'. Different models of 'treatment' can also be considered from the same perspective - essentially, the right approach is the one which the client finds relevant.

This is not an argument for ignoring theoretical developments but for reconceptualising their role. The therapist who has a thorough understanding of the different models of alcoholism, and the different types of intervention, is potentially in a position to develop a highly empathetic relationship with the client, whereas therapists who are committed to one model and one approach may well find themselves unable to form such a relationship. All the points made above can be applied to the individual or one-to-one relationship, the therapeutic group, treatment milieus or self-help situations.

CONCLUSIONS

In this chapter an attempt has been made to describe two different philosophical approaches to the treatment of alcohol abusers. On the one hand, there is a model which is based upon the assumption that treatment can best be understood in essentially mechanistic terms. The basic assumption of this model is that the treatment technique is, in principle, separate from the 'treater' and the 'patient'. 'Personality' factors are embarrassing errors to be 'controlled out'. Treatment so conceived is something which differs from events which occur outside of the treatment environment.

There is little evidence that treatment delivered within the confines of this model is effective. Indeed, one might claim that treatment research has evaluated, not treatment itself, but the model which has been used to evaluate treatment. It is the model, not the treatment, which needs to be discarded.

The alternative model is based upon the assumption that it is alcohol abusers' experiences of the relationship which emerges between themselves and the 'treater' which is the core therapeutic experience, and that 'treatment techniques' are only effective in that they build upon and reinforce that 'relationship'. Thus the 'personality' of the therapist or the 'ethos' of the therapeutic environment are central factors in change. The only real difference between therapeutic experiences and those which occur outside of the treatment environment is likely to be the skill of the therapist, which is based upon the capacity to understand and respond to the client's needs and bring about and maintain the relevant conditions. The evidence provided in this paper suggests that when this occurs the treatment situation may have considerable influence on the alcohol abuser's subsequent experience. As the Maudsley Alcohol Pilot Project (Shaw et al., 1978) demonstrated, when a client with a long-standing drinking problem encounters a professional, the conceptual and relationship skills demanded may be considerable and, as Miller's study shows, when they are lacking the client may be better without such 'help'.

These different philosophical models have implications which reach beyond the design of research projects. From the perspective of the medically-based model, there is little point in investing money in treatment facilities which are clearly not cost-effective, and it would be better spent on fundamental research which might eventually bring about a cure. Similarly, training for treatment personnel is a pointless exercise and can justifiably be restricted to enhancing their awareness of the nature of alcohol problems, thus enabling them to provide advice. From the alternative point of view these priorities are changed. Treatment situations can provide useful help to the drinker provided they are staffed by selected and trained personnel who possess skills relevant to the client's needs. Thus, a greater investment in skills-orientated training is indicated, with research studies designed to help us understand the complexity of the therapeutic process.

REFERENCES

Carkhuff, R.R. and Berenson, B.G. (1977) Beyond Counselling and Therapy, 2nd Edition, New York: Holt Rinehart & Winston

Cartwright, A.K.J. (1981) 'Are different therapeutic perspectives important in the treatment of alcoholism?', British Journal of Addiction, 76, 347-61

____ (1980) 'The attitudes of helping agents towards the alcoholic client: the Influence of experience, support, training and self-esteem', British Journal of Addiction, 75, 413-31

____ (1981) 'Future directions in the training of agents to work with alcoholic clients', New Directions in the Study of Alcohol Group, Members' Booklet No.2, 11-24

Edwards, G., Orford, J., Egert, S., Guthrie, S., Hawker, A., Hensman, C., Mitcheson, M., Oppenheimer, E. and Taylor, C. (1977) 'Alcoholism - a controlled trial of treatment and advice', Journal of Studies on Alcohol, 38, 1004-31

Emrick, C.D. (1975) 'A review of psychologically orientated

treatments of alcoholism: II The relative effectiveness of different treatment approaches and the effectiveness of treatment versus no treatment, Journal of Studies on Alcohol, 36, 88-108

Glaser, S.B. (1980) 'Anybody got a match? Treatment research and the matching hypothesis' in G. Edwards and M. Grant (eds), Alcoholism Treatment in Transition, London: Croom Helm

Goldberg, D (1973) The Detection of Psychiatric Illness by Questionnaire, London: Oxford University Press

Heather, N. and Robertson, I. (1981) Controlled Drinking, London: Methuen

Kiesler, D., Mathine, P. and Klein, M. (1967) 'A summary of issues and conclusions' in C.R. Rogers (ed.), The Therapeutic Relationship and Its Impact, Madison: Wisconsin Press

Kohut, H. (1959) 'Introspection, empathy and psychoanalysis: an examination of the relationship between mode of observation and theory', Journal of the American Psychoanalytic Association, 7, 459-83

____ (1971) The Analysis of the Self, New York: International University Press

Luborsky, L. (1978) Individual Treatment Manual for Supportive/ Expressive Psychoanalytically Orientated Psychotherapy: Special Adaption For the Treatment of Drug Dependence, available from Piersol Building, Room 203, Hospital of University of Pennsylvania, 36th & Spruce Sts., Philadelphia, Pennsylvania, 19104

Malan, D. (1979) Individual Psychotherapy and the Science of Psychodynamics, Butterworths: London

Miller, W.R., Taylor, Cheryl A. and West, Joanne (1980) 'Focused versus broad-spectrum behavior therapy for problem drinkers', Journal of Consulting and Clinical Psychology, 48, 5, 590-601

____ and Baca (1983) 'Two-year follow-up of bibliotherapy and therapist-directed controlled drinking training for problem drinkers', Behaviour Therapy, 14, 441-8

Shaw, S., Cartwright, A.K.J., Spratley, T.A. and Harwin, J. (1978) Responding to Drinking Problems, London: Croom Helm

Shostrom, E.L. (1974) An Inventory for the Measurement of Self Actualisation, San Diego, Calfornia 92107: Educational and Industrial Testing Service

Stockwell, T., Hodgson, R., Edwards, G., Taylor, C. and Rankin, H.A. (1979) 'The development of a questionnaire to measure severity of alcohol dependence', British Journal of Addiction, 74, 79-87

Truax, Charles B. and Carkhuff, Robert R. (1973) Towards Effective Counselling and Psychotherapy, Chicago: Aldine

Valle, Steven K. (1981) 'Inter-personal functioning of alcoholism counsellors and treatment outcome', Journal of Studies on Alcohol, 42, 783-90

Yalom, Irvin D. (1975) The Theory and Practice of Group Psychotherapy, (second edition) New York: Basic Books

____ (1980) Existential Psychotherapy, New York: Basic Books

Chapter 8

THE VALUE OF A COGNITIVE-BEHAVIOURAL APPROACH TO THE TREATMENT OF PROBLEM DRINKERS

Steve Rollnick

'Does treatment work?' is a question which has been diligently addressed in the alcohol field (e.g. Emrick, 1974; Armor, Polich and Stambul, 1978). Armed with the largely pessimistic conclusions of these major reviews it would be fairly easy for an experienced therapist to dampen enthusiasm in a newcomer to the field. Because of the more optimistic tone about treatment in this chapter, it is necessary to explain from the outset why such pessimistic conclusions could be misleading. In the first place, a promising range of cognitive-behavioural strategies has been developed in recent years which remain to be applied and properly evaluated among problem drinkers, particularly those receiving abstinence treatment: until this is done it would be premature to conclude that treatment does not work. The main aim of this chapter is to describe some of these strategies and review some of the evidence available for their effectiveness. Secondly, we still know far too little about treatment process to jump to any dogmatic and pessimistic conclusions. Until we have understood why treatment so often fails to make an impact on the lives of problem drinkers, it would be premature to become too despondent about our work.

This chapter will begin with an analysis of traditional treatment process in which it will be argued that the problems of lack of motivation, denial and resistance are not resolved by focusing treatment mainly around enhancing willpower among problem drinkers. In suggesting the use of a more dynamic model of motivation, it will be seen that there are a number of constructive strategies that can be used both to engage clients in the treatment process and to promote behaviour change. Among these are the problem-solving strategies derived from social learning theory, which are described in the second half of the chapter.

TRADITIONAL TREATMENT - A CRITIQUE

Unfortunately, clinical researchers in this field have almost completely neglected the study of treatment process in favour of evaluating treatment outcome. There are at present few answers to such questions as 'What do therapists and their clients talk about in treatment and what are the areas of disagreement?'; 'Why are the problems of resistance, denial and feelings of hopelessness so frequently encountered?'; 'How are these problems dealt with?'; 'How do the clients change in treatment and with what relation to future outcome?'. Davies (1979) provides one of the few examples of this kind of research. His findings indicate that what goes on in the psychiatric treatment of alcoholism is very different to what happens in the treatment of other problems, like depression and anxiety. Something of a battle seems to take place between clinician and client which revolves around the issues of motivation, willpower and responsibility for resolving the problem. An analysis of treatment process offers the possibility of suggesting new ways of dealing with these issues.

It is the same kind of psychiatric treatment described by Davies and evaluated in outcome studies like the Rand Report (Armor et al., 1978) which will be termed 'traditional treatment' and analysed below. Such an analysis is not without its pitfalls. Besides the scarcity of supporting empirical evidence about treatment process, there is the problem of defining traditional treatment. Even within the psychiatric setting there is a wide range of treatments offered to problem drinkers, ranging from 'antabuse therapy' to insight-oriented psychotherapy and family therapy (see Miller, 1980). The approach adopted here will be to focus upon the common elements of most approaches while ignoring the more subtle differences between them.

Faith, Hope and a Dose of Willpower?

That traditional alcoholism treatment is likely to have elements in common with psychotherapy as a whole is self-evident. What is more difficult to assess is how important factors like faith, hope and persuasive communication are (see Hodgson, 1980). Alan Cartwright has shown how empathy and genuineness in the therapist and a belief in the effectiveness of treatment are crucially important features of all psychological interventions (see Chapter 7). Despite the relevance of these 'non-specific' factors to an understanding of alcoholism treatment, however, there are obviously limits on the degree to which explanations can be borrowed from broader psychotherapy research since so much of what goes on in alcoholism treatment concerns drinking. As noted above, the problems of resistance to treatment, apparent lack of motivation and denial seem to appear more frequently among alcoholics than, for example, among people with other anxiety-based problems. Against the background of poor success rates in traditional alcoholism treatment, non-specific factors are best viewed as necessary, but not sufficient, conditions for successful treatment.

Although limited to the initial consultation sessions only, the two reports that have emerged from Davies' research (1979 and 1981) provide a useful platform for exploring the treatment process and the nature of therapist-client interaction. From most of the sessions Davies observed came the notion that the client should take responsibility for resolving the problem. Although therapists and clients were apparently in agreement about this, Davies points out that,

> the one aspect of treatment on which ... (they) ... were seen to diverge ... concerns the offering of advice, guidance and direction by therapists. From the patient's point of view this constitutes the expertise of therapists and something to expect from consultation ... From the therapist's point of view, however, the offering of direct advice and guidance often appears to be out of keeping with the psychiatric practice of helping patients to help themselves. (1981, p. 172)

What the patients seemed to be left with was the requirement that they take responsibility for their problems and develop sufficient motivation to stop drinking. In this kind of treatment environment, as Miller (1983) has pointed out, lack of motivation and denial tend to be viewed as personality characteristics of the alcoholic which present clinicians with immediate problems in the early stage of treatment. The failure of personality research to construct a profile of the typical 'alcoholic personality' does not seem to have permeated through to the clinical arena. Alcoholics are usually regarded as difficult to engage in treatment because they 'exhibit' lack of motivation and denial. Such a view can always be justified by making the simple observation that, since neurotic clients do not present with these problems, they must therefore be peculiar characteristics of the alcoholic population.

Before turning to an alternative explanation, it is worth considering how these issues are dealt with in the later stages of treatment. Despite the complete absence of research evidence on this question it seems reasonable to suggest that the most important feature of traditional treatment is persuading clients to stop drinking by developing sufficient willpower to achieve this goal. In the pursuit of this end, the content of therapy sessions is likely to vary in a number of ways: Disulfiram might be used as a booster to the maintenance of willpower; some therapists might see the attainment of 'insight' as an important task; while others might encourage the use of group therapy to enable alcoholics to publicly review their drinking careers and reaffirm their commitment to change. If this is an accurate picture of the basic elements of traditional treatment then the problems pinpointed by Davies in the early stages of treatment are unlikely to be very different later on. If the crucial outcome of successful treatment is the development of sufficient willpower to stop drinking then the problems of resistance and denial are likely to be interpreted by therapists as reflecting a lack of willpower and commitment to change in the clients. It is difficult to predict the outcome of this rather confusing state of affairs. Some alcoholics do seem able to work towards change within this kind of treatment setting which has many of the features of the AA approach. For the patient who does not get on well in treatment the outcome is obviously more worrying. Being faced with his or her apparent lack of willpower or even 'weakness of character' is unlikely to lead to the development of a good therapeutic relationship. It is now clearly time for process and outcome research to be merged into a single enterprise, one in which problems in treatment are identified and their effect upon subsequent outcome are evaluated.

The only conclusions that can be reached from this brief review are that problems in the treatment process appear to revolve around the issues of self-responsibility and the marshalling of willpower and that, as Davies (1979) has shown, some clients might want more concrete advice and direction than they are given. The number of clients adversely affected by this kind of experience remains to be determined. If someone does fail to make progress in treatment this is likely to be attributed to their own lack of motivation, willpower or denial (see Miller, 1983). What needs to be considered is whether these problems can be dealt with in a more productive manner.

New Approaches to Old Problems

A useful starting point will be to move away from viewing a concept like motivation as a simple, all-embracing characteristic which alcoholics have different amounts of and which determines whether or not they are likely to succeed in overcoming their problems. A more complex explanation outlined below will include the suggestion that there is more than one kind of motivational problem encountered in treatment and that a clinician's approach to these problems could have a marked influence on the progress of clients. Seen in this light, a problem like motivation is best understood as the product of an interaction between the background and expectations of clients on the one hand and the model of treatment used by clinicians on the other (Rollnick and Heather, 1982; Miller, 1983).

In his writing on the subject of psychological treatment, Bandura (1977a) has noted two reasons why clients might have difficulty in changing their behaviour: first, they might not believe that the goal or outcome of treatment is worthwhile (an outcome expectation) and secondly, they might not feel able to achieve this goal (an efficacy expectation). While the way in which these two kinds of expectation interact with one another remains to be fully elucidated, the distinction between them could help to clarify some of the problems in alcoholism treatment described above (see Rollnick and Heather, 1982). It suggests that there are two kinds of motivational problem each containing different implications for treatment.

The <u>first motivational problem</u> concerns the alcoholic who does not have entirely positive expectations about the goal of treatment, regardless of whether he or she feels able to achieve this goal. This should not come as too much of a surprise to treatment personnel, given the large changes in lifestyle implied by a shift from drinking to complete abstinence. Such a shift is likely to have both positive and negative consequences for the individual, for example, while it might lead to better health and improvement in a marriage, it could also result in social isolation from workmates. Clinicians would be wrong to interpret this kind of ambivalence as reflecting resistance to treatment per se; similarly, it has little or nothing to do with the alcoholic lacking willpower, and it would only confuse matters if clinicians were to unwittingly use the willpower notion as a platform for supposedly therapeutic intervention. If they do make this mistake, and Davies' (1979) study suggests that sometimes they do, then it is not surprising that the alcoholic appears to resist treatment or complain about the lack of direction given by therapists. If the client is concerned about the goal of treatment then this should be the initial focus of discussion, not whether he has the ability or willpower to achieve this goal. Concrete guidelines for structuring this kind of discussion using a 'decision matrix' (Marlatt and Parks, 1982) or pay-off matrix' (Hodgson, 1984) have emerged from the application of social learning principles to addictive behaviours and can be used to help the alcoholic examine the 'pros and cons' of abstinence. An important first step should be for the therapist to accept this as a problem in its own right and to communicate this acceptance to the client in a non-judgmental manner as early as possible in treatment. Using this approach to engaging alcoholics in treatment, the therapist thus regards ambivalence about abstinence as normal and acceptable and does not use this to question the person's motivation, willpower or attitude to treatment.

Along similar lines Miller (1983) has examined the concept of denial, a term often used to describe the alcoholic who appears to resist treatment or who lacks motivation. His analysis leads him to conclude that 'denial is not inherent in the alcoholic individual but, rather, is the product of the way in which counsellers have chosen to interact with problem drinkers' (p.150). As an alternative to focusing discussion on issues like 'you are an alcoholic' or 'you must abstain for the rest of your life' - assertions which are likely to elicit denial from the client - Miller describes a range of strategies which can be used to examine the positive and negative aspects of drinking and abstinence. The purpose of this 'motivational inverviewing' is to tip the balance in favour of abstinence without labelling the client or pursuing a counter-productive discussion about motivation, denial or resistance to treatment.

In conclusion, there is reason to believe that traditional treatment has overlooked the kind of possibilities described above by assuming that clients should somehow enter treatment with little ambivalence about returning to abstinence. An important part of treatment should be to deal directly with this issue before attempting to promote behaviour change. In this sense treatment contains more stages than is usually accepted.

A second motivational problem and source of ambivalence among alcoholics concerns their expectations about actually achieving the goal of treatment, or in Bandura's terms, developing a feeling of self-efficacy about their ability to achieve this goal. The analysis of traditional treatment suggested that enhancing willpower was the main method used for developing this sense of mastery over abstinence. One of the most important implications of social learning theory is that there is quite a lot that therapists and alcoholics can actually do to develop these efficacy expectations, thereby avoiding the potentially crippling concept of willpower. As Mahoney and Arnkoff (1978) have pointed out, this concept is problematic because it is something which a person apparently has which contains no implications for action. The alcoholic who is led to believe that he or she does not have enough willpower cannot be blamed for wondering what to do about it. Some of the cognitive-behavioural strategies described below attempt to tackle this problem by adopting an active problem-solving approach to these issues.

COGNITIVE-BEHAVIOURAL STRATEGIES
Once the client has moved some way through the process of examining the feasibility of the treatment goal and the need for a change in lifestyle, the whole question of implementing desired behaviour change comes to the fore. Here social learning theory has a considerable theoretical and technological base upon which to draw and it is the author's contention that, until this base is properly developed and evaluated with respect to alcohol problems, the question 'Does treatment work?' cannot be answered. It is not within the scope of this chapter to describe this theory and technology and the reader is referred to such writers as Hodgson (1983), Wilson (1978), Marlatt and Parks (1982), Bandura (1977a, 1977b) and Thoresen and Mahoney (1974) for such a description. One major conclusion which can be drawn from this literature however is that performance-based interventions more readily achieve both behaviour and attitude change than do purely verbal procedures. In other words, the problem drinker should have practice in doing the things necessary for a change in lifestyle. Of course, practice must be supplemented by discussion but traditional treatment has over-emphasised the verbal process and largely neglected behavioural performance. Rather than describe the whole cognitive-behavioural literature on alcohol problems, a few key outcome studies will be described and the treatment approaches used, outlined.

Skill Training Approaches
Hunt and Azrin developed what they called a community-reinforcement approach (Hunt and Azrin, 1973; Azrin, 1976). Their aim was to make the consequences of drinking less palatable to the alcoholic by building up a series of reinforcements for being sober, which were then either withdrawn or made less accessible if the person started drinking again. The highly successful treatment package developed by these authors contained vocational counselling, marital and family counselling with various agreements and positive changes contingent upon sobriety, social counselling which encouraged the development of new friendships and membership of a self-supporting social club, as well as numerous other incentives for remaining sober such as the purchase of a telephone, television or newspaper subscription - some of the down-

payments being paid for by the treatment agency! A subsequent package (Azrin, 1976) included other features like the use of a 'Buddy system' to provide additional support and counselling outside treatment; Antabuse with an accompanying system for ensuring that it was taken regularly; a daily report mailed to the therapist to act as an early warning system; and a problem-solving procedure rehearsed by clients under the guidance of the therapist. In both studies the experimental group fared dramatically better than the control group on measures of both drinking and social stability.

These results certainly provide confirmation of the principle that activating alcoholics to change as many aspects of their lives as possible can produce definite improvements, though it is by no means certain that operant conditioning was responsible for these treatment gains.

While this expensive package would be out of the reach of most treatment services, it is also possible to apply the same principle while using fewer financial and personal resources: marital therapy, vocational counselling and providing recreational and companionship outlets are just some of the things which any service could potentially offer. In this context motivation is therefore not seen as residing entirely within the individual but is seen as the result of interaction between the person and his or her environment.

A second promising study was that by Chaney, O'Leary and Marlatt (1978), who used a social learning approach to design a treatment package for helping problem drinkers anticipate and deal with the kind of situations likely to precipitate a return to drinking. In the experimental group clients were trained to use a problem-solving strategy (D'Zurilla and Goldfried, 1971) for coping with problem situations which were presented to them by the therapist. To begin with, the therapist first modelled a response that did not involve drinking; for example, in dealing with dangerous situations involving other people like social pressure to have a drink, the therapist chose an alternative response, explained his choice to the group members and then modelled this response. Clients then decided about their own way of dealing with the problem, rehearsed it in front of the group and then received feedback from them about the appropriateness of their responses. At the end of each exercise one group member was required to summarise the method used for generating and evaluating these new strategies. In this way, over a period of eight 1½-hour sessions, a wide range of interpersonal and intrapersonal problem situations were examined.

The rationale behind such a skill training approach is that, having repeatedly responded to a wide range of situations by drinking, the problem drinker needs to identify and practice new strategies which will be more successful and satisfying than drinking. It is interesting to note that Chaney's clients simply practised these skills in an artificial role-play situation for a limited period of time and were then left to their own devices. Treatment did not involve any real-life practice. Nevertheless, at the one-year follow-up these clients had experienced less severe relapse episodes, and of shorter duration, than subjects from two control groups. One of these groups received the regular service offered at the treatment centre, while the other, called a 'discussion group', spent the same amount of time discussing the problem situations used in the experimental group but without the use of role-playing, modelling and coaching; instead, they merely discussed their feelings about these situations. These results come very close to confirming Bandura's (1977a) hypothesis that performance-based treatments are more likely to raise self-efficacy and promote behaviour change than those simply relying upon verbal persuasion and discussion. This methodologically sound study (lack of blind follow-up being its only major weakness) clearly needs to be replicated and extended. One difficulty in interpreting the results is the fact that experimental and control groups did not differ in the number of abstinent days following treatment, despite the differences in severity and duration of relapse episodes. Future controlled outcome studies of this kind might also consider extending and improving the treatment package by giving clients real-life practice in dealing with problem situations, an approach already incorporated into the cue exposure and relapse prevention techniques to be described below.

Along similar lines to the Chaney study, Oei and Jackson (1980, 1982) investigated the value of a social skills training package, but also combined this in one group with a cognitive-restructuring approach. Derived from the treatment of depressed people, this method is based on the assumption that irrational beliefs and attitudes have a marked influence on people's ability to change their behaviour; treatment thus involves examining these distorted beliefs and persuading clients to alter their perceptions and behaviour accordingly; for example, among problem drinkers it can be hypothesised that beliefs and expectations about control could strongly influence their behaviour (see Heather, Rollnick and Winton, 1983). Oei and Jackson found that a combined social skills/cognitive restructuring approach was related to better outcome than either approach used on its own, with clients in all three experimental groups faring significantly better than those in a traditional/supportive control group. Unfortunately, the selection of a biased sample for treatment, non-random assignment to groups and a lack of blind follow-up cautions against generalising from these results.

One of the most interesting applications of social learning principles comes from an attempt in Toronto to teach coping skills to a population of severely dependent and socially unstable alcoholics living in a half-way house (Sanchez-Craig and Walker, 1982; Walker, Sanchez-Craig and Bornet, 1982). All residents attended an initial ten hours of group meetings which centred around identifying realistic goals, pinpointing assets and obstacles to achieving these goals, formulating concrete plans of action and then reporting back on progress. After this introduction clients were assigned to one of three conditions for a further 20 hours: a coping skills programme in which they were taught how to use a functional analysis and problem-solving approach to interpersonal and drink-related problems; a covert sensitisation programme which involved relaxation and the pairing of alcohol scenes with aversive imagery (see Cautela, 1967); and a discussion control group. At 6, 12 and 18-month follow-up there were no differences between clients in any of these groups. One of the likely reasons for this finding is that clients in the coping skills group subsequently forgot many of the strategies which were taught to them during treatment, as the authors themselves point out, probably because they were taught general principles rather than specific strategies for specific problems. In contrast, the control group appears to have contained a fair amount of individually-tailored discussion. Coupled with the fact that all groups received the goal-setting procedure to begin with, the authors have clearly minimised the differences between their treatment conditions from the start. Although improvement rates among the group as a whole were apparently better than expected in this kind of setting, it was not possible to attribute this to the treatment experience because the use of a second half-way house as a no-treatment control condition fell away unexpectedly. One important problem noted by these authors which needs to be considered in future studies is that chronic alcoholics with some degree of cognitive impairment might have difficulting in recalling ideas and strategies taught to them during treatment.

Relapse Prevention and Cue Exposure

The tendency of treatment gains to gradually decrease over time is a problem encountered in most of the studies described thus far. A number of related factors could be responsible for this: treatment tends to be viewed as time-limited, lasting a given number of weeks in which clients learn new coping strategies and are then left to their own devices; in some cases they are taught general principles rather than specific, individually-tailored skills; and even when this is not the case, specific skills are modelled and rehearsed in an artificial role-play situation without any structured real-life application. Some of the more recent developments in this field indicate that strategies derived from social learning theory do not necessarily need to be restricted in these ways. The relapse prevention procedures outlined by Marlatt (Marlatt, 1978; Marlatt and Parks, 1982) contain many of the better features of the skill-training techniques described above. The rationale of this approach is that problem drinkers frequently relapse and that treatment should be concerned with anticipating and identifying future high-risk situations and teaching appropriate coping strategies. The likelihood of skills generalising and persisting over time can be increased with the aid of 'dry run' practice sessions in which the client is actually taken into difficult situations to practice new coping strategies for avoiding alcohol.

Relapse-prevention techniques are also able to help clients deal with a return to drinking and prevent the possibility of a lapse developing into a full-blown relapse. Marlatt has hypothesised that the guilt reaction which follows the initial violation of abstinence (the 'abstinence violation effect') will increase the likelihood of further drinking and that a number of strategies can be used to counteract this effect; for example, cognitive restructuring can be used to persuade the client not to view a lapse as a personal disaster which will inevitably lead to relapse. The client can also be given a set of reminder cards in a sealed envelope which is only opened after a lapse has occurred. An even more direct method called the 'programmed relapse technique' involves helping the person to drink under the supervision of the therapist so as to encourage the rehearsal of strategies geared towards returning the person to abstinence as soon as possible. A useful description of the way in which relapse prevention techniques can be integrated into a treatment service can be found in Goldman and Klisz (1982).

Similar in many ways to relapse prevention is cue exposure, a strategy derived from the treatment of phobias (de Silva and Rachman, 1981) and obsessive-compulsive disorders (Rachman and Hodgson, 1980) which has recently been applied to problem drinkers. The single-case studies reported by Blakey and Baker (1980) and Hodgson and Rankin (1982) present the rationale for exposing clients to a wide range of stimuli that usually elicit drinking. One of these cues could be alcohol itself, in which case the client is taught to stop drinking after having just one or two drinks. Hodgson and Rankin have described the treatment and five-year follow-up of a chronic alcoholic who believed that one drink meant complete relapse, and who was encouraged to break this compulsion by taking only a limited amount of alcohol and then stopping altogether. The client attributed the marked reduction in his drinking over a six-year period to this procedure and the authors themselves discuss this success in terms of the gradual enhancement of self-efficacy.

Strategies like relapse prevention and cue exposure do not only offer the possibility of overcoming the problem of maintaining behaviour change, but also succeed in breaking a taboo which has been pervasive in traditional treatment: that clients on an abstinence goal should not be encouraged to think or talk about curtailing drinking episodes. What these preliminary reports indicate is that helping even chronic alcoholics to prevent the onslaught of a full-blown relapse is not the same thing as advising them to pursue a controlled drinking goal. Although these techniques remain to be properly evaluated they could well change the face of abstinence treatment quite dramatically.

The focus of this chapter upon abstinence treatment should obviously not be taken to mean that controlled drinking treatment is a separate clinical enterprise to be practised among an altogether different group of clients. Many of the techniques described above can and have been used to teach controlled drinking. A number of other more specialised strategies have also been developed in this field, for example, BAC discrimination training, regulated drinking practice and bibliotherapy. One review has distinguished between two kinds of client who receive controlled drinking treatment, clinic alcoholics and problem drinkers, each likely to benefit from different approaches to treatment (Heather and Robertson, 1981). Other reviews of this subject can be found in Miller (1982) and

Nathan and Briddel (1977).

CONCLUSION

In conclusion, the prevailing pessimism about the effectiveness of alcoholism treatment is not unlike a state of learned helplessness. This chapter has argued that it should be possible to produce better outcomes by adopting an active cognitive-behavioural approach to treatment. To begin with, this would involve avoiding the use of a static model of motivation in which treatment centres around whether or not clients have sufficient willpower to stop drinking. A more dynamic model would entail dealing with two motivational problems in treatment: in the early stages of treatment ambivalence about the abstinence goal should not be overlooked by clinicians or used to question a client's motivation or attitude to treatment. Instead, this should be regarded as normal and acceptable and some time should be spent examining the 'pros and cons' of abstinence in a non-judgmental atmosphere. This is likely to be a more successful method of engaging clients in the treatment process. In a later stage of treatment, attention could then be turned to the other major problem, that of actually achieving the abstinence goal. Although many of the cognitive-behavioural strategies derived from social learning theory remain to be properly evaluated they offer the promise of producing greater behaviour change than verbally-based treatment methods. Until these possibilities have been fully explored it would be premature to conclude that treatment does not work.

REFERENCES

Armor, D.J., Polich, J.M. and Stambul, H.B. (1978) Alcoholism and Treatment, New York: Wiley

Azrin, N. (1976) 'Improvements in the community-reinforcement approach to alcoholism', Behaviour Research and Therapy, 14, 339-48

Bandura, A. (1977a) 'Self-efficacy: toward a unifying theory of behavioural change', Psychological Review, 84, 191-215
____ (1977b) Social Learning Theory, New Jersey: Prentice Hall

Blakey, R. and Baker, R. (1980) 'An exposure approach to alcohol abuse', Behaviour Research and Therapy, 18, 319-25

Cautela, J.R. (1967) 'Covert sensitisation', Psychological Reports, 20, 459-68

Chaney, E.F., O'Leary, R. and Marlatt, G.A. (1978) 'Skill training with alcoholics', Journal of Consulting and Clinical Psychology, 46, 1092-104

Davies, P. (1979) 'Motivation, responsibility and sickness in the psychiatric treatment of alcoholism', British Journal of Psychiatry, 134, 449-58
____ (1981) 'Expectations and therapeutic practices in out-patient clinics for alcohol problems', British Journal of Addiction, 76, 159-73

De Silva, P. and Rachman, S. (1981) 'Is exposure a necessary condition for fear-reduction?', Behaviour Research and Therapy, 19, 227-32

D'Zurilla, T.J. and Goldfried, M. (1971) 'Problem-solving and behaviour modification', Journal of Abnormal Psychology, 78, 107-26

Emrick, C.D. (1974) 'A review of psychologically orientated treatment of alcoholism', Quarterly Journal of Studies on Alcohol, 35, 523-49

Goldman, M.S. and Klisz, D.K. (1982) 'Behavioural treatment of alcoholism: the unvarnished story' in N. Hays and P.E. Nathan (eds), Clinical Case Studies in the Behavioural Treatment of Alcoholism, New York: Plenum

Heather, N. and Robertson, I. (1981) Controlled Drinking, London: Methuen

____ Rollnick, S. and Winton, M. (1983) 'A comparison of objective and subjective measures of alcohol dependence as predictors of relapse following treatment', British Journal of Clinical Psychology, 22, 11-17

Hodgson, R. (1980) 'Treatment strategies for the early problem drinker' in G. Edwards and M. Grant (eds), Alcoholism Treatment in Transition, London: Croom Helm

____ (1984) 'Social Learning Theory' in P. McGuffin, M. Shanks, and R.J. Hodgson (eds), The Scientific Principles of Psychopathology, London: Academic Press

____ and Rankin, H. (1982) 'Cue exposure and relapse prevention' in W.M. Hay and P.E. Nathan, Clinical Case Studies in the Behavioural Treatment of Alcoholism, New York: Plenum

Hunt, G. and Azrin, N. (1973) 'A community-reinforcement approach to alcoholism', Behaviour Research and Therapy, 11, 91-104

Mahoney, M.J. and Arnkoff, D. (1978) 'Cognitive and Self-Control Therapies' in S.H. Garfield and A.E. Bergin (eds), Handbook of Psychotherapy and Behaviour Change, New York: Wiley

Marlatt, G.A. (1978) 'Craving for alcohol, loss of control and relapse' in P.E. Nathan, G.A. Marlatt and T. Loberg (eds), Alcoholism: New Directions in Behavioural Research and Treatment, New York: Plenum

____ and Parks, G.A. (1982) 'Self-management of addictive disorders' in P. Karoly and F.H. Kanfer (eds), Self-Management and Behaviour Change, New York: Pergamon

Miller, P.M. (1982) 'Behavioural treatment of binge drinking' in W.M. Hay and P.E. Nathan (eds), Clinical Case Studies in the Behavioural Treatment of Alcoholism, New York: Plenum

Miller, W. (ed.) (1980) The Addictive Behaviours: Treatment of Alcoholism, Drug Abuse, Smoking and Obesity, New York: Pergamon

____ (1983) 'Motivational interviewing with problem drinkers', Behavioural Psychotherapy, 11, 147-72

Nathan, P. E. and Briddel, D. (1977) 'Behavioural assessment and treatment of alcoholism' in B. Kissen and A. Begleiter (eds), The Biology of Alcoholism, Vol. 5, New York: Plenum

Oei, T. and Jackson, P. (1980) 'Long-term effects of group and individual social skills training with alcoholics', Addictive Behaviours, 5, 129-36
___ (1982) 'Social skills and cognitive-behavioural approaches to the treatment of problem drinking', Journal of Studies on Alcohol, 43, 5, 532-47
Rachman, S. and Hodgson, R.J. (1980) Obsessions and Compulsions, Englewood Cliffs: Prentice Hall
Rollnick, S. and Heather, N. (1982) 'The application of Bandura's self-efficacy theory to abstinence-oriented alcoholism treatment', Addictive Behaviours, 7, 243-50
Sanchez-Craig, M. and Walker, K. (1982) 'Teaching coping skills to chronic alcoholics in a co-educational halfway house: 1. Assessment of programme effects', British Journal of Addiction, 77, 35-50
Thoresen, C.E. and Mahoney, M.J. (1974) Behavioural Self-Control, New York: Holt, Rinehart & Winston
Walker, K., Sanchez-Craig, M. and Bornet, A. (1982) 'Teaching coping skills to chronic alcoholics in a co-eductional halfway house: 2. Assessment |of |outcome and |identification of outcome predictors', British Journal of Addiction, 77, 185-96
Wilson, G.T. (1978) 'Booze, beliefs and behaviour: cognitive processes in alcohol use and abuse' in P.E. Nathan, G.A. Marlatt and T. Loberg (eds), Alcoholism: New Directions in Behavioural Research and Treatment, New York: Plenum

Chapter 9

DOES TREATMENT WORK?
YES, BUT NOT ALWAYS IN THE WAY WE PLAN IT

Fred Yates

It is a disturbing fact about our knowledge of alcoholism treatment that the question which heads this chapter cannot be dismissed as a provocative impertinence. Those familiar with the evaluative literature are compelled to take the question seriously because of evidence from several major studies casting doubt on the efficacy of treatment (Emrick, 1975; Edwards, Orford, Egert, Guthrie, Hawker, Hensman, Mitcheson, Oppenheimer and Taylor, 1977; Armor, Polich and Stambul, 1976). These studies were not able to attribute differences in drinking outcome to measured characteristics, and there was evidence from all three studies that minimal treatment was as effective as much longer periods in treatment.

There has been an understandable reluctance on the part of workers in the field to accept these findings as valid because of their apparent negative implications for treatment policy - economy of delivery should be a higher priority than the development and evaluation of new therapeutic techniques. The studies are not without their methodological faults (Yates and Norris, 1981), nor is it too difficult to find contradictory evidence of some statistical ingenuity claiming measurable treatment effects (Costello, 1975a, 1975b; Cronkite and Moos, 1980), but the general conclusion that there is a uniformity of outcome across many different treatment experiences has been largely substantiated.

In admitting this interpretation, I would resist the charge by implication of 'therapeutic nihilism'. On the contrary, the rest of this contribution will unfold the positive consequences which can follow from taking these negative results seriously. My optimistic response to the simple question, 'Does treatment work?' might be briefly formulated as, 'Yes, but not in the way we plan it'.

THE ACTUARIAL RESPONSE
It is first necessary to emphasise that the existing work has addressed the matter of treatment effectiveness as a purely actuarial one. Evaluators have mainly been interested in the curative action of treatment to alleviate a drinking problem. In consequence, the variables considered crucial in answering the question, 'Does treatment work?' were type and amount of

treatment, and pre- and post-treatment measures of drinking problems. As an answer to the general question of how treatment works, these outcome figures are as grossly uninformative as scrutinising goal scores to understand how a game of football is played. The number of successfully rehabilitated cases following a 'dose' of treatment tell the treatment researcher little about the processes going on within treatment. Nevertheless, the plain fact about programmes for problem drinkers demonstrated by these kinds of results is that, when they are conceived of as pharmaceutical-type interventions, then different alcoholism treatments do not explain differences in outcome.

THE CLIENT'S ROLE IN TREATMENT

The Rand Report (Armor et al., 1976) includes the following concluding comment on its failure to demonstrate a difference in outcome attributable to type of treatment: 'These results strongly suggest that the key ingredient in remission may be a client's decision to seek and remain in treatment rather than the specific nature of the treatment received' (p.160).

Acknowledgement of client influences on treatment outcome is frequently made in the literature but rarely taken up explicitly as a major determinant of change after treatment. To do so requires a wider interpretation of treatment than the conventional evaluative model allows. In this section I want to look at some pieces of evidence from outside the traditional investigations of treatment to obtain some measure of the client's contribution to treatment. I hope to show that it is precisely because treatment-specific factors are not crucial to its success, as found in the evaluative studies already mentioned, that treatment can work in non-clinical ways. The client can take the initiative and adapt the general features of any treatment experience to his own individual purpose.

The absence of any clearly defined therapeutic authority in the treatment encounter has been pointed out by Davies in a careful analysis of the interactions between client and therapists in three out-patient clinics (Davies, 1981). In these interactions he found that patients' high expectations about expert guidance were not fulfilled by therapists who made use of 'elicitation strategies' to shift therapeutic responsibility back onto the client. Such questions as, 'So what do you feel is the main problem?', 'Would you call yourself an alcoholic?', 'Do you think drink is a factor?' were intended to assess client motivation and emphasise his involvement in the treatment process. Davies (1981) has remarked on this outstanding feature of the interviews:

> In none of the cases observed and recorded however, did therapists go further ... and tell patients what was the cause of their alcohol problems. To do so would be out of keeping with the psychiatric model of helping patients help themselves, though it might be more in keeping with what the majority of patients expect from treatment. (p. 166)

Does Treatment Work?

The fact that these interviews were recorded across three treatment locations points towards a general reticence on the part of practitioners to assume a directive role in alcoholism treatment.

Over the course of treatment, the model client will be expected to take on the management of his drinking problem himself with agency support, but this invitation may be used in other ways by many clients who find themselves in treatment with needs which do not correspond with the therapeutic ideal, or fall in some way short of it. It is these other, unofficial treatment uses taken up by clients to which I now wish to draw attention in the following fragments of interviews with clients. These extracts were taken from post-treatment interviews with five different clients who passed through the same residential programme with a controlled drinking objective (see Gilligan, Norris and Yates, 1983, for a full treatment description).

1. But I think when you go to T......, you've got to sincerely want to have treatment, not use it to get off a lighter sentence or to please a family. You've got to want it to work because it won't otherwise.
2. I don't know whether I'd made that personal decision or whether I wanted to be patched up so I could do it (drink) all over again. But the last time when I went into hospital I certainly wanted to give it up.
3. Several contacts have tried to help me before but never had the same approach as at T......, going into the reasons why we were drinking. Nobody had ever gone into that underlying question. Everybody was telling me I should stop it (drinking) but not how to do it.
4. Well I thought that T. .. . was the help I needed but I was just a little too sure of myself. When I was there I took the advantage of controlled drinking, mastered it earlier than anybody else.
5. Obviously I can't say they completely cured me because the only complete cure would be myself. Well, I'm not ready to accept complete stopping of drinking. I don't want to stop completely because I like to have a drink. That's all there is to it.

In contrast to Davies' material, these views belong to clients who had passed through at least one treatment episode and were able to reflect on its significance for themselves and others. It should be immediately evident that these accounts give no suggestion whatever of a common treatment experience. It should also be noted that only client 3 refers to a treatment-use congruent with a simple clinical conception of treatment as a course of instruction to cure a drinking problem. All the other interviewees stress their own and others' active role in taking from treatment what they wanted with no mention of the details of treatment content, the main treatment variable attended to in conventional evaluative work. Clients 2 and 4 express an uncertainty about their motives at the beginning of treatment and, in both cases, its resolution is perceived as a personal achievement and not the result of any direct influence from treatment. The picture presented by Davies of treatment in its early stages without any clearly defined area of therapeutic responsibility is completed by these observations. They suggest that more often it is clients who come to control general facilities in treatment for their own ends.

Implicit in these accounts is a self-conscious and general use of a treatment episode by clients which calls for a redefinition of the traditional view of treatment as it applies to drinking problems. Using treatment in the way it is planned to work by treatment-providers is only one among a number of client-determined uses. It is enlightening to look again at some of the conventional evaluative work from this new position because a rather different view of treatment success presents itself. Costello (1975a, 1975b), in search of treatment characteristics associated with favourable results, carried out a statistical survey of over 80 reported studies. Using the technique of cluster analysis, it was possible to divide treatments into several main groups related to their outcome performance. His efforts to identify the effective constituents of treatment were to some extent frustrated because they were confounded with selection procedure. In particular, successful treatments not only shared certain treatment characteristics but were also characterised by a restrictive admission procedure. Within a treatment-use perspective which does not give pre-eminence to treatment content, this finding is interesting and not just a statistical irritation. It suggests that some treatments are successful because they are able to eliminate unpromising client-users or misusers of their treatment at the admission stage. From the range of possible uses, Costello's group of successful treatment regimes may have been especially effective in selecting those kinds of ideal uses exemplified in interview number 3 above which correspond most closely with the official, therapeutic function of treatment. A treatment-use perspective would also predict that those treatments not operating any strict selection criteria run the risk of having their service substantially defined by the types of users who come forward; in so far as some of these uses do not give primacy to the official treatment aim of a successful drinking outcome, then their results will be unfavourable by conventional measures. The abuses of treatment referred to in interview 1 above, for example, 'to get off a lighter sentence or to please a family' would be more common in this treatment group. This is, in fact, what Costello's work shows - the treatment group with the poorest outcome in his study included those treatments with no screening procedure or active programme. In other words, the initiative in establishing the character of the service was with the users.

Another distinct group of less successful treatments in this study were those with few intake restrictions but a positive therapeutic orientation. Costello noted that the typical length of stay was between 1 and 8 weeks, which differed markedly from the stays of up to 40 weeks reported for the best-outcome group of treatments. This difference is nicely accounted for by a treatment-use model which would predict early withdrawal by those users who could not adapt their specific needs to a rigid treatment policy. It is a real possibility that better-than-average treatment results have more to do with the elimination of treatment misuses at selection than the treatment factors which follow.

We should then recognise that treatment may work in client-oriented ways which do not conform to its orthodox, clinical mode of operation. We have, in an earlier paper (Yates and Norris, 1981), noted some of these uses and would like to set them out here more formally with some evidence from the literature.

POSITIVE TREATMENT USE

Logically the list should begin with a hidden group who never enter into the actuarial calculation of treatment efficacy. Technically we may refer to them as non-users since they do not actually come into contact with any of the therapeutic factors which constitute the treatment experience. Yet this group may benefit in an indirect way simply because of the availability of a treatment service. Those people with drinking difficulties for whom treatment becomes a practical course of action on offer must justify to themselves or others why they do not require it, and may be encouraged to concentrate their efforts and succeed in the personal management of their drinking problem. It is a subtle and immeasurable treatment effect which extends to the general population of problem drinkers and is not just confined to those actively seeking treatment. Something akin to this process may explain the failure of evaluative studies to establish a clear relationship between outcome and amount of treatment. The Rand Report (Armor et al., 1976) found that those who had not begun treatment were as successful as those given small amounts, with slightly greater than 50 per cent reporting abstinent or harm-free drinking outcomes. The recovery of this group of non-users, otherwise mysteriously referred to as cases of spontaneous remission, may be attributable to the simple act of enlisting on a course of treatment without any further involvement. It declares a drinking problem which may have been denied, and makes real the fearful possibility of relinquishing absolute personal control of drinking. Withdrawal from treatment may not be an indication of poor motivation, rather it may be an indication of a strengthened resolve to cope on one's own, acquired prior to treatment rather than during treatment. The public agency here sets in motion a process of recovery which can evidently be completed by the problem drinker himself.

I would therefore argue that there is some evidence for the existence of an inestimable number of potential users for whom 'treatment works', even though they never take on the course of antabuse, turn up at out-patient appointments, or attend group therapy sessions. For them it is more precisely the prospect of treatment which works.

I want next to draw attention to that most important user-group who conspicuously demonstrate that treatment works in the normal therapeutic sense. They follow the treatment plan assiduously, complete the course and afterwards give much credit to the treatment experience as a positive turning point in the management of their drinking problem. The third speaker in the interview extracts exemplifies this type of user. Upholders of conventional treatment doctrine would point to the specific attributes within treatment, such as therapist factors or therapeutic techniques, in order to account for these successes. The evidence for a uniformity of outcome across different types of treatment already noted suggests, however, that there are important general features of treatment to be found of which these users are taking advantage. What engages this particular group in treatment and wins such full commitment, yet fails to attract the previous group of non-users? The answer, 'a determination to succeed in a treatment setting', may be less than satisfactory, but further specification would not do justice to the many reasons why some problem drinkers will reach a moment in their lives when treatment becomes the best available option. In general though, this group do not possess the private resources to tackle their drinking unaided though their resolve may be firm. Domestic conditions may be too impoverished to give purpose and impetus to a major life change. Treatment can provide the foundation of an orderly life style to replace the private chaos of unpaid bills, irregular work routine and general household neglect to which sustained, excessive drinking can lead. Robin Room has characterised a treatment-seeking population of 'spare people' who find themselves socially isolated after exhausting their 'moral credit' with employers, families and friends (Room, 1980). The decision to make a public declaration of a drinking problem and resolutely follow a treatment programme may be a conciliatory act to re-establish relationships, and at the same time qualify for professional concern to replace the sympathy they have lost in their private lives. The etiology of alcoholism is also still sufficiently confused for treatment to be conceived of and used as a short, sharp, medical cure for a chronic illness which discharges all moral responsibility for a drinking problem as long as treatment advice is observed.

The significant point to note about this group of treatment users is that their success may be properly credited to a high initial motivation to change which is facilitated by very general features of treatment. This motivation would be the crucial client quality discerned at intake by treatment workers in Costello's most successful treatment groups. Such clients would be expected to be enthusiastic participants in any treatment programme. Recovery may be speeded up or made more comfortable for those users fortunate enough to find a regime compatible with their personal philosophy of treatment, but these are enhancements to a process which can work in any genuinely therapeutic environment. The function of treatment suggested here is summed up in a remark made in one of the earlier interview extracts - 'you've got to want it to work because it won't otherwise'.

TREATMENT MISUSE
I have so far concentrated on two ways in which treatment works to

produce a favourable outcome. I want now to present in less detail several ways in which treatment works for the user, but not in bringing about a positive or long-term change in harmful patterns of drinking. There are some users, mainly in residential services for homeless alcoholics, who need protection from the natural drinking environment. They lack the social and/or personal resources to control their drinking, and use treatment as a shelter from which to practise a code of abstinence they could not otherwise sustain. These are long-term users whose weak resolve to change their drinking habits is augmented only over the duration of treatment and not beyond it, with no real change resulting from the treatment experience. Workers in the field of vagrant alcoholic rehabilitation recognise the 'dry drunk' in treatment who may remain sober for long periods but does not learn to cope with his drinking problem independently:

> Real sobriety is kicking all the crutches away. Take Micky, for example. He's got no insight at all into his problem and he's been off the beer for a long time now but he's still got social workers running around after him, writing letters for him when he's trying to get a job ... he is very dependent (Archard, 1979, p.139).

The vagrant classes also exhibit a clearly instrumental use of alcoholism treatment as a rest before resuming a harmful drinking pattern. This was alluded to in one of the earlier interviews where it was presented as 'wanting to be patched up so I could do it all over again'.

Staff are usually well aware of their exploitation by this type of user:

> Ideally I would like to feel that men think sobriety has a lot to offer in terms of their future ... that sobriety is worthwhile ... but the majority of residents who pass through here are not sincere. For these men this place gives them a chance to build up physically and mentally so that they can cope with their next bout on skid row (Archard, 1979, p.138).

It should not be forgotten that there are many treatment places occupied by people who would not be there of their own volition but who undergo the experience to satisfy other parties. In another paper we were able to compare referral networks to different residential services and the interests of third parties in the process of referral were clearly influential in the probability of clients reaching the final stages of assessment (Yates and Norris, 1983). The client who is merely compliant will respond indifferently to the type of treatment in which he finds himself. In such cases the completion of treatment is an end in itself at the insistence of a wife, GP or Probation Officer, and not an indication of any serious intent to beat a drinking problem.

IMPLICATIONS FOR RESEARCH AND TREATMENT DELIVERY

In practice, I believe many of these other modes of treatment operation are well known amongst treatment workers who are able to respond in a positive way to clients whose use of treatment deviates from its official therapeutic function. Experienced workers are quick to recognise clients without any serious intention of using treatment to change their drinking. What concerns me is that this significant area of treatment activity is ignored by conventional research and evaluation, which insists on narrowly defining treatment qua treatment, and attributes follow-up results exclusively to the planned features of programmes. I want to follow through some important implications of the wider view of treatment I have presented here. Workers in the field may already have informally incorporated these suggestions in their treatment routine.

Firstly, a major empirical study of alcoholism treatment is required in order to extend and elaborate the rudimentary typology of treatment-user submitted here. I have only been able to document the more obvious uses and misuses but a number of less frequently encountered uses awaits some systematic description. For example, I have heard reports of model clients who, after substantial progress in treatment, suddenly relapse without any warning signs. I would like to speculate that at least some of these spectacular and inexplicable reversals conceal a fear of losing an identity and being swallowed up by the system as a conventional treatment success. The treatment event is an object of sabotage in a rebellious act.

This empirical groundwork to expand our knowledge of treatment processes should be essential preparation for a more self-conscious style of treatment delivery which I wish to propose. At the moment, practitioners pay lip service to a clinical mode of treatment which is applied indiscriminately to all treatment arrivals, even though it represents only one form of use. Other less legitimate uses may be taken up regardless though outwardly the clinical mode will be enacted. Poorly motivated clients will be those who observe the minimum requirements of a programme in order to remain in treatment long enough to satisfy their own individual ends. For instance, some clients will stay in treatment as unresponsive attenders of group sessions until their physical recovery is complete and then they will resume drinking. I would like to see these other uses openly acknowledged so that this explicitness can become a therapeutic resource in a wider model of treatment. Both therapist and client should be aware that each treatment encounter begins as a fresh opportunity for the user to accomplish a genuine shift in attitude towards the natural drinking environment.

This possibility becomes more remote over the course of a single treatment episode, and with each successive encounter as other deviant uses develop. Left unchallenged, these deviant patterns can only divert the therapeutic efforts of treatment staff into unproductive areas. Time spent with poorly motivated clients, the unedifying influence of examples of treatment misuse on sincere users and the disruptive effect of every drinking lapse in a treatment setting can all be traced to the improper use of treatment. The early detection of these uses to correct or eliminate them would be possible if treatment research took a wider view of the treatment experience in the lives of users and passed on this knowledge to treatment workers.

I have been compelled to reply very generally to the abstract question, 'Does treatment work?', but it has presented a welcome opportunity to consider uniform features of all treatment services. Too often treatment evaluation has been satisfied to ask the question, 'Does this or that treatment work?', and the answer presupposes that treatment is the seat of a mysterious therapeutic power. The actual state of affairs is a more common place one in which the client holds the therapeutic initiative and may discard it and use the treatment service for other purposes. If practitioners and researchers could collaborate and build up an expertise of knowledge in these other uses then there is a better chance that the client could be directed to the right one.

REFERENCES

Archard, P. (1979) Vagrancy, Alcoholism and Social Control, London: The Macmillan Press Limited

Armor, D.J., Polich, J.M. and Stambul, H.B. (1976) Alcoholism and Treatment, Santa Monica, California: The Rand Corporation

Costello, R.M. (1975a) 'Alcoholism treatment and evaluation: in search of methods', International Journal of the Addictions, 10, 251-75

_____ (1975b) 'Alcoholism treatment and evaluation: in search of methods. II. Collation of 2-year follow-up studies', International Journal of the Addictions, 10, 857-67

Cronkite, R.C. and Moos, R.H. (1980) 'Determinants of the post-treatment functioning of alcoholic patients: a conceptual framework', Journal of Consulting and Clinical Psychology, 48, 305-16

Davies, P. (1981) 'Expectations and therapeutic practices in outpatient clinics for alcohol problems', British Journal of Addiction, 76, 159-73

Edwards, G., Orford, J., Egert, S., Guthrie, S., Hawker, A., Hensman, C., Mitcheson, M., Oppenheimer, E. and Taylor, C. (1977) 'Alcoholism: a controlled trial of "treatment" and "advice" ', Journal of Studies on Alcohol, 38, 1004-31

Emrick, C.D. (1975) 'A review of psychologically orientated treatment of alcoholism. II. The relative effectiveness of different treatment approaches and the effectiveness of treatment versus no treatment', Journal of Studies on Alcohol, 36, 88-108

Gilligan, T., Norris, H. and Yates, F.E. (1984) 'Management problems in a small hostel with a controlled drinking programme', British

Journal of Addiction, 78, 277-91
Room, R. (1980) 'Treatment-seeking populations and larger realities' in G. Edwards and M. Grant (eds), Alcoholism Treatment in Transition, London: Croom Helm
Yates, F.E. and Norris, H. (1981) 'The use made of treatment: an alternative approach to the evaluation of alcoholism services', Behavioural Psychotherapy, 9, 291-309
___ (1983) 'An investigation of pre-admission referral activity to 3 residential units with a related commentary on the Pattern and Range of Services for Problem Drinkers', British Journal of Addiction, 78, 391-402

Chapter 10

DOES TREATMENT WORK? A SOCIOLOGICAL PERSPECTIVE

Phil Davies

The answer to the question, 'Does treatment work?' hinges upon qualifying elements such as what one means by 'treatment' and what one means by 'work'. Treatment can refer to quite different types of intervention, such as the management of acute intoxication and withdrawal, the provision of individual or group therapy on an in-patient, day-patient or out-patient basis (Ministry of Health, 1962, 1968; DHSS, 1973, 1975), psychoanalysis (Knight, 1937; Menninger, 1938), behaviour therapy (Nathan, Marlatt and Loberg, 1978; Heather and Robertson, 1981) and environmental manipulation (Hunt and Azrin, 1973). These interventions differ from each other not only in terms of how they define abusive drinking and what they offer problem drinkers, but also in terms of what counts as 'working'. Some interventions, such as the 'community-reinforcement' approach reported by Hunt and Azrin (1973), are so radically different from most hospital or clinic-based treatments that some researchers (see Saunders, Chapter 6) would not consider them to be treatment at all. Such a viewpoint is unfortunately narrow, and fails to appreciate how a number of treatable conditions, such as physical impairments, require considerable community-based support and environmental manipulation. However, the point is that if one is prepared to count contingency management and other behavioural strategies (Heather and Robertson, 1981) as treatment, then these appear to work in terms of reducing harmful drinking and improving other areas of functioning, and they seem to do so better than many other interventions (Sobell and Sobell, 1976).

By the same token, if one considers the management of acute intoxication and withdrawal as 'treatment' then this appears to work quite well, at least in terms of restoring some degree of sobriety and normal functioning, however short term this might be. Moreover, even the most critical reader of evaluation studies would have to concede that the so-called 'conventional treatments' offered in British and American treatment units do work, according to varying criteria, for between 10 per cent (Hayman, 1956) and 73 per cent (Armor, Polich and Stambul, 1978) of clients.

Criteria of whether or not treatment works are no less problematic than what counts as treatment. For adherents of the

AA philosophy nothing less than total abstinence counts as a measure of success for treatment or some other intervention. In recent years, however, a wider set of outcome criteria has been used by alcohol researchers to include behavioural and social adjustment factors such as job status, marital status, domestic lifestyles and relationships. None the less, despite the inclusion of such factors in outcome criteria, it is drinking patterns and drinking-related behaviours that are given primacy in treatment evaluations (cf. Armor, et al., 1978, p.51).

A noticeable absence in studies of treatment effectiveness is a consideration of therapists' and patients' criteria of success and failure of treatment. In the pursuit of so-called 'objective' indicators of treatment effectiveness, the subjective dimension of what therapists and patients define as treatment and outcome has either been ignored or dealt with in terms of ratings on variables determined deductively by researchers rather than inductively from treatment participants themselves. This is perhaps unfortunate in an area of therapy in which the relationship between therapist and client is held to be of considerable importance. As Edwards (1982) has recently pointed out: 'The clumsy therapist is like someone who tries to carve a piece of wood without respect for the grain. The basic work of treatment requires immense respect for that grain, and therapy must always be matched to individual needs'. (p.198)

In this chapter I shall focus on what therapists and patients bring to treatment for alcohol problems in terms of their respective ideas and expectations about treatment and their respective criteria of success. In doing so I hope to demonstrate that treatment is most likely to 'work', albeit in terms of rather more modest criteria than those measured by most treatment evaluation studies, when patients' perceived needs and expectations of treatment are recognised and accommodated by therapists and treatment programmes.

THE EVALUATION LITERATURE
Before I present some data on therapists' and patients' views of treatment and of treatment success I want to highlight three themes which emerge from the literature on treatment evaluation. First, it has been suggested (Tuchfeld, 1976; Saunders, Chapter 6) that treatment is not necessary for recovery from harmful drinking to occur, and that it is changes in a problem drinker's social and domestic situation or environment that bring about spontaneous recovery. There can be little doubt that factors such as getting married, divorced, re-uniting or leaving a partner, changing a job or moving to a new locale or environment can and do bring about significant changes in an individual's level and pattern of drinking. This should come as no surprise to anyone familiar with the mental health field, where these factors have been shown to be of considerable importance in the aetiology of, and recovery from depression of schizophrenia (Brown, et al., 1973; Brown and Birley, 1968). However, whilst treatment may not be necessary for these factors to occur it is logically and empirically (Davies, 1983) the

case that treatment might help patients make decisions to change their lifestyles and environments in such a way as to bring about so-called spontaneous remission. This seems to be an essential component of many behavioural approaches to treatment (Nathan et al., 1978; Heather and Robertson, 1981) and of the community reinforcement approach reported by Hunt and Azrin (1973). One way in which we might consider treatment to have worked (or failed), then, is the extent to which it facilitates or militates against such changes in a problem drinker's lifestyle or environment.

Secondly, the treatment evaluation literature also suggests that, whilst no particular treatment approach works better than others, a problem drinker's participation in treatment of any kind is likely to enhance recovery more than non-participation (Emrick, 1975; Armor et al., 1978). The first RAND study suggested that 'at 18 months, about 67 per cent of the treatment clients are in remission compared with only 53 per cent of those making a single contact with the treatment centre' (Armor et al., 1978, pp.116-17). This study concluded that 'alcoholism treatment is effective to a moderate extent ... [in that] clients who receive treatment experience remission at higher rates than those who remain untreated ... [and] a higher amount of treatment leads to higher remission rates' (Armor et al., 1978, p.150). Such observations have led Emrick to conclude that 'a wiser expenditure of resources might be in the area of developing strategies to involve alcoholics in therapy, any kind of therapy, since all approaches seem generally helpful to the majority of patients' (Emrick, 1975, pp.94-5, my emphasis). According to this evidence treatment can be said to have worked to the extent that it engages and maintains patients in therapy for more than one visit.

Thirdly, the above observation seems to conflict with a major contribution to the treatment evaluation literature (Orford and Edwards, 1977) which suggests that minimal treatment intervention, based on a comprehensive assessment and a single counselling session, works as well as more intensive, conventional treatment. This would seem to suggest that a single contact with a treatment agency, which was regarded by the RAND researchers to constitute non-treatment, may be of considerable therapeutic benefit to problem drinkers. At the same time, Orford and Edwards reported that prolonged treatment 'had succeeded in engaging patients in therapy' (Orford and Edwards, 1977) which, as we have seen, is considered by some researchers to enhance recovery from harmful drinking.

The apparent contradiction between these three positions from within the treatment evaluation literature may be resolved if one accepts, notwithstanding the RAND researchers' opinion that 'the specific type of treatment is largely irrelevant to the client's prospect for remission' (Armor et al., 1978, p.151), that 'rather than seek an outstanding treatment, therapists might give attention to matching each alcoholic with the setting and approach which meshes best with his views on the causes, nature and treatment of alcoholism' (Emrick, 1975, p.95). This, it will be noted, concurs with my suggestion that treatment is more likely to work when patients' perceived needs and expectations of treatment are recognised and accommodated by therapists and treatment programmes. The focus of attention then becomes therapists' and clients' views on treatment and treatment success and how these are dealt with during treatment encounters.

METHODOLOGY AND DATA
For the most part, treatment evaluation studies are based on input-output models of the treatment process, whereby the complexities involved are reduced for analytical purposes by subsuming them under aggregate categories such as 'client inputs' and 'treatment inputs' (e.g. Armor et al., 1978, pp.49-56). One consequence of this is that the process of treatment, its 'throughput', is largely neglected. The data generated by such studies are mostly correlational rather than interactional. This is not to deny the importance of aggregate, correlational data in the study of treatment effectiveness or, for that matter, in health service research in general. They are clearly crucial in taking research and analysis away from the particular and providing general trends and overall perspectives. The corollary of this is that aggregate data are relatively insensitive to qualitative factors which structure the process of treatment at the micro level of therapist-client interaction.

In an attempt to redress this imbalance I have been studying treatment for alcohol problems by focusing on the treatment experiences of 50 clients referred to the out-patient services of (a) a general psychiatric hospital, and (b) a specialist alcoholism treatment unit. The aim of this research was to examine what clients and therapists bring to treatment in terms of expectations and views of the treatment process, and to examine the extent to which these factors influence or structure the interaction between clients and therapists. A further aim of the research was to identify what clients and therapists consider to be of therapeutic value over a course of treatment.

Two sorts of data were collected, interview and observational. Eleven psychiatrists at the consultant or senior registrar level at the general psychiatric hospital, and the four principal therapists (one consultant psychiatrist, two senior registrars and a clinical psychologist) at the specialist alcoholism treatment unit were interviewed. A 37-item interview schedule was administered to elicit therapists' views on the nature of alcohol problems, the role of psychiatry in their treatment, and the role of therapists and clients in the treatment process. Therapists were also interviewed about particular clients, cases and consultations over the course of treatment. Therapists' reponses to a selection of these interview questions will be presented in this chapter. A more detailed and comprehensive presentation of these interview materials will be found elsewhere (Davies, 1983).

Clients were interviewed each time they visited the out-patient services. They were interviewed before and after each consultation.

The pre-consultation interviews with clients asked about why they had been referred, what they identified as their main problem(s), who had referred them, and what they expected from their visit to out-patient services. A detailed drinking history was also taken before their consultations with therapists. Post-consultation interviews were based on a nine-item interview schedule. This covered issues such as their views of the consultation they had just had, whether or not they were satisfied with it, whether or not it had helped them with their alcohol problem and their expectations about future treatment. All clients, including those who discontinued treatment after one visit, were additionally interviewed twelve weeks after their initial visit to out-patient services. A selection of clients' interview responses will be presented in this chapter.

Each client's consultations with a therapist over a course of treatment were observed by me and audio-recorded. A selection of consultations was video-taped. These recordings allow the interaction between therapists and clients to be retrieved and extensively analysed. Elsewhere (Davies, 1983), I present a detailed analysis of these consultations. In this chapter I use these observational and recorded data to present two case studies of therapeutic style and therapist-client interaction. It is important to stress that in this chapter I am only able to use these data illustratively. They are clearly not an exhaustive analysis of the minutia or variation in therapist-client interaction.

THERAPISTS' VIEWS OF TREATMENT
Two of the questions addressed to therapists were:

(1) What in your view does treatment for alcohol problems consist of?
(2) By what criteria do you view the success or failure of treatment for alcohol problems?

Table 10.1 presents the responses to the first question of the 15 therapists interviewed. It shows that therapists most often mentioned counselling (i.e. advice-giving, explanation, providing guidelines) and detoxification/management of withdrawal in response to the first question. The fact that all four therapists at the specialist alcoholism treatment unit mentioned advice-giving and counselling is perhaps not surprising given that this unit organises its treatment programme around a four-week day-hospital course of alcohol education and information. The pursuit of abstinence and the treatment of primary problems such as depression and psychosis were mentioned by only three of the therapists, and these were all psychiatrists in the general psychiatric hospital.

Table 10.2 presents the responses of these 15 therapists to the question, 'by what criteria do you view success or failure in the treatment of alcohol problems?'. The outstanding feature of Table 10.2 is that 12 of the 15 therapists mentioned 'social and personal adjustment' factors such as a change in primary relationships, marital status, employment, return to normal social functioning and

Table 10.1: Therapists' Views About Treatment for Alcohol Problems

	General psychiatric hospital therapists (n = 11)	Specialist ATU therapists (n = 4)	All therapists (n = 15)
Counselling (advice-giving, explanation, guidelines)	8	4	12
Detoxification (management of withdrawal)	6	2	8
Working with spouse and families	3	2	5
Pursuing abstinence	3	0	3
Treatment of primary problems (psychosis, depression)	3	0	3
Behavioural methods	1	2	3

personal growth as criteria for success of treatment. Eight therapists mentioned 'return to non-harmful drinking', which may include abstinence, but only two therapists mentioned abstinence specifically as a criterion for treatment success. These two therapists, one from each unit, differed considerably in their views about abstinence. One was quite definite, if not dogmatic, in his view that 'the only measure of success is the ability [of the patient] to remain off alcohol, that's the only target'. The other therapist who mentioned abstinence as a criterion of treatment success, thought that 'abstinence for a period of time can do nobody any harm, so if we can encourage people to do that I think we're doing very well'. Although none of the other therapists mentioned abstinence specifically in response to this question, their responses to other questions on the interview schedule suggest that the latter therapists' opinion is quite commonly held by many, if not most therapists who work with problem drinkers.

Table 10.2: Therapists' Criteria of Success or Failure of Treatment for Alcohol Problems

	General psychiatric hospital therapists (n = 11)	Specialist ATU therapists (n = 4)	All therapists (n = 15)
Social and personal adjustment (primary relationships, job, marriage, social functioning, growth)	8	4	12
Return to non-harmful drinking	4	4	8
Patients' or families' criteria	1	3	4
Attainment of short-term goals	0	2	2
Getting patients to return for more than one visit	1	1	2
Abstinence	1	1	2

These views about treatment and treatment success are consistent with therapists' responses to other questions on the interview schedule. For instance, when asked, 'what do you believe to be the causes of alcohol problems?' the vast majority of therapists (14 out of 15) mentioned people's lifestyles and environmental factors, and a slightly smaller majority (10 out of 15) mentioned the availability of alcohol. Whilst as many therapists who mentioned availability of alcohol mentioned psychiatric illness or personality factors, in most cases this seemed almost a token, or taken for granted response for psychiatrists to make, and in most instances was qualified by reference to lifestyle factors and/or availability. For instance, one psychiatrist at the general psychiatric hospital said, 'A lot of it has to do with availability and subcultural drinking habits. I think these are the overwhelming things. I mean there must be some personality attribute, but I don't think that's enough.' Another psychiatrist responded to this question by saying that 'alcohol problems are caused by how much you drink, for how long. And that tends to be determined by people's environment, the situations they find themselves in. I really don't think it's particularly a matter of personality of psychological make-up. It's about how people respond to their environment.'

Furthermore, the vast majority of therapists (11 out of 15) did not think that psychiatry is the most appropriate discipline or service for dealing with alcohol problems. Some of the grounds that were given for this position were: 'many people have far more skills to offer than a pure medical or psychiatric approach'; 'anybody who has knowledge of alcoholism, or who can listen and give sound advice can do just as well'; 'it's not an illness or even a psychiatric problem'; 'it's important to deal with it out in the community, where it belongs'.

In sum, then, these interview responses suggest that for these therapists at least, treatment for alcohol problems consists of giving advice, providing an explanation and information, pointing out the role of lifestyles and environmental factors which lead to harmful drinking, and providing detoxification and withdrawal facilities where necessary. Moreover, for these therapists treatment along these lines is not restricted to psychiatrists and psychiatric services. Success or failure of treatment was seen by these therapists in terms of the extent to which clients make adjustments to their personal and social lives, reduce their drinking to non-harmful levels and, to a lesser extent, achieve at least some degree of short-term abstinence. Other criteria for success or failure of treatment that were mentioned by the therapists interviewed were the opinions and judgements of clients and their families, the attainment of short-term goals, and getting patients back for more than one visit.

CLIENTS' VIEWS OF TREATMENT

Clients were not asked directly what they thought treatment for alcohol problems consisted of, nor about their criteria for treatment success or failure. However, certain questions which were addressed to clients do provide indirect indications of their views on these matters.

One question was: 'What do you expect to happen when you see the doctor/therapist today?' Elsewhere (Davies 1980, 1981) I have reported clients' answers to this question when it was put to another sample of 34 new patients in out-patient clinics of alcoholism treatment units. In that study the majority of clients (22 out of 34) said that they expected an interview from their initial visit. By way of contrast only six clients said that they expected a physical examination or some medical procedure such as a blood test.

The other expectation mentioned by 22 of the 34 clients was that they would be given an explanation, advice or guidance from therapists. Six clients said that they expected to be given practical advice and information about alcohol and ways of curtailing its use.

A further six clients said that they expected to be given 'some sort of guidelines', or simply 'guidance' about their alcohol use and/or problems which they thought caused them to drink excessively. The remaining ten patients indicated that they expected the therapists to give them some explanation for their drinking problems.

Table 10.3 presents the responses of the 50 clients interviewed in my current research project. It also indicates that the most frequently expressed expectation (by 26 out of the 50 clients) was that therapists would provide advice, guidance and help about drinking and/or some explanation for their drinking behaviour. The next most often mentioned expectation was that their visit would consist of 'questions' and 'talking'. Only four clients said that they expected some sort of psychiatric treatment – for example, 'I hear voices and I want to find out what these voices are' – and only two clients expected a physical examination. It is important to note that 11 of the clients interviewed said that they did not know what to expect from their visit to the out-patient clinic, and these eleven were so-classified after they had been prompted with the possibilities presented in Table 10.3.

Table 10.3: Patients' Expectations of Treatment
for Alcohol Problems

	General psychiatric hospital therapists (n = 25)	Specialist ATU therapists (n = 25)	All therapists (n = 50)
Advice, direction explanation, help with drinking	12	14	26
Questions and talking	8	6	14
Psychiatry group therapy	0	4	4
Medications	0	3	3
Physical examination	1	1	2
Other (controlled drinking, occupy time, be locked up)	2	3	5
Don't know	6	5	11

It will be recalled that advice-giving, explanation and providing guidelines were the treatment factors most often mentioned by therapists when asked about treatment for alcohol problems (Table 10.1). This would seem to indicate that clients' expectations of treatment tend to converge with therapists' views on treatment. At the same time there were therapists and clients whose views and expectations about treatment were not in keeping with these general trends, and one may assume that these views and expectations might well diverge rather than converge.

Although clients were not asked directly about their criteria for treatment success or failure, three other questions asked after their initial session with a therapist provide indirect indicators. The first post-consultation question that clients were asked was a general and open-ended one: 'What are your views of the consultation you have just had?' Clients' responses were grouped as 'favourable', 'unfavourable' and 'neutral' according to the criteria given at the bottom of Table 10.4. Table 10.4 indicates that the majority of clients (32 out of 50) had generally favourable views about their

Table 10.4: Patients' Views of their Initial Consultation

	Favourable	Unfavourable	Neutral	N/A
General psychiatric hospital patients	11	4	8	2
Specialist ATU patients	21	0	0	4
All patients	32	4	8	6

Criteria of classification

Favourable

Found it helpful
Pleased
Was told something
Not disappointed
To my liking
What I wanted/expected
Good
Factual
Learned something
Received an opinion
Surprised (favourably)
It allowed relief

Unfavourable

Disappointed
Haven't learned anything
I gave more than I received
Not very helpful
A bloody waste of time

Neutral

Alright/OK
Straightforward
Uncomplicated
What anyone would have
    asked me
Just a question and answer
    session

initial consultations with therapists. Only four clients had unfavourable views, and these were all from the general psychiatric hospital. The eight neutral responses were also from clients at the general psychiatric hospital.

Clients were then asked whether they were satisfied or dissatisfied with their initial consultation. Table 10.5 indicates that the vast majority of these clients were satisfied. The two clients who expressed dissatisfaction were both at the general psychiatric hospital.

Table 10.5: Clients' Satisfaction/Dissatisfaction
with Consultation

	Satisfied	Dissatisfied	D.K.	N/A
General psychiatric hospital clients	19	2	2	2
Specialist ATU clients	21	0	1	3
All clients	40	2	3	5

One might infer from the data in Tables 10.4 and 10.5 that the treatment offered in both of these facilities 'worked' to the extent that it satisfied the expectations of the majority of clients. Alternatively, one might justifiably say that this is a rather narrow conception of treatment having 'worked', and that clients may express satisfaction with what was offered without having been helped with their alcohol problems. Anticipating this objection clients were also asked whether or not the consultation they had just had had helped them with their alcohol problem. Again, the majority of clients (Table 10.6) said that their initial consultation had helped, though there were more of these clients in the specialist alcoholism out-patient clinic than in the out-patient service of the general psychiatric hospital. The generally more favoured and helpful service that is apparently provided by the out-patients clinic of the specialist alcoholism treatment unit may be attributable to its policy and emphasis of providing 'treatment' on the basis of a four-week day-hospital course of alcohol education and information. Consequently, the initial consultation offers clients a follow-up service which is explicitly informative and educational and generally in keeping with their expectations. These data also support the underlying theme of this chapter which is that treatment is more likely to 'work' when clients' perceived needs and expectations of treatment are recognised and accommodated by therapists and treatment programmes.

Table 10.6: Clients' Views on Whether the Consultation Helped

	Yes	No	D.K.	N/A
General psychiatric hospital clients	14	8	2	2
Specialist ATU clients	20	1	1	3
All clients	34	9	3	5

CASE-STUDY EVIDENCE

So far I have focused on interviews with therapists and with clients and on the general pattern of relationships between their respective viewpoints. I now want to briefly address the proposition that treatment is more likely to work when it converges with and accommodates clients' perceived needs and expectations, by comparing the treatment experiences of two clients at the out-patient service of the general psychiatric hospital. I acknowledge that the case-study method is limited in terms of its generalisability, though its value in this context is as a heuristic device and as a means of illustrating qualitative differences in treatment approaches.

Client A. This client was a 45-year-old male who readily acknowledged that his drinking was problematic. He claimed not to have drunk alcohol within the last seven days, though his reported alcohol consumption when he was drinking was 112 units a week. Client A said that he had come to the out-patient clinic following 'yet another heavy binge' which had inspired him to 'get on and do something about it'. He said that he didn't know what to expect from his visit, though he repeatedly said that he was seeking 'help to keep me off alcohol'.

Client A was seen by the psychiatrist (Therapist A) who took the rather definite view (see above) that 'the only measure of success is the ability to remain off alcohol, that's the only target'. However, this therapist said that he distinguished between primary and secondary alcoholism. The former he sees as a condition in which the client cannot control his drinking behaviour because he/she is addicted to alcohol, whereas the latter is seen as an excessive intake of alcohol associated with the client's primary psychiatric illness (e.g. manic-depression, schizophrenia, personality disorder). Therapist A added that in his experience more than 95 per cent of clients referred to him for drinking problems are 'primary' alcoholics. To these clients he offers, without exception, the advice: 'You are an alcoholic. You must become one hundred per cent dry and you must immediately make contact with Alcoholics Anonymous.' He also explained that 'my techniques constantly face them [clients] with what they are doing, not in a critical way, but I never let them escape from the word alcohol'.

Therapist A's style of therapy is confrontational, aggressive, and rather like that of a lawyer cross-examining a witness in a court case. His interviews with clients are distinctly formal in that he and the clients sit at opposite sides of a desk, the therapist always wears a white coat and he addresses clients by their surnames (prefixed by Miss, Mr or Mrs) throughout the interview. Moreover, he constantly draws upon information in the medical records to challenge the client's statements and claims, again very much like a cross-examination lawyer. This description is not a criticism of Therapist A's style for it is readily acknowledged that a confrontational, aggressive approach to clients is seen by many psychiatrists to be a useful and rewarding way of breaking down clients' resistance, defences and denial mechanisms.

This approach, however, is not always successful with patients, at least not in the sense of establishing a good therapist-client relationship. In client A's case it resulted in friction between the therapist and client and did little to provide the help that the client was seeking. Consider the closing sequences of the consultation, after Therapist A had told the client that he was 'suffering from chronic alcoholism' and that he should go immediately and every night henceforth to Alcoholics Anonymous:

C: OK. I'll go and see them. I take it we're finished.

T: Well, now you're running off from me.

C: No. I take it that is your advice, so I'd better go.

T: Ah, but you haven't said what you think of the advice, or whether you feel it's any help to you.

C: I said I would take it. My own thoughts about it I'll no doubt pass on at a future date. But I'll take it. I'll keep an open mind. I'll go now.

T: That leads me on to the next point. You say you're going to be here (in the city) for at least a month.

C: I should imagine so.

T: Well, what I should suggest is that I make an appointment to see you in two weeks' time.

C: I very much doubt if I'll make it, but you never know. I'll let you know.

Immediately following the consultation I interviewed the client, who said that he was dissatisfied with the consultation and that it had not helped him with his search for ways of keeping off alcohol. Moreover, when I asked him how long he anticipated treatment lasting he replied: 'If the first interview is anything to go by I doubt if there'll be a second.' Indeed, this client did not return for additional consultations and at 12-weeks follow-up he was still drinking at or about a level of 112 units of alcohol a week.

It is difficult to see how this treatment approach 'worked' with this client. Since the client did not return for additional consultations one could not say that the treatment experience worked at getting the client to remain in treatment. Nor could one say that as a single counselling session it worked in terms of satisfying the client's expectations, helping the client with his drinking problem or getting the client to face his drinking problem in a way which would reduce his alcohol consumption. Nor did it appear to have inspired or stimulated the client to change his lifestyle in a way which would bring about less harmful drinking.

It could be argued that this was a particularly belligerent client who was 'poorly motivated' and had little genuine desire to change his drinking habits. This, however, would not be consistent with his expressed desires and expectations during the pre-consultation interview or during the early sequences of his consultation with the therapist. Even if this were the case, the issue remains as to whether or not therapists should go about inducing clients' motivation, changing their perceptions of their problems and situation, and modifying their expectations of treatment (Sterne and Pitman, 1965; Davies, 1979). The majority of therapists interviewed in this study thought that this is a role for therapists. On this question Therapist A said:

> I must say that I am extremely forthright with patients if it's an alcohol problem and if I make a diagnosis of alcoholism. And I say that frequently and rigidly. And you have all the arguments about it, so I think you've got to be absolutely crystal clear and hold your front. It may take six months for a person to get around to agreeing with you.

Changing clients' perceptions of their problem, then, takes time and requires them to continue with treatment. This, however, may depend upon therapeutic style and therapist-client interaction. Of the three clients in this sample who were seen by Therapist A none of them continued in treatment after their first visits and their alcohol consumption at 3-months follow-up was not reduced.

Client B. This client was a 41-year-old male who also readily acknowledged that his drinking was problematic, though he also identified depression and an inferiority complex as his main problems. He also claimed not to have drunk alcohol during the past seven days (corroborated by his spouse) and his alcohol consumption when he was drinking was 84 units a week.

Client B had come to the out-patient service because his involvement with a day-care centre for problem drinkers 'wasn't helping me with what I felt was my problem, my inferiority complex'. His strongest expectation was that the therapist would 'be asking me questions which could be hurtful, but if it's going to help me that's alright'. His expectation so far as his drinking was concerned was that he could be helped to return to 'social drinking'.

Client B's psychiatrist (Therapist B) contrasted with Therapist A considerably. He has what he calls 'an eclectic point of view' about treatment for alcohol problems, one which allows him to use several different methods. This reflects his view that alcohol problems are multi-causal and occur amongst people who are not uniform. His objective for treatment is 'to try and understand what starts off heavy or abusive drinking and to rearrange the situation so that these [sic] are less likely to affect them'. This might involve 'establishing or arranging for some stable situation to be set up where there are social difficulties such as accommodation, debt or job loss'. Alternatively, Therapist B said that he 'might refer some patients to a clinical psychologist who might use behaviour-therapy methods to bolster up their ability to refuse drinks in certain situations'. For other clients Therapist B said that he would 'spend a lot of time explaining or discussing various strategies for avoiding alcohol, especially around Christmas and New Year, with a spouse if possible'. In sum, Therapist B has a generally more flexible approach to treating alcohol problems and one which explicitly acknowledges the situated, or environmental nature of alcohol problems.

Therapist B's style of therapy and of therapist-client interaction also contrasts with that of Therapist A. His interviews are less formal in that, although he sits at his desk, clients sit adjacent to him in armchairs. This therapist never wears a white coat (he does not own one), and he occasionally addresses clients by their Christian names during the consultation. It would be false to say that Therapist B does not confront or challenge clients, though when doing so he is more indirect, persuasive and generally attentive to clients' viewpoints. He counsels clients rather than cross-examines them. Consider the following extract from his first meeting client B:

T: What's your, have you got some sort of aim? What you want to do about your drinking. You know, your plan. Your objectives.

C: I want to have it under control.

T: You want controlled drinking?

C: Possibly that's what I want, but then I don't know if I can do it. I can control it up to a level and then all of a sudden I get under stress and then I go back.

T: Say somebody said to you 'Your solution is to stop drinking altogether. There's no half measure on this.' How would you feel about that?

C: Upset (laughs).

T: You would really be upset at the prospect of stopping drinking?

C: I'd probably take it very hard.

T: Are you doubting whether you can be a social drinker?

C: Uh-huh.

The end of client B's initial interview was much smoother and apparently more satisfactory to the client than was the ending of client A's consultation:

T: Now, you see, for instance we could, if you're afraid of going off to drink impulsively and you want to avoid drink for a while, we could give you Abstem or Antabuse. Which would mean you'd be pretty ill once you started to drink. A sort of prop. If that's what you want. It's not a substitute, but it stops you being caught, or it makes it less likely that you are going to be caught on an impulse.

C: I find this, being honest with you, I find this Valium very helpful. You know, it never crosses my mind to go in and have a drink.

T: So you're saying that you think you can manage until we see you next, without a drink?

C: Yes.

T: I think that ought to be your intention. We can maybe discuss longer term goals then, but I would think in the meantime you should be aiming for that. OK, we'll not tinker with the existing situation till we discuss things more. OK? See you then.

C: OK. Thank you very much doctor.

T: Thank you. Bye-bye.

When interviewed immediately following the consultation client B said that he was most satisfied with the consultation, though he said that although it had been generally beneficial it was not of immediate help. He added, however, that 'I didn't expect anything wonderful immediately. It's not an overnight thing. I know that, and I've got enough intelligence to know he's not going to come out and say "That's you cured", you know.' When asked how long he envisaged his treatment lasting he said, 'Just as long as it takes. It could be six months, it could be two years. If we're going to really get to the root of the problem. I mean, maybe the drink is the main thing and I maybe won't accept it.'

What is particularly interesting about client B is that he had acquired a reputation of being a 'non-compliant' patient. By his own account he was 'a difficult customer', and he readily acknowledged that he had problems with authority figures such as doctors and managers at work. None the less, he did return for a second and many more visits to the out-patient clinic, and was still in treatment twelve months later. At that time he reported non-interrupted abstinence since the week before commencing treatment, which was corroborated by his wife. It could be said, therefore, that this treatment experience 'worked' in terms of getting the client to remain in treatment, to attain abstinence and, since the treatment went on to consider more suitable employment for the client, in helping him make adjustments to his lifestyle which would help him with both his inferiority complex and his harmful drinking. This, however, might be too generous to the treatment approach of Therapist B. The client had, after all, stopped drinking the week before commencing treatment, and he had certain non-treatment factors, especially an involved and supporting wife and family, working in his favour. This was something the client was quick to point out at three months follow-up. None the less, he also mentioned the importance of Therapist B to his recovery from harmful drinking:

> He's given me the support I need, if only to the extent
> that he's another person I'd be letting down if I started
> drinking again. It's somebody else to consider. And
> maybe it's because I've got somebody, the feeling that
> I'm speaking to him and he is going to help me with my
> problems, and therefore I'm OK. So that's maybe what
> has made me more at ease and I'll maybe come to
> terms with myself a lot more than before.

These two case studies demonstrate that treatment for alcohol problems can look quite different and have quite different consequences within even a single treatment setting. Whilst these case studies cannot possibly represent the wide variation that exists in therapeutic practice and styles of therapist-client interaction, they do suggest that these factors may be of greater importance than is apparent or acknowledged in input-output studies of treatment. One implication of this is that a particular client's chances of remission, and hence whether treatment works for him or her, may well depend upon the matching of his or her needs and expectations with the treatment approach of a particular therapist.

CONCLUSIONS

There is a sense in which the question 'Does treatment work?' is the wrong one to ask, for it implies a yes/no answer to an issue which is surrounded by contingencies. In this chapter I have suggested that these contingencies include what one means by treatment and what one means by work. On these issues I have introduced the perspectives of therapists and clients in two out-patient facilities for the treatment of alcohol problems. In addition I have identified three major themes from within the treatment evaluation literature: (1) that treatment may be said to have worked to the extent that it inspires or activates clients to change their lifestyles and/or environments; (2) that treatment may be said to have worked to the extent that it engages and maintains clients in treatment for more than one consultation; (3) that treatment may be said to have worked to the extent that in a single counselling session it identifies the nature of a client's alcohol problems and provides appropriate advice, guidance and direction to clients and their families. Having taken these issues into consideration, a more pertinent question to ask might be 'under what conditions does treatment for alcohol problems work?'. I have argued that treatment is more likely to work when clients' perceived needs and expectations are recognised and accommodated by therapists.

I have presented data from interviews with therapists and clients which suggest that in two out-patient treatment settings at least clients' expectations of treatment for alcohol problems have much in common with the views about treatment held by the majority of therapists. For the majority of therapists, treatment of alcohol problems consists of giving advice, providing an explanation and information, pointing out the role of lifestyles and environmental factors which lead to harmful drinking and, to a lesser extent, providing detoxification and withdrawal facilities where necessary. Success or failure of treatment was seen by the majority of therapists in terms of the extent to which clients make adjustments to their personal and social lives, reduce their drinking to non-harmful levels and, to a lesser extent, achieve at least some degree of short-term abstinence.

The most frequently expressed expectation of clients was that therapists would provide advice, guidance and help about drinking and/or some explanation for their drinking behaviour. The majority of clients indicated that they expected 'talking' therapies rather than the procedures and treatments of physical medicine. Interviews with clients immediately following their initial consultations indicate that the majority viewed them favourably, were satisfied with them and found them helpful. This suggests that the majority of clients found that what therapists actually did was in keeping with what they expected from treatment. However, it was noted that the treatment offered in the out-patient service of the specialist Alcoholism Treatment Unit tended to be viewed more favourably and was more helpful to clients than the treatment offered in the out-patient service of the general psychiatric hospital. This may have been attributable to the fact that treatment at the Alcoholism Treatment Unit is built around a four-week day-hospital course of alcohol education and information. It was concluded that the interview data generally supported the argument that treatment is more likely to work when clients' perceived needs and expectations of treatment are recognised and accommodated by therapists.

Two case studies were presented in order to demonstrate that treatment for alcohol problems can look quite different and have quite different consequences within a single treatment setting. It was argued that whether or not treatment works for particular clients may depend upon the therapist's and client's views about alcohol problems and their treatment, the therapist's therapeutic style and the therapist-client relationship that is established during the initial consultation. It was concluded that these factors may be of greater importance than is apparent or acknowledged in input-output studies of treatment.

REFERENCES

Armor, D.J., Polich, J.M. and Stambul, H.G. (1978) Alcoholism and Treatment, New York: John Wiley & Sons

Brown, G.W. and Birley, J.L.T. (1968) 'Crisis, life changes and the onset of schizophrenia', Journal of Health and Social Behaviour, 9, 203-14

Brown, G.W., Sklair, F., Harris, T.O. and Birley, J.L.T. (1973) 'Life events and psychiatric disorder', Psychological Medicine, 3, 74-87

Davies, P. (1979) 'Motivation, responsibility and sickness in the psychiatric treatment of alcohol problems', British Journal of Psychiatry, 134, 449-59

_____ (1980) The Identification and Management of Alcohol Problems, Report to the Scottish Home and Health Department, Health Services Research Committee

_____ (1981) 'Expectations and therapeutic practices in outpatient clinics for alcohol problems', British Journal of Addiction, 76, 159-73

_____ (1983) An Intensive Study of Certain Key Aspects of Psychiatric Treatment for Alcohol Problems, Report to the Scottish Home and Health Department, Health Service Research Committee

DHSS (1973) Alcoholism, Report of the Standard Medical Advisory Committee for the Central Health Services Council, the Secretary of State for Social Services and the Secretary of State for Wales, London: Department of Health and Social Security

_____ (1975) Better Services for the Mentally Ill, London: HMSO

Edwards, G. (1982) The Treatment of Drinking Problems: A Guide for the Helping Professions, London: Grant McIntyre

Emrick, C.D. (1975) 'A review of psychologically orientated treatment of alcoholism. II. The relative effectiveness of different treatment approaches and the effectiveness of treatment vs. no treatment', Journal of Studies on Alcohol, 36, 1, 88-108

Hayman, M. (1956) 'Current attitudes to alcoholism of psychiatrists in Southern California', American Journal of Psychiatry, 112, 484-93

Heather, N. and Robertson, I. (1981) Controlled Drinking, London: Methuen

Hunt, G.M. and Azrin, N.H. (1973) 'A community reinforcement approach to alcoholism', Behaviour Research and Therapy, 11, 91-104

Knight, R.P. (1937) 'The dynamics and treatment of chronic alcohol addiction', Bulletin of the Menninger Clinic, 1, 7, 233-50

Menninger, W.C. (1938) 'The treatment of chronic alcohol addiction', Bulletin of the Menninger Clinic, 2, 101-12

Ministry of Health (1962) National Health Service: Health Treatment of Alcoholism, HM (62) 43, London: HMSO

———(1968) National Health Service: The Treatment of Alcoholism, HM (68) 37, London: HMSO

Nathan, P.E., Marlatt, G.A. and Loberg, T. (1978) Alcoholism: New Directions in Behavioural Research and Treatment, New York: Plenum

Orford, J. and Edwards, G. (1977) Alcoholism: A Comparison of Treatment and Advice, with a Study of the Influence of Marriage, London: Oxford University Press

Sobell, M.G. and Sobell, L.C. (1976) 'Second year treatment outcome of alcoholics treated by individualised behaviour therapy', Behaviour Research and Therapy, 14, 195-215

Sterne, M.W. and Pitman, D.J. (1965) 'The concept of motivation: a source of institutional and professional blockage in the treatment of alcoholics', Quarterly Journal of Studies on Alcohol, 26, 41-57

Tuchfeld, B. (1976) Changes in Patterns of Alcohol Use Without Formal Treatment, North Carolina: Research Triangle Institute

THE ANATOMY OF ORGANISATIONAL MELANCHOLIA, OR WHY TREATMENT WORKS ON SOME OCCASIONS AND NOT ON OTHERS

George Gawlinski and Shirley Otto

Treatment is generally only as good as the vehicle which delivers it. Central government, local health services, social services, voluntary agencies, professional groups and consumers all contribute to the creation and maintenance of this vehicle. This chapter will review some of the lessons we have learnt while working with or within a large number of agencies concerned with 'people work', as trainers or management consultants. We will conclude that the current concentration of research and training on 'treatment methodology' may be misplaced while scant attention is given to the vehicle which delivers these services.

Our overall approach will be to:

(1) examine why an understanding of the organisation and pattern of services to problem drinkers has become more important in recent years;
(2) describe our experience of 'organisational melancholia' and some of the factors which create it;
(3) outline some organisational principles which may be applied when trying to understand why treatment fails;
(4) draw out some of the implications of these factors for research.

CONTEXT

Concepts of service delivery in helping agencies have changed dramatically in the last decade and especially so for services to problem drinkers. Early theories of alcoholism were clear and simple with the not inconsiderable virtues of being easy to state, understand, publicise and enact, concentrating as they did on self-help and the disease model as determinants of treatment services. Thus, to quote from Kessel and Walton (1965): 'The alcoholic has to appreciate that he is an alcoholic and that he must stop drinking.'

Unfortunately, during the last ten years increasing doubt has been cast on this simple presentation, and it has been criticised at a number of levels and in particular on a philosophical level. Douglas Cameron (1981) is one of its most outspoken critics, and he has argued the following: 'There are a number of us who argue in individual ideographic humanist terms about people with problems of alcohol abuse and who will settle for nothing less than an acceptance of individuals as unique. To us, therefore, concepts of alcoholism and alcohol dependence are inadequate as explanations.' Similarly, at a practical level, the method of helping has shifted from the American Medical Association's view in 1935 that 'alcoholics are valid patients' (see Kessel and Walton, 1965, p.21) to the view of Dr J.S. Madden, a distinguished psychiatrist writing in 1980: 'Concentration on the sickness concept can now mitigate against further development of ideas supplied by the non-medical profession.' (Madden, 1980)

It is not surprising in the light of these trends that in the last decade the organisational and professional structures that grew from the sickness model have come under increasing scrutiny (Shaw, Cartwright, Spratley and Harwin, 1978). Participants in the field have been deeply divided as to philosophy and methodology and multidisciplinary teams have fought to survive the tensions created by the growing confidence of psychologists, social workers and nurses in challenging the methods, styles and assumptions of medical colleagues.

Politicians, policy makers and government ministers have expressed open confusion as to where and how our services should be deployed, while admitting to a greatly increased need for intervention. Theories of prevention and fiscal control have become popular in government circles (DHSS, 1981) and coincided with increasing comment, both professional and lay, as to the ineffectiveness of treatment services (Edwards, Orford, Egert, Guthrie, Hawker, Hensman, Mitcheson, Oppenheimer and Taylor 1977; National Council for Voluntary Organisations, 1982). Strict control and curtailment of central and local government expenditure has further hastened the demise of 'uncertain or ineffective agencies', without much concern for who or what replaces them.

THE EXPERIENCE OF ORGANISATIONAL MELANCHOLIA

'I used to enjoy my work. Where has the feeling gone?'
'How can we make a success of a new venture when morale is low and leadership lacking?'
'Our management is indifferent to anything other than bureaucratic criteria i.e. paper work and social control.'
'Departmentalisation is inefficient and divisive.'
'What are we expected to achieve?'
'I experience lack of consultation in decision-making processes at all levels, not knowing what is going on now or in the future.'
'There is more interest at times in this organisation on trivial happenings instead of dealing with items of importance.'
'I feel patronised and stigmatised by virtue of having low-prestige qualifications.'
'There is no praise or recognition for work well done.'
'There is disagreement and uncertainty and lack of clarity about the philosophy in this team.'
'I feel lonely most of the time with little support from anyone else.'

'There is a lack of trust and respect which emanates from management, and as such has been reciprocated with interest.'

These comments are taken from a random selection of meetings in which workers from social work, nursing, teaching and medicine were expressing views about their own agencies, and they are in our view frighteningly typical of many working teams. This phenomenon which we labelled 'organisational melancholia' can be observed at a number of levels in the organisation.

One of the major lessons of the last decade has been the acceptance that consumers may need access to a wide range of resources and treatment methods while seeking help for complex problems related to alcohol abuse (Gawlinski and Robertshaw, 1978), and that how agencies and different professionals collaborate together can have a profound effect on long-term treatment progress. Sadly, intra-professional and inter-agency rivalry, distrust or misunderstanding can lead to clients being (metaphorically) carved up by contradictory treatment advice or poor continuity of help (Department of Health and Social Security, 1978). Inter-agency planning groups often fail to confront the real issues inherent in using resources flexibly and manpower creatively to meet local needs, and prefer on occasions to use these forums as a battleground for increasing or protecting their own boundaries or resources. The result of this, in our view, is often a considerable waste of resources in terms of people, time, money, opportunity, appropriate investment and credibility. Man hours and finance are sometimes invested without regard to the real need or to the practicability of the schemes concerned. The results are costly both for the workers who have to implement the ill-thought-out project and for the recipients who are once again robbed of appropriate services.

We have found surprisingly often that organisations small and large have no clear goals and simply respond to whatever comes in the door. Others started with clear goals, but over the passage of years failed to adapt these to changed circumstances (Otto and Armstrong, 1977). Workers and management often sense something is wrong when the referrals dry up, or clients come and go confused and angry that their expectations have not been fulfilled. Often the blame for this is projected onto the state of the economy, poor publicity or more usually onto the unfortunate population who need help and who get blamed for not appreciating what this particular agency has to offer. Not surprisingly, many agencies grow into hybrids in terms of staff, structure and administration which bear little relationship to the task and services they are there to fulfil.

A characteristic of many 'people work' agencies is a vulnerability to constant change; they are often 'a feather in every wind that blows'. Moreover, fluctuations in quality of work, approach and staff morale appear largely to be due to factors out of the agencies' control; the most obvious and most significant is the way in which they are funded. Regular uncertainty about the likelihood of funding, the disproportionate amount of time necessary to raise funds or respond to central government initiatives, and the administration required to manage multiple funding all contrive to undermine the qualities essential to good management, continuity of policy and strategic planning. The only realistic approach is therefore for their managers to think no further ahead than twelve months and to allow development to occur reactively either in response to government initiatives to which money is attached or in response to ideas which happen to appeal to a charitable trust. This kind of entrepreneurism is much celebrated, especially amongst voluntary-sector workers, and no doubt is responsible for many vital services being made available; however, it has negative consequences also. There is a well-worked tradition when going for funding of implying that a piece of work can achieve more than is realistically possible, owing to either limited resources or because the problems to be tackled are intractable. The tendency of funding bodies to be more interested in being seen to provide than in the quality or outcome of the service has contributed to a low priority being given to project evaluation and monitoring, especially with regard to consumer feedback. Moreover, the criteria which determine the continuance of a project will often have little to do with any measurable impact on the consumer and rather more on the project's political value or promotional capacity.

The pressure on projects to be seen to be doing something new and interesting and to be flexible in meeting government statutory demands, however inconsistent and elusive, has created an ethos whereby the development of new work is regarded as good for its own sake. Some projects also need to expand to survive, thereby being able to meet increasing costs and to cover non-service functions (e.g. research, in-service training and some administration) which are regarded by the funders as of low priority. A not uncommon effect of this emphasis on expansion is an imbalance of what organisational theorists call maintenance and adaptive capacities (Dale Lovelock, 1975). In other words, agencies experience too long periods of change and therefore of instability, and too little consolidation, in particular for ensuring that there is sufficient administrative and management support for the growing numbers of staff and clients.

The adoption of large numbers of community enterprise project workers through the Manpower Services Commission (this scheme provides the unemployed with short-term work on a fixed and low wage) gave many projects the opportunity to do much needed work, and yet brought some into chaos and near ruin. One project serves as an extreme example. An advice service almost doubled in size by this means, thereby giving some young people invaluable experience, only to find it impossible to support and supervise them adequately. As a consequence there was considerable staff unrest, 'attempted coups' and a decline in the quality of service to clients. The project, as well as the staff, 'burnt out' and took 18 months to stabilise and to recover credibility. A key factor in this project's trauma was the lack of support and supervision provided, the importance of which has not always been fully appreciated. In some cases, this has been deliberately rejected along with hierarchical styles of management.

Agencies whose aim is to help individuals suffering from stress-related problems often give scant attention to their own workers' mental health, and frequently manage to create structures which demoralise and disable the workers concerned. In these conditions, it is not surprising that we have observed tired and dispirited workers who eventually give a higher priority to their own survival than to the needs of the people they are supposed to be there to help. Sadly, it is only now being generally recognised how stressful work with under-privileged people can be, especially if combined with pressure from limited and/or uncertain resources. The low status given to much of the work with problem drinkers and the homeless has inhibited the growth of structures to train and support workers, especially in-service training and the induction of new staff. The lack of the essential elements of good staff management has tended to reinforce the traditional voluntary, and in many cases, statutory notions of self-sacrifice and indifference to conditions of service. To the extent that value is placed on 'baptism by fire' and 'survival of the fittest', services often end up being staffed by those who tolerate bad conditions (or feed on them) and yet who may not necessarily be best at the work in hand.

The major cause of projects being so varied in approach and quality and so prone to periods of instability and isolation lies, in our view, largely with the piper who calls the tune, i.e. with their financial masters (local and central government, health authorities and charitable trusts). However, it is also true that project staff are party to some of this unreasonable funding policy, given an ultimate commitment to self-preservation on their part.

THE ANATOMY OF ORGANISATIONAL MELANCHOLIA
Theories abound about what makes for effective organisations, but few concentrate on service delivery in 'people work' agencies. However, our work has allowed us to identify some of the ingredients that help to ensure good practice (Table 11.1) and those which mitigate against it (Table 11.2). We hope it may present some helpful guidelines when trying to understand why organisations fail to deliver treatment services effectively.

THE IMPLICATIONS FOR EVALUATION RESEARCH
The classical approach to the evaluation of 'people work' projects is to assess them in terms of formally or explicitly stated goals. It is not usually the business of the researcher to reflect on why a project is or is not achieving its objectives. There are a number of drawbacks to this position:

(1) Not every project is able to be sufficiently clear and specific about its goals and priorities.
(2) Knowing that a project does not do what it originally said it would (which is often the case), it is not of very great value to staff, managers or policy makers etc. (except when they are keen to close it down) unless it is accompanied by a sound analysis of the reason why it fails. Failure due to poor management has quite different implications from failure because the model of provision adopted

Table 11.1 Core Conditions for Effective Service Delivery

Organisational	Core condition	Client/Worker
The agency has effectively researched and understood client need. It is clear about its goals and working methods	CLARITY	Good assessment. Clear agreement as to goals of intervention, time scale and working methods
Other people, especially consumers, understand what the agency is offering	CONGRUENCE	The intervention being used is appropriate
Recruitment, training and staffing levels are correct	COMPETENCE	The worker is skilled, knowledgeable and experienced
The worker is well supervised and supported with adequate working conditions	CONFIDENCE	The customer is willing to be helped, believes she will be helped, and trusts the worker concerned. The worker is confident about her role/task
Local services are co-ordinated and planned effectively. Some element or agreement exists vis-à-vis working methods and core philosophy, agencies trust and respect each other's work	CONTINUITY	Long-term support is available to those who need it. The customer can move/ be referred between agencies without disrupting his or her confidence or progress

Table 11.2:   Barriers to Good Practice, or 'I Did Everything
You Suggested and it Still Didn't Work'

Politics	Central government is confused or ambivalent about services. Speaks with forked tongue; i.e. expects much, gives too little, changes mind often
Policy	There is an absence of agreed policy about services at a national regional and local level
Planning	No clear plan exists for services nationally, regionally or locally. Investment in buildings, people and services is haphazard
Professional	Different professional groups are competing for power, mystique, status and collectively devaluing clients' views, needs and opinions.
People	Managers Uncommitted Planners are Disenchanted Researchers personally Tired Fieldworkers Cynical
Practice	Working methods are ill-defined. Research findings are ignored and no good theoretical basis for work exists. Training is poor or non-existent

↓

Intervention is likely to
be misplaced, confused,
inappropriate or non-existent

was inappropriate to the problems being tackled.

(3) If the findings of a piece of research are to be generalised beyond its subject, then the project concerned must be true to some type or model of approach that is recognised and clearly stated. Hence, given the eclectic approach to treatment programmes in alcohol units, studies of them can only be said to comment on the effectiveness of the regime in question.

(4) An agency must have sufficient resources to be able to function as an effective organisation with its particular goals. If it has not, then all the research can reasonably conclude is that the agency lacks the means to be able to attempt to achieve its goals; paradoxically, the research may often cost more than the amount needed for the project to do its job properly.

Given the very individualistic nature of many projects, and given the lack of conceptual models with which to understand residential and day-care services in particular, the majority of agencies are inappropriate subjects for evaluation studies in the traditional mode. Research resources would be more usefully devoted to systematically describing the work being done, and to assessing the relationship between the various organisational and political factors described above.

CONCLUSIONS

In summary, we would like to amend the quotation from Kessel and Walton which was cited at the beginning of the chapter in the following way:

> It would be nice to say that the answer to "organisational melancholia" is that the organisation must first recognise that it is melancholic and then stop working with clients or patients.

In many cases such drastic treatment may in fact benefit clients, though in reality we propose no more than that those who allocate resources, manage staff, or work directly with human beings should recognise the complexity of the task they are undertaking. When, as is often the case, agencies fail, they should refrain from immediately jumping to the conclusion that the method is at fault or that further training or more expertise would automatically make it better next time. Funders, managers and practitioners should be willing to look at themselves as individuals, their organisational structure and the pattern of service within which they work, as powerful determinants of treatment effectiveness.

REFERENCES

Cameron, D. (1981) 'Is dependence a necessary explanatory concept?', New Directions in the Study of Alcohol Group, Members' Booklet, No. 1

Charles, H. (1976) Bibliography: Understanding Organisations, Harmondsworth: Penguin Books

Dale Lovelock Associates (1975) Organisation Development Manual, London: Dale Lovelock Associates

Department of Health and Social Security/Welsh Office (1978) The Pattern and Range of Services for Problem Drinkers, Report by the Advisory Committee on Alcoholism, London: DHSS

Department of Health and Social Security (1981) Drinking Sensibly, London: HMSO

Edwards, G., Orford, J., Egert, S., Guthrie, S., Hawker, A., Hensman, C., Mitcheson, M., Oppenheimer, E. and Taylor, C. (1977) 'Alcoholism: a controlled trial of "treatment" and "advice" ', Journal of Studies on Alcohol, 38, 1004-31

Gawlinski, G. and Robertshaw, S. (1980) 'Differential approaches to the problem drinker within a framework of personal growth' in J.S. Madden, R. Walker and W.H. Kenyon (eds), Aspects of Alcohol and Drug Dependence, Tunbridge Wells: Pitman Medical

Kessel, N. and Walton, H. (1965) Alcoholism, London: Penguin Books

Madden, J.S. (1980) 'Controversy and development' in J.S. Madden, R. Walker and W.H. Kenyon (eds), Aspects of Alcohol and Drug Dependence, Tunbridge Wells: Pitman Medical

National Council for Voluntary Organisations (1982) National Voluntary Organisations and Alcohol Misuse 1982, London: NCVO

Otto, S. and Armstrong, F. (1977) The Action Research Experiment: A Report of Two Years' Work by the Consortium Action Research Team 1975-1977, London: South East London Consortium

Shaw, S., Cartwright, A., Spratley, T. and Harwin, J. (1978) Responding to Drinking Problems, London: Croom Helm

BIBLIOGRAPHY

Friend, J., Hall, R. and Wiseman, C. (1978) Alcohol Related Problems: A Study of Inter-Organisational Relations, Edinburgh: Scottish Institute for Operational Research

Handy, C. (1982) Improving Effectiveness in Voluntary Organisation, Report of NCVO Working Party, London: National Council for Voluntary Organisations

Martin, P.J. and Segal, B. (1977) 'Bureaucracy, size and staff expectations for client independence in halfway houses', Journal of Health and Social Behaviour, 18, 376-90

McDonald, J. and Otto, S.J. (1978) 'A way to ensure that research is meaningful to the practitioner', Health and Social Services Journal

Silverman, D., March (1970) The Theory of Organisations, London: Heinemann

Wilmot, R. and Ogborne, A. (1981) 'Conflicts and contradictions in a halfway house for alcoholics - inside the black box', Journal of Drug Issues, 7, 151-62

PART THREE

WHAT IS EFFECTIVE PREVENTION?

INTRODUCTION

Phil Davies

Prevention, rather like mother love, is something that few people would doubt to be of positive value. Our everyday language abounds with aphorisms such as 'prevention is better than cure' and 'tis better to be safe than sorry', the pithiness of which is only surpassed by the elements of truism and commonsense wisdom contained within them. None the less, the general consensus and approval that I am claiming for the concept of prevention should not hide the fact that in many areas, such as that pertaining to alcohol use and misuse, there is a noticeable lack of agreement as to what constitutes prevention or even what it is that should be prevented (Grant and Ritson, 1983).

The problem is not a new one. The history of prevention in the field of alcohol is one of shifting foci concerning what is to be prevented and how preventive activity should be organised. In Britain an Act of 1552 first gave justices of the peace the power to issue and withdraw licences for the sale and serving of alcoholic beverages. This was done with the explicit aim of preventing public intoxication as a result of alcohol use, and it established the principle of preventing alcohol-related consequences by controlling the terms and conditions under which alcohol is made available.

In the nineteenth century there was a noticeable change of emphasis whereby alcohol-related problems were seen less as a consequence of the availability of alcohol and more in terms of the weakness of character of certain drinkers. Consequently, prevention was directed towards individuals, and took the form of evangelical salvation and moral crusades (thereby establishing the foundations of contemporary health education).

In other countries, such as the United States, Canada, Finland, and Norway, the focus of concern became alcohol itself, rather than the individuals who used it or the conditions under which it was made available for consumption. The appropriate response was to direct prevention towards the 'demon drink' in the form of prohibition. Whilst appearing to be the extreme form of the control of availability approach to prevention, prohibition was, and is, quite distinct. For whereas in the former the thing to be prevented is certain consequences of alcohol use, with prohibition it is the very substance of alcohol itself which is to be prevented. Also, whereas with the control-of-availability approach it is readily acknowledged that there are positive aspects of alcohol use which must be preserved and promoted, no such acknowledgement or accommodation is conceivable from a prohibition perspective.

In the past decade or so yet another approach to the prevention of alcohol-related problems has developed, one which has become known as the problem-prevention approach (Room, 1974, 1981). This again focuses on preventing the consequences of alcohol use but without particular regard to controlling individuals or the availability of alcohol. Instead, the emphasis is placed on manipulating the physical and social environments so as to make them less hostile to drinkers. This involves measures such as making cars, roads, houses and machines less dangerous in the hands of people who are intoxicated, encouraging third parties to be more responsible for people who are intoxicated, and providing alternative means of transport to and from pubs, bars and other drinking places (Gusfield, 1976; Moore and Gerstein, 1981).

This is a greatly condensed version of the historical backdrop against which contemporary discussions and debates concerning the prevention of alcohol problems are carried out. Thus, one of the burning and most controversial issues in alcohol studies today is whether alcohol-related problems, or undesirable consequences of drinking alcohol, are related to the amount of alcohol consumed in a society. The implication of this is that to prevent alcohol problems one must control the availability and per capita consumption of alcohol. This principle has enjoyed renewed currency in recent years following the publication in 1975 of Alcohol Control Policies in Public Health Perspective by Kettil Bruun and a distinguished group of international alcohol researchers. However, it is challenged on a number of grounds (see below), including the arguments of those who claim that the most effective way of preventing alcohol problems is to influence individuals by informing and educating them about alcohol and its effects. Others argue that alcohol problems can best be prevented by manipulating the social and physical environments, as proposed by Room and others.

Another contemporary issue which runs across each of these perspectives asks whether or not meaningful and effective prevention measures can be formulated and mobilised at the national government level or at the local community based level. There is little doubt, then, that a central question in alcohol studies today, and one which provides the main theme for this section, is 'What is effective prevention?'.

The discerning reader may detect a logical flaw in this seemingly innocuous, yet very important question. For, logically, one can only have effective prevention; ineffective prevention is logically not possible. This logical teaser once again brings us back to what one means by 'prevention', what one means by 'effective', and what it is that is to be prevented. Ron McKechnie (Chapter 12) presents an extensive review and analysis of these issues and provides three distinct meanings to the term 'prevention'. These are

(i) stopping, or to keep from coming to pass; (ii) hindering, to make it difficult for the phenomenon to come about; and (iii) curtailing, or holding steady the frequency of occurrences to their present level. If one accepts McKechnie's distinctions, and they are by no means exhaustive of the conceptual possibilities associated with the term prevention, then the above logical objection to the question of what is effective prevention becomes less convincing empirically. For instance, prohibition in the United States can be said to have been ineffective in terms of stopping the availability of alcohol, not to mention its effects on criminality, but somewhat effective at hindering alcohol availability and curtailing, indeed reducing, per capita alcohol consumption and deaths from 'alcoholism' and from alcohol-induced liver cirrhosis (Moore and Gerstein, 1981, pp.34-5).

McKechnie also distinguishes between things that are a direct consequence of alcohol use (e.g. liver cirrhosis, intoxication), things that are a consequence of the contexts within which drinking occurs (e.g. family distress as a result of a member of an abstinent family drinking alcohol), and the interaction of alcohol use with certain contexts (e.g. drinking and driving). McKechnie prefers the term 'drinking-related consequences' to 'alcohol-related problems' on the grounds that not all drinking nor its consequences are necessarily problematic, nor are all undesirable consequences of drinking necessarily caused by alcohol per se. By bringing his two sets of distinctions together, McKechnie provides an interesting typology with which we might organise our thinking about appropriate and effective prevention strategies.

The conceptual framework provided by McKechnie suggests that some drinking-related consequences may be prevented by controlling the availability of alcoholic beverages and per capita alcohol consumption, whilst others require measures to influence individuals' knowledge and behaviour (e.g. health education), and yet others require the manipulation of the contexts within which drinking takes place and undesirable consequences emerge. As has already been noted, the first of these possibilities has received much criticism from alcohol researchers (see McKechnie, Chapter 12; Yates and Hebblethwaite, Chapter 15; Tuck, 1980; Pittman, 1980). Much, if not most of this criticism challenges the empirical basis for the assertion that the proportion of heavy drinkers and overall levels of alcohol-related harm in a community are related to that community's per capita alcohol consumption. More specifically, the empirical arguments, assumptions and evidence of Ledermann (1964) and of Bruun et al. (1975) have been rigorously called into question (Duffy, 1977; Duffy and Cohen, 1978; Miller and Agnew, 1974; Pittman, 1980; Tuck, 1980). Notwithstanding these criticisms, there are empirical grounds for wanting to prevent per capita alcohol consumption from rising, if not bringing about its decline, and these are reviewed by Bill Saunders in Chapter 13.

Closely related to the issue of preventing alcohol-related problems by controlling per capita alcohol consumption is the question of how this might best be achieved. All too often the complexity of the relationships involved is ignored, and particular strategies, such as price and taxation manipulation, or advertising restrictions, are invoked as panaceas for all manner of alcohol-related problems and drinking-related consequences. In Chapter 14 Alan Maynard takes a more critical look at the available evidence concerning the economics of alcohol. He concludes that there is some scope for using tax-price increases to affect the consumption of alcoholic beverages. This, however, is limited, and varies according to beverage type (i.e. beers, wines, spirits). So far as advertising of alcoholic beverages is concerned, Maynard concludes that its effects are rather small and incompletely understood. What is required from research, says Maynard, is 'an analysis of preference formation over the life cycle and an appraisal of all aspects of the media on this process, not just advertising'.

The issues and measures covered in Chapters 13 and 14 are for the most part concerned with preventing drinking problems at the level of national policy. In Chapter 15 Yates and Hebblethwaite make the case for utilising natural resources within communities for preventing drinking problems. In their view 'the distinctive character of any preventive work is the central place it must occupy in the ordinary life of the community'. Accordingly, say Yates and Hebblethwaite, 'a primary source of usable material for the prevention strategist will be the ordinary efforts of individuals, families, social groups and non-specialist agencies to absorb and repair those drinking problems which never emerge in a clinical setting'. A substantial part of their chapter is given to illustrating how such community based prevention initiatives have been developed in two towns in the north-east of England. This approach is seen by Yates and Hebblethwaite as an alternative to the problem prevention approach developed by Room (1974, 1981) and others (Gusfield, 1976) which was briefly outlined above. However, Yates and Hebblethwaite conclude their chapter by acknowledging that 'in the end the empirical, community-oriented programme we are advocating does not radically depart from the problem-oriented approach'. This is fortunate, for there are a number of empirical examples of prevention initiatives which have emerged spontaneously from within communities and which are the embodiment of the problem prevention approach. One such example is the practice in north-east Scotland whereby the hosts of wedding receptions provide a bus service to and from peoples' homes and the reception. This allows guests to enjoy alcohol without the worry or the risk of driving under the influence. The notable feature of this indigenous initiative is that guests quite readily use this facility and are apparently quite happy to leave their cars at home. Thus, it would appear that problem prevention and community based initiatives can and do work together and may, in the final analysis, be the same thing.

The importance of developing prevention strategies that are meaningful to individuals and groups within particular communities is taken up by Anthony Thorley in his discussion of the role of mass media campaigns in health education work (Chapter 16). Thorley argues that a great deal of mass media work which has sought to prevent drinking problems has tended to communicate only negative images and messages about alcohol, and has failed to appreciate, and thereby build upon, the ways in which alcohol is positively valued in most communities. Thorley notes that health education programmes in California (Wallack and Barrows, 1981) have similarly failed to acknowledge and develop culturally apposite mass media campaigns.

As an alternative to these predominantly negative approaches, a mass media campaign was launched in the north-east of England which readily acknowledged the positive aspects of alcohol and offered guidelines for harm-free drinking. Moreover, the campaign's messages were presented to the north-east public by a well-known television personality with whom they identified. In this way, says Thorley, a positive approach to health education was taken which was culturally meaningful in this particular part of England. The implication of Thorley's chapter is that scarce health education resources might be utilised most beneficially if other communities were to seek ways of portraying positive images and messages about alcohol which are culturally apposite.

To claim that the chapters in this section definitively answer the question, 'what is effective prevention?', would be misleading. What they show is that the number of answers to this question appears to be proportional to the number and diverse types of alcohol problems that are identifiable. Certainly, it would be wrong to suggest that there is one answer to this question - a panacea for all undesirable consequences of drinking alcohol. It is this which makes the prevention of alcohol problems such a controversial, stimulating and intellectually challenging area of inquiry. Elsewhere (Davies, 1982; Davies and Walsh, 1983) I have suggested that there is nothing incompatible with wanting to prevent per capita alcohol consumption from rising, promoting moderate drinking practices, preserving the positive aspects of alcohol use and minimising its negative consequences. It remains to be seen how many, if any, fellow travellers I have in this journey towards synthesis and eclecticism.

REFERENCES

Bruun, K., Edwards, G., Luncio, M., Madelei, K., Pan, L., Popham, R.E., Room, R., Schmidt, W., Skog, O., Sulkunen, P. and Osterberg, E. (1975) Alcohol Control Policies in Public Health Perspective, Helsinki: The Finnish Foundation for Alcohol Studies

Davies, P.T. (1982) 'A public health perspective on alcohol problems', British Journal on Alcohol and Alcoholism, 17, 128-34

___ and Walsh, D. (1983) Alcohol Problems and Alcohol Control in Europe, London: Croom Helm

Duffy, J.C. (1977) 'Estimating the proportion of heavy drinkers' in D.L. Davies (ed.), The Ledermann Curve, London: Alcohol

Education Centre
____ and Cohen, G.R. (1978) 'Total alcohol consumption and excessive drinking', British Journal of Addiction, 73, 259-64

Grant, M. and Ritson, B. (1983) Alcohol: The Prevention Debate, London: Croom Helm

Gusfield, J. (1976) 'The prevention of drinking problems' in W. Filstead (ed.), Alcohol and Alcohol Problems: New Thinking and New Directions, New York: Ballinger

Ledermann, S. (1964) Alcool, alcoolism, alcoolisation, mortalité, morbidité, accidents du travail, Paris: Institut d'Etudes Demographiques

Miller, G.H. and Agnew, N. (1974) 'The Ledermann model of alcohol consumption', Quarterly Journal of Studies on Alcohol, 35, 877-98

Moore, M. and Gerstein, D. (1981) Alcohol and Public Policy: Beyond the Shadow of Prohibition, Washington DC: National Academy Press

Pittman, D.J. (1980) Primary Prevention of Alcohol Abuse and Alcoholism: An Evaluation of the Control of Consumption Policy, St. Louis: Washington University

Room, R. (1974) 'Minimising alcohol problems', Alcohol Health and Research World, 3, 12-77

____ (1981) 'The case for a problem prevention approach to alcohol, drug and mental problems', Public Health Reports, 96, 26-33

Tuck, M. (1980) Alcoholism and Social Policy: Are We On the Right Lines?, Home Office Research Study No. 26, London: HMSO

Wallack, L.M. and Barrows, D.C. (1981) Preventing Alcohol Problems in California: Evaluation of the 3-Year 'Winners' Program, Berkeley: Social Research Group

Chapter 12

ALCOHOL, CONTEXTS AND UNDESIRABLE CONSEQUENCES: WHAT IS TO BE PREVENTED?

Ron McKechnie

The word 'prevention' derives from two roots. The first is 'pre' which is the Latin for 'before'; the second part either derives from the Latin 'venire' meaning coming or the French 'venue' meaning event. So prevention means 'coming before' or 'before event'. Given this derivation there obviously cannot be secondary or tertiary prevention, but only what is referred to tautologically as primary prevention.

Since prevention is therefore activity focusing on what occurs before the event, then it must attend to the processes involved in the causation of events. We thus need to know something, or at least have theories, about what causes the events we would wish to prevent.

The word prevention is also used in a variety of ways, and it is necessary to distinguish these uses from each other since they represent different aims of preventative effort.

Stopping In its absolute sense prevention means 'to stop' or 'to keep from coming to pass', that is, to stop any occurrence of what is the focus of preventative action, to eradicate the problem.
Hindering Prevention can also mean 'to hinder', that is, to make it difficult for the event or phenomenon to come about, without necessarily being aimed at reducing its frequency to zero.
Curtailing Prevention is also used in the sense of 'curtailing the progress of'. Whilst this is similar to 'hindering', it is usually meant in the sense of curtailing increases or holding steady the frequency of occurrences at their present level.

Although the word prevention embodies all three levels of meaning, each meaning in fact gives rise to different goals. In order to achieve these goals, intervention can be aimed at different processes or factors which contribute to the appearance of a problem. For example, to 'stop' consequences in the absolute sense, it is almost certainly necessary that prevention should be aimed at the central causative processes which give rise to the consequences: that is, a direct strategy has to be adopted. Whereas if the aim of prevention was to 'hinder' or 'curtail' consequences, it would be possible to interfere indirectly in peripheral, as distinct from central, processes or factors which give rise to the consequence. 'Stopping' requires direct strategies, whereas 'hindering' could use either direct and/or indirect strategies and 'curtailing' would use indirect strategies.

What we know about the nature and development of drinking-related consequences is extremely limited. One consequence of this limitation of knowledge is the tendency to lump together drinking-related consequences as though they shared common processes of development and were amenable to the same influences of intervention. In avoiding this over-simplification, it is not assumed that the factors or processes involved in the development of different consequences are the same. Nor is it assumed that these processes are the same as those which give rise to increases in the frequency of consequences.

For example, the processes involved in the development of liver cirrhosis are not the same as those that give rise to increases in the frequency of liver cirrhosis. Thus, it is important to distinguish factors involved in the nature of the consequences and those which contribute to their frequency. Some consequences are problems because of their nature, others because of their frequency, and some because of both. For example, although liver cirrhosis is a serious and debilitating disorder, we would not consider it to be a major drinking-related problem if its frequency were extremely low. Such a distinction opens up the possibility of different strategies for tackling consequences, with one set aimed primarily at factors involved in the nature of consequences and the other aimed at factors involved in their frequency.

A prevention programme could include direct and indirect activity at more than one level, and it is thus important to clarify the aim of preventative action at each level to avoid confusion and possible contradiction.

DRINKING AND DRINKING-RELATED CONSEQUENCES

It would appear reasonable to assume that people drink for benefits which are included in the pharmacological, psychological and social spheres. These benefits or consequences are pursued despite the fact that their attainments frequently extract a price, again usually in the pharmacological, psychological or social spheres. Drinkers drink for the benefits, usually with full knowledge of the costs, and believe that the benefits outweigh the costs. When the costs, that is the undesirable consequences, outweigh the benefits, people alter their drinking behaviour in order to achieve the benefits at lesser cost. This is true of all drinkers, whether their drinking is viewed as problematic or not. (For a fuller analysis of such a balance sheet model with regard to drinking, see Robertson, Hodgson, Orford and McKechnie, 1984).

The view being adopted here is that the consumption of alcohol has consequences, some good and some bad. These consequences include what are often referred to as 'alcohol problems'. However, there is no particular reason or evidence to suggest that because there is evidence of an alcohol-related consequence there is also an underlying pathological process producing the drinking. For example, the presence of alcohol liver cirrhosis does not mean that the sufferer has manifested any of the pathology usually thought of as 'alcoholism' or 'alcohol abuse'. Too often authors talk as though liver cirrhosis was synonomous with alcohol addiction or alcoholism.

The use of the word 'consequence' in preference to 'problem' avoids the value judgement inherent in identifying an event as a problem. It also emphasises, as does the balance-sheet model, the positive consequences of drinking. Research has by no means been impartial in its investigation of consequences, as the research focuses almost exclusively on the negative consequences (see Turner, Bennett and Hermandez, 1981 for the exception). At the individual level only the drinker can evaluate the balance of desirable against the undesirable, but at a national level there is likely to be a large consensus as to what constitutes undesirable consequences.

The term 'drinking-related consequences' has been adopted in this paper in preference to 'alcoholism' and 'alcohol-related problems' for the following reasons. If there is such a thing as alcoholism, with its emphasis on physical addiction and/or psychological dependence, then it is only one of a number of consequences and by no means accounts for the range of consequences which it might be thought desirable to prevent.

'Alcohol-related problem' also tends to focus attention on alcohol as a substance rather than on the activity of drinking, which also may have undesirable consequences not attributable to the ingestion of alcohol. The term 'alcohol-related problem' has also been rejected since it appears to have taken on many of the associations of the terms it replaced, namely alcoholism, alcohol abuse etc. This has been unfortunate as it leads to the tendency to assume that all undesirable drinking-related consequences are due to underlying biological or psychopathological processes. Such an assumption accounts for the reluctance of general practitioners and physicians to ask patients about their drinking or to carry out investigations (Dubach and Schneider, 1980), although it also reflects society's ambivalent attitude towards drinking in general.

It is only when a consequence is viewed as undesirable that it constitutes a problem. We shall see that undesirability is not simply a function of the consequence itself, but depends largely on the circumstances or context within which it is experienced. Therefore, the same consequence may be beneficial in one situation but problematic in another.

Under the more usual heading of 'alcohol-related problem' one finds listed a range of more or less serious problems, ranging from liver cirrhosis, delirium tremens, hangover, drunken driving, other drunken offences, marital and financial problems, wife and child beating, aggression and a host of other events in which alcohol might feature as an ingredient. It is clear from this list that they have remarkably different frequencies and they also differ in terms of their nature. It is the combination of nature and frequency which brings a consequence to awareness. Once attending to a consequence we, as a society, tend to label it as an 'alcohol-related problem' if alcohol is involved in or around the problem. This everyday bias mirrors a bias seen also in the alcohol literature which focuses on the negative effects of alcohol use to the exclusion of the positive. The balance-sheet model of drinking attempts to avoid this bias. This labelling, however, arises not simply due to bias, but due to some inadequate causal thinking which infers that anything which follows after the consumption of alcohol must have been caused by alcohol.

A closer analysis of drinking-related consequences reveals that it is possible to divide them into three types on the basis of the kind of factors involved in their development.

Type 1 - Alcohol-related Consequences

Alcohol-related consequences are those consequences which are a direct result of the consumption of alcohol: for example, alcohol-induced liver cirrhosis, intoxication and alcoholic poisoning. These might be called alcohol-related consequences. They are those which come about as a direct consequence of the consumption of alcohol. That is, they are clearly the consequences of or the effects of consumption per se. Here straightforward, linear, causal thinking is appropriate. We can view the sequence of events that lead to the consequence as beginning at the point of consumption. Although this type of linear or Humean causal thinking is appropriate to this type of consequence, it is not necessarily appropriate to the others. Unfortunately, scientific thinking is dominated by this Humean view of causality based on temporal contiguity, which does not do justice to many instances of human behaviour where more teleological thinking is required.

Type 2 - Context-related Consequences

Context-related consequences are those which arise from the context or situation within which the drinking occurs. It is important to note here that the context or situation can be defined on a cultural, social, interpersonal or individual level. These might be called context-related consequences. For example, any drinking by a member of an abstinent family may be viewed as a drinking problem, yet arises from the attitudes of the family towards drinking and towards individual freedom. The resulting family distress will usually be blamed on drinking and not on the family's attitudes.

Another example might be of those individuals who allow themselves to experience, recall or relive certain emotional events only when they have been drinking. The ensuing distress and discomfort is frequently attributed to alcohol, rather than to the initial experience with which the individuals have no other method of coping. To punctuate this sequence of events as beginning with consumption and leading to distress is to eliminate important causal events from the sequence, as well as the intention of the drinker. These two examples have been given to illustrate that the situation or context can be taken at different levels.

Type 3 - Interaction-related Consequences

Interaction-related consequences are those which arise from the interaction of the effects of alcohol and the context or situation within which these effects are experienced: for example, drinking and driving or Monday morning absenteeism due to hangover.

Interaction-related consequences arise from a combination of processes involved in the other two types and are best illustrated by drunken driving. Consumption of alcohol beyond certain levels impairs judgement and produces motor inco-ordination. Whilst these effects are not of themselves a problem (some drinkers view them as benefits), in the context of driving they give rise to a dangerous set of circumstances. There is no good reason why they should be called 'drinking' problems rather than 'driving' problems. Consequently, it would be possible to aim intervention at either drinking or driving or both. To view these consequences as drinking problems may restrict the range of solutions to be considered for a prevention programme; the same applies if they are viewed simply as driving problems. An interactional view might raise questions regarding the distribution and location of drinking settings and the provision of transport to and from them. This example helps to illustrate the importance of the typology in general, since its relevance becomes clear when you have to decide on preventative strategies or, to be more precise, to decide in what causative process we wish to intervene. The choices are to interfere in the drinking process per se, the driving process, or in the larger drinking/driving interaction. Current fashion in the prevention of drinking-related consequences is to intervene in the drinking process rather than the problem-development phase. This follows from assuming that all drinking-related consequences are of Type 1, namely alcohol-related. Whilst it appears to be appropriate for Type 1 problems, it is by no means obvious that it should be the preferred tactic in dealing with Types 2 and 3. Although the phenomena included in each group may overlap with each other, the distinction is important since it distinguishes consequences of different natures, that is, due to different processes or combinations of processes.

We have seen that consequences have to be viewed as undesirable before they are conceptualised as a problem. However, we should note that 'undesirability' is likely to be defined relative to the cultural norms and expectations which prevail in that situation. Thus, the undesirability of consequences is culturally relative. This imposes on us the need to seek solutions to undesirable consequences which are culturally relative. The idea that there may be a universal solution rests on the notion that there is some common pathological process going on. Although it may be assumed that alcohol has some constant effects across different cultures, these would appear to be limited to motor inco-ordination and eventual narcosis. The bulk of other effects appear to be extremely variable across time and place (MacAndrew and Edgerton, 1970).

Having spelled out the differences between these different types of drinking-related consequences, let us consider what implications this typology has in relation to our three levels of preventative intervention.

PREVENTION OF UNDESIRABLE DRINKING-RELATED CONSEQUENCES

As noted above, it is only when consequences are undesirable that they constitute a problem and it is those problems which we seek to prevent. We should not be concerned with preventing beneficial consequences. It has already been noted that different strategies can aim at altering or intervening in the nature of consequences or their frequency. Inevitably, to interfere with the nature of a consequence will almost certainly lead to an alteration in its frequency. However, the same is not true in the other direction. Thus, it would be possible to have interventions which attempt to alter the frequency of problems without in any way altering their nature. We shall see in more detail how this applies when we consider specific examples in relation to each of the cells contained within Table 12.1. The value of this framework is that it raises specific questions about identified problems and clarifies which strategies might be possible or realistic, depending on the level of intervention being proposed. It also brings greater coherence to the 'problem prevention' approach (Room, 1981) which is accused of being too fragmented.

Each culture may wish to consider a different range of drinking-related problems, and also bring to the prevention field a unique set of attitudes to drinking and its consequences. In the absence of a theoretical or empirical base for making decisions regarding preferred strategies, these culturally related values become extremely important and constitute another strength of the proposed framework.

The preceding comments imply that there is no universally appropriate strategy for prevention of drinking-related problems but, rather, that this framework would be used to help preventative thinking for any given set of problems or circumstances. For the purpose of illustration the framework will be discussed in relation to the situation prevailing in the United Kingdom. As such its suggestions and conclusions are offered as appropriate to that country and not as universally valid.

PREVENTING TYPE 1 CONSEQUENCES: ALCOHOL-RELATED PROBLEMS

Type 1 consequences are those which arise directly as a result of consumption and are the only ones which should properly be called alcohol-related.

(a) Stopping Alcohol-related Problems

In order to stop these problems in the absolute sense, it is necessary to intervene in the consumption process by stopping drinking or altering alcohol so that it does not have damaging properties. In the past such interventions as prohibition have been used. Usually this has been enforced prohibition and has proved not only undesirable, but also ineffective (Coffey, 1975).

An alternative approach to enforce prohibition would be to

Table 12.1 A Framework for Prevention of Drinking-related Problems

Problem	Type 1: Alcohol-related	Type 2: Context-related	Type 3: Interaction-related
Aim of prevention			
Stop	Prohibition Abstention Non-harmful Minimal integrated consumption	Utopia Perfect people's lives Relabel	Impossible without either 1 or 2 being stopped
Hinder	Safer alcohols Safer drinking practices Antidotes Antabuse More damaging alcohols Rationing Restrict availability Safe limits Food	Conceptualise alcohol use and meaning Tackle cultural drug reliance Coping, living skills, training Find new scapegoat Special drinking contexts	Special drinking contexts Ease transitions Safer cars, roads for pedestrians, drivers Combination of previous Location of and transport to and from drinking settings Insulation of drinking contexts Combat alcohol/aggression myth Increase natural constraints
Curtail progress	Unemployment Conflicting attitudes Poverty Affluence	Living standards Harmonious living Integrate drinking	Combination of previous

embark on an educational campaign to encourage abstention as our cultural view towards drinking. This would not appear to have any likelihood of success, there being no major lobby in this country for a move in this direction. Another possibility might be to encourage extremely low levels of consumption. This would be unlikely to succeed also as it would appear that the experience of intoxication achieved by drinking more than minimal amounts is a desirable consequence. To abandon this would be to abandon alcohol. Too often alcohologists speak as though people should drink without getting intoxicated, which is a contradiction in terms.

The implications also of this policy would be to reduce revenue from the sale of alcohol to extremely small amounts and obviously governments at this point in time are not interested in this (DHSS, 1981). It would appear, therefore, that there is no real possibility of stopping this type of drinking problem by stopping or severely curtailing drinking. The alternative of altering alcohol such that it did not have damaging consequences also seems unrealistic in its absolute sense, since the nature of alcohol would have to change so radically that it would be unlikely to fulfil the needs for which it is currently used.

(b) Hindering Alcohol-related Problems
Under hindering, it is possible to think of two types of intervention, one which interferes directly in the causative process and one which has an indirect influence via altering the frequency of problems.

It has been previously advocated (Royal College of Psychiatrists, 1979) that drinking problems could be reduced by reducing per capita consumption. Reducing per capita consumption is the soft form of prohibition. It represents the same type of thinking as does stopping drinking and, as such, represents common sense. Whilst it is likely to be true in extremes that there will be more problems given greater consumption, this is in no way an inevitable outcome and ignores the wide variation possible within extremes. Thus, in our consideration of preventative strategies, the focus will be on limiting problems and not necessarily on limiting consumption. Such a perspective allows for the possibility of reducing problems in spite of, or independently of, increased consumption.

Even in relation to Type 1 problems, there are serious limitations of a prevention programme which attempts to limit consumption and therefore reduce the frequency of problems. Limiting per capita consumption has become the main strategy offered in preventative thinking for drinking-related problems generally. Its popularity arises from the apparent demonstration of a relationship between levels of consumption, levels of mortality from liver cirrhosis and other indices of drinking-related consequences. The data to support this relationship are predominantly cross-cultural, and thus there is a feeling of having discovered a prevention strategy that should apply universally. While this generality holds many attractions, its applicability to the United Kingdom is not so straightforward. The following objections to the argument arise from considering Britain's position in detail and should not necessarily be viewed as a criticism of the argument in general.

(1) Whilst it is true that alcohol consumption has been rising steadily for the last 20 to 30 years, this increase is from an all-time low since records were kept in the late sixteenth century (Spring and Buss, 1977). The present level of consumption is lower than the mean for the last 300 years, and will probably continue to regress towards that mean. This recent increase coincides with an even greater increase in the consumption of other psychotropic substances. To radically alter such a trend by price control, if possible, would require massive increases which would be unacceptable to the public and counter-productive to the government. In order to be effective, price controls would have to be extremely severe. Government would lose vast amounts of income through loss of duty, if effective. In a realistic world government will offer price increases that will attempt to contain consumption rather than reduce it. They will only be interested in 'hindering' or 'curtailing the progress of', as preventative aims.

(2) The proponents of the policy to limit consumption argue that they do not want to stop drinking but wish to stop the 'harm that results from drinking'. Note that the 'harm that results from drinking' invokes linear causality. Let us assume that what they are referring to are the physical consequences of drinking. The argument presented here is that a statistical relationship between per capita consumption and rates of liver cirrhosis there has been demonstrated, and that the way to reduce liver cirrhosis is by attacking per capita consumption. The cross-cultural data on which this relationship is based are worthy of closer attention. Not only have the suggested relationships and the predictions based on them for preventative purposes been criticised (Duffy, 1977; McKechnie, 1977; Miller and Agnew, 1974), but the data with reference to the United Kingdom are highly atypical. Whilst UK consumption lies in the mid-range, its liver cirrhosis rate is lowest of the 20 countries cited by Sulkenen (1976) and is 20 per cent lower than its nearest rival which is Ireland, whose consumption is only 72 per cent that of the UK. Canada has similar consumption to the UK but three times as much cirrhosis, and the USA, where consumption is slightly lower than in Britain, has almost five times as much cirrhosis. Thus, UK is extremely successful at limiting cirrhosis, but not by limiting per capita consumption.

Other factors are obviously important which, as yet, have not been investigated. As Skog (1973) argues, 'the existing data are not sufficient to prove that a change in average consumption is the instrument of choice in the fight against alcoholism. The causal relationships relevant to the problem of alcoholism are much too complicated for that to be the case'. This view is supported by Edwards (1973) who suggests that 'it is unlikely that any unifactorial preventative policy will be widely effective', in view of the multivariate nature and determination of alcohol problems.

Despite these injunctions, the limitation of _per capita_ consumption has become the main thrust of preventative efforts in the field of drinking problems. The argument seems to be that other problems are similar to that of cirrhosis, so limiting _per capita_ consumption will be effective in controlling other problems, thus ruling out differences in the nature of their causation. Given the UK's outstanding record of limiting the level of deaths from liver cirrhosis, it is unlikely that gains are going to be made in this domain. Indeed, it is more likely that liver cirrhosis rates will regress towards the mean regardless of what happens to consumption levels. Although it is argued that the relationship between levels of consumption and levels of cirrhosis has been established, there is little evidence on changes in level of consumption in a downward direction. As a society, we have to decide what level of cost we are prepared to tolerate for the benefits of drinking. This is implied in our balance sheet model, but needs to be fully recognised and acknowledged.

(3) Alcohol is frequently implicated in a number of other physical disorders and these also, it is argued, could be reduced if alcohol were not consumed. What is never answered seriously is what physical disorders might increase in the absence of alcohol. Or what price we might have to pay for giving it up. Thus, the limitation of _per capita_ consumption lobby sounds like an anti-alcohol lobby rather than anti-harm lobby. The suggestion is sometimes refuted by arguing that there may be a safe limit to drinking, but this safe limit refers only to the increase in the risk of liver damage, and has no implications for any other types of problem unless it is accepted that all drinking-related problems are of similar type.

The 'safe limit' is a two-edged instrument. It is hoped that those drinkers who consume more than the safe limit will reduce their consumption to a safe level. What, of course, might happen is that those who drink below the safe limit may feel that they can increase their consumption with safety; since _per capita_ consumption is already much lower than the safe limit, any move in this direction would increase _per capita_ consumption in this country.

How then are we to embark on attempting to hinder Type 1 problems? Another solution that has been offered is to encourage the consumption of weaker alcohols, i.e. to lower the strength of alcohols that are available for sale. This inevitably raises the question of whether or not there might, in fact, be safer alcohols - alcohols which might allow some of the same intoxicating effects, for which many people appear to drink, and yet would not have the same physically damaging properties. Along these lines too, one might think about antidotes to alcohol, something to be consumed after having been drinking which might counteract some of the more damaging effects.

Further possibilities highlight our ambivalence in this whole area and our lack of understanding of what is likely to be effective. Consider for a moment the problem of hangovers. It is frequently argued that hangovers arise from certain impurities in alcoholic beverages. It may be possible, therefore, to make alcohols which would give even worse hangovers. This might have the effect of people reducing their consumption. On the other hand, making alcohols which did not produce hangovers would actually reduce hangover problems, hangovers being one example of Type 1 problems. Our dilemma here is seen clearly, in that we have no theoretical basis for deciding which of these two contradictory solutions would be most advantageous. A decision is likely to be made on the basis of attitudes to drinking held by the community making the decision, rather than drinkers in general. There are more indirect approaches which would involve rationing or limiting availability by means other than price control with a view to reducing overall levels of consumption. Again, there is some evidence here which runs in contradictory directions. The general argument is that the less alcohol that is available, the fewer problems that will arise and vice versa. In Scotland, there is recent evidence to suggest that the opposite has happened by making alcohol more available through longer drinking hours (Bruce, 1979; Wann and Bruce, 1979).

There is a need to investigate much more clearly what safer drinking practices there might be. It is clear that Scotland has many more Type 1 problems than England and Wales, and yet Scottish per capita consumption appears to be the same as that for England and Wales (Dight, 1976; Wilson, 1980). The proportion of the alcohol diet which is consumed in Scotland in the form of spirits is higher than in England, and people frequently suggest that this is why Scotland suffers more for its drinking than England and Wales. It has also been suggested that it is the proportion of wine which contributes to high liver cirrhosis (Whitlock, 1974). It is necessary to define drinking practices in ways other than simply quantity and frequency, and to locate those practices more properly in their context in order to understand more clearly what safe drinking practices might be. This applies also to notions of safe limits. Safe limits need to be spelled out very clearly, including what the limits are safe from.

(c) **Curtailing Alcohol-related Problems**

In considering the 'curtailing the progess of' aspects of prevention, we notice that these need not be primarily aimed at the nature of the problems, but are more usually aimed at contributing factors which give rise to fluctuations in an upward direction of the problem being focused upon. This strategy attempts to limit factors which help increase the frequency of problem drinking, or the development of problems, or any factors that push drinking practices in the direction of unsafe or risky practices. This can be done, not only by stopping or limiting certain things, but by actually advocating other alternatives. Thus, it is possible, even in the preventative field, to make positive moves towards enhancement and enrichment rather than restriction. The identification of safe practices would lay the foundation of a programme of promotion of these moves. They would, of course, have to be identified in terms wider than amount consumed.

It is noteworthy that liver cirrhosis increases in times of unemployment and poverty, and reducing these would affect the incidence of Type 1 problems. It is also true that the recent increases in drinking problems are associated with a number of other changes in our society, and these should be investigated more fully towards developing a broader base from which to consider preventative efforts (e.g. consumption of tranquillisers and antidepressants, decline in major recreational activities such as cinema and football matches).

PREVENTING TYPE 2 CONSEQUENCES: CONTEXT-RELATED PROBLEMS
(a) Stopping Context-related Problems
Type 2 problems arise from the context within which drinking occurs rather than from the drinking per se. This, of course, represents an ideal type as drinking always occurs in a context.

It is not particularly helpful to say that there would not be a problem if there were no drinking. The kinds of problems which are considered here may well arise whether or not drinking occurs. They would not be called drinking problems if drinking was not occurring. The main problem here is that these problems have been wrongly labelled. They have been labelled as drinking-related problems when, in fact, they should be considered much more as context-related problems.

The context can be defined at three different levels, the cultural level, the social or interpersonal level, and at an individual level. When one considers the implications of trying to stop these kinds of problems in their absolute sense, what is required is Utopia - a Utopia in which people's lives are perfect. This would lead to perfect contexts within which drinking could occur. Notice the assumptions here that people would continue to drink even though they had perfect lives. The idea that people only drink because they have problems is totally rejected. The creation of Utopia is an unrealistic target, and therefore it is more appropriate to consider how these kinds of problems may be hindered.

(b) Hindering Context-related Problems
It has been argued above that most of these problems come about because of wrong labelling. This wrong labelling arises because of current conceptualisations of alcohol. It is necessary to attempt to change society's views of alcohol in order to relieve alcohol from its scapegoat image, to give it new or different meanings, or to emphasise more strongly some of its current meanings. For example, there is a common reliance on alcohol in times of crisis. Any attempts which weaken the cultural view of alcohol as a panacea would help clarify those consequences which arise because people have got problems or are in predicaments during which they happen to drink. It is also important to notice here that many of the problems, particularly those of family aggression, violence, financial difficulties etc. arise not simply because of drinking, but because of poor coping mechanisms for other aspects of living. Therefore, the introduction of parenthood, social skills training, preparation for

marriage, the handling of violence and aggression, conflict within marriage and families, money management etc. would be vital aspects of an educational programme conducted in schools.

It is also necessary to ask what factors give rise to harmonious living and freedom from trouble? For example, one might ask, what is the role of religion in the development of drinking-related problems, and what aspects of religious contact protect people from developing problems?

We also require to consider what contexts for drinking might be thought to be relatively harm-free and try, if possible, to create such contexts within our society or find ways of insulating those contexts such that any trouble which arises is contained within them rather than carried over into other contexts. Japanese drinking houses which tolerate violent and aggressive behaviour within a caring environment are one example of this.

(c) Curtailing Context-related Problems

Regardless of whether problems are Type 1 or Type 2, the same factors apply, so any factors indicated under Type 1 problems should also apply here. Consequently, there is little difference between 'hindering' and 'curtailing' context-related problems since the strategies have to be indirect and not aimed at drinking but at the context.

PREVENTING TYPE 3 CONSEQUENCES: INTERACTION-RELATED PROBLEMS

(a) Stopping Interaction-related Problems

Any effective strategy dealing with either Type 1 or Type 2 problems will contribute to alleviating those which arise from the interaction of the processes involved in either Type 1 or Type 2. Since it is not possible or realistic to stop, in the absolute sense, either Type 1 problems or Type 2 problems, it is not possible to stop Type 3 problems in an absolute sense either. Therefore, attention focuses on the lesser aims of hindering and curtailing Type 3 problems.

(b) Hindering Interaction-related Problems

The value of safer alcohols and safer contexts under Types 1 and 2 obviously applies here. It is important to notice, as Room (1975) indicates, that many of these interactional problems arise when a drinker moves from a drinking context to a non-drinking context, and any efforts to ease this transition may alleviate the problem. Problems here appear to arise when behaviour appropriate to one context is carried over into another. In essence the problem here centres on the mutability of 'drunken' behaviour.

There is a tendency to believe that drunken behaviour is immutable, and this highlights another way in which our current belief system requires a major overhaul. Any prevention programme which does not tackle the belief that alcohol causes certain behaviours in an inevitable manner perpetuates the myth that alcohol is responsible for many behaviours of which it is innocent. One may wish to continue with a high level of merriment and jocularity derived from a party atmosphere, but it does not have to continue when one moves to a more serious or sober environment. This point touches on the question of personal responsibility and accountability when under the influence of alcohol. If bad behaviour is excused on the grounds of intoxication, then we must expect people to behave badly when intoxicated and to get intoxicated in order to behave badly.

It is also important to note that many problems of this type are not dose-related as are Type 1 problems. The implication of this is that reducing consumption may have little to offer by way of prevention, and there is therefore a need to focus on the beliefs and attitudes which surround the activity of drinking.

To view these problems as interactive problems is also to create another field or level or intervention which can be illustrated by considering drinking and driving. It has been agreed that drinking and driving problems can be viewed as 'drinking' or 'driving' problems, and there is merit in each view. If viewed as drinking problems suggested solutions would focus on weaker alcohols, antidotes to the effects of alcohol, only drinking in moderation and with food, etc. If viewed as driving or 'road safety' problems, suggestions would focus on safer cars designed externally to reduce damage on impact and internally to reduce the damage from secondary impact. (Secondary impact is when a passenger or driver bangs into the equipment or structure inside the vehicle.) Safer roads are also required, not only for drivers but also for pedestrians. If there is an accident risk from drinkers emerging from pubs onto the street at closing time, then perhaps we require crash barriers on footpaths similar to those used at schools. Such proposals have already been put forward much more fully by Wilkinson (1970).

When an interactional view is considered a number of other strategies become obvious. We know that alcohol slows reaction time, especially in choice conditions, thus impairing an essential skill required for driving. It would be possible to build a complex ignition switch requiring a choice to be made within a particular time in order to start the car. Such a device would not just stop those whose ability is affected by alcohol, but those who are slow for other reasons and this may be a general contribution to road safety.

Within an interactional view one should give serious thought to the question of location of drinking establishments. This becomes a town-planning issue. We have seen instances of large housing estates, with populations equivalent in size to many small towns, without facilities including public drinking places. We also see hotels and pubs being built in locations which obviously necessitate travel and with the provision of car parks, hence condoning vehicular travel of some kind.

Too often permission for pubs or inns is rejected because the road access is considered inadequate for the increased traffic. We thus build drinking and driving into the structure of our society. Such a concern would also raise questions concerning the role of city-centre pubs in the evenings where there is no living population but only those who have travelled into town for cinema or theatre etc. What is being raised here is not simply the location of pubs but the transport arrangements to and from them. It may even be possible for landlords to supply transport for groups of regulars from particular areas or for informal arrangements to be made.

One solution might be to encourage people to drink at home. This has never been an attractive proposition to those who work with problem drinkers since they tend to be suspicious of home drinking. Their suspicion is unwarranted. There is evidence from Dight (1976) to suggest that home-based drinking is extremely moderate, whereas most pub, club and hotel drinking amongst males will carry them over the drink-driving limit.

Any help aimed at improving personal and social interaction would be likely to alleviate problems in this area, as would the development of our understandings of everyday alcohol use.

(c) Curtailing Interaction-related Problems

Again, the same factors which apply to Types 1 and 2 are appropriate here, but also a wide range of other measures to improve the quality of the interaction between people's drinking and the rest of their lives. Perhaps of more relevance in Scotland than in England is the nature of the public house, where the predominance of males continues largely unabated and there is a great resistance to move towards more general-purpose settings such as cafeteria bars or family bars. The integration of drinking into the mainstream of other aspects of life would seem to be very important, without wishing to deny the importance of 'drinking' as a means of 'time out' from that mainstream.

CONCLUSION

Table 12.1 summarises the kinds of preventative strategies that are being suggested. It should be noted that there is much information not available with regard to such things as safe drinking practices or whether or not there might be safer alcohols. Therefore, there is a great deal of research work which requires to be done. Within Table 12.1, it is important to come away with the conclusion that prevention in the field of drinking-related problems is not aimed at stopping drinking problems in an absolute sense. The best that can or should be done is to hinder or curtail the progress of drinking-related problems in our community. When embarking on preventing drinking-related problems it is important to suit preventative strategies to what is seen specifically as the problem, rather than attempting one global solution. If one is concerned about people throwing beer cans at goal-keepers at football matches, then perhaps alcohol should be sold in plastic cups, rather than beer cans, at football matches. At a research level the question, 'What is it about football matches which produces violence which does not happen to the same degree at cricket matches or rugby matches despite the fact that alcohol is frequently available?' needs to be answered.

If a health education process is adopted, it is important to have specific messages aimed at specific problems, rather than global vague messages about cutting down, keeping below the safe limit, etc., at the same time spelling out very clearly what is to be prevented and why it is viewed as a problem. Table 12.1 has given a few examples of the kind of thinking that is required. It is difficult at this point to go much further without some further research being done.

The overall aim of a preventative programme should be to create the conditions and attitudes which will minimise undesirable related consequences.

REFERENCES

Bacon, S. (1978) 'On the prevention of alcohol problems and alcoholism', Journal of Studies on Alcohol, 39, 1125-47

Bruce, D. (1979) Timing and Number of Drink Related Offences and Road Accidents, Edinburgh: Scottish Office

Coffey, T.M. (1975) The Long Thirst, London: Hamilton

DHSS (1981) Drinking Sensibly, London: HMSO

Dight, S. (1976) Scottish Drinking Habits, Edinburgh: HMSO

Dubach, U.C. and Schneider, J. (1980) 'Screening for alcoholism', Lancet, 2, 1374-6

Duffy, J.C. (1977) 'Estimating the proportion of heavy drinkers in the Ledermann Curve' in D.L. Davies (ed.), The Ledermann Curve, London: Alcohol Education Centre

Edwards, G. (1973) 'Epidemiology applied to alcoholism: a review and examination of purposes', Quarterly Journal of Studies on Alcohol, 34, 28-35

MacAndrew, C. and Edgerton, R.B. (1970) Drunken Comportment, London: Nelson

McKechnie, R.J. (1977) 'How important is alcohol in alcoholism?' in J.S. Madden, R. Walker and W.H. Kenyon (eds), Alcoholism and Drug Dependence: A Multidisciplinary View, London: Plenum

Miller, G.H. and Agnew, M. (1974) 'The Ledermann model of alcohol consumption', Quarterly Journal of Studies on Alcohol, 35, 877-98

Robertson, I., Hodgson, R., Orford, J. and McKechnie, R. (1984) Psychology and Problem Drinking, Leicester: British Psychological Society

Room, R. (1975) 'Normative perspectives on alcohol use and problems', Journal of Drug Issues, 5, 358-68

____ (1981) 'The case for a problem prevention approach to alcohol, drug and mental problems', Public Health Reports, 96, 26-33

Royal College of Psychiatrists (1979) Alcohol and Alcoholism, London: Tavistock

Skog, O.J. (1973) 'Less alcohol - fewer alcoholics?', Drinking and Drug Practices Surveyor, 7, 7-14

Spring, J.A. and Buss, D.H. (1977) 'Three centuries of alcohol in the British diet', Nature, 270, 567-72

Sulkenen, P. (1976) 'Drinking patterns and the level of alcohol consumption: an overview', in Y. Israel et al. (ed), Research Advances in Alcohol and Drug Problems, Vol.III, New York:

Wiley

Turner, B.T., Bennett, V. and Hermandez, H. (1981) 'The beneficial side of moderate alcohol use', John Hopkins Medical Journal, 148, 53-63

Wann, D.M. and Bruce, D. (1979) Survey of Licensed Premises, Edinburgh: Scottish Office

Whitlock, F.A. (1974) 'Liver cirrhosis, alcoholism and alcohol consumption', Quarterly Journal of Studies on Alcohol, 35, 586-605

Wilkinson, R. (1970) The Prevention of Drinking Problems, New York: Oxford University Press

Wilson, P. (1980) Drinking in England and Wales, London: HMSO

Chapter 13

THE CASE FOR CONTROLLING ALCOHOL CONSUMPTION

Bill Saunders

Alcohol is the most popular and widely used psychoactive drug in the world. In many societies alcohol has been incorporated into the fabric of everyday life, with its use being an integral part of the most joyous and the most distressing of human occasions. Alcohol is used as a stimulant, a tranquilliser, an anaesthetic, a celebrant, a medicine, a social lubricant, a religious symbol, a food, a fuel and as an indicator of the transition from work to play. The functions of its use are so diverse that at times they are contradictory, and at normal dosages our expectations about the value and effects of alcohol influence our behaviour to a far greater extent than do the psycho-pharmacological properties of the drug.

That alcohol fulfils such a plethora of functions has ensured that it is not a neutral substance, and discussions about alcohol, and the problems associated with its use, provoke a diversity, and often a conflict of opinion. One of the most contentious and acrimonious of these debates is the significance of the level of per capita consumption of any given society. In this chapter it is contended that, in terms of the prevention of alcohol problems, attention should be directed to the overall level of alcohol consumption in a society. This contention is based on the empirical evidence which shows that levels of per capita consumption and alcohol-related problems are positively linked.

The essential message of this statement is that if, in any given society, the amount of alcohol consumed per head of population increases, then there will in all probability be an increase in the amount of alcohol-related damage in that society. Similarly, a fall in per capita consumption will in general be associated with a decrease in the indices of alcohol-related harm. This philosophy has been encapsulated by Bruun et al. (1975) who noted: 'Changes in the overall consumption of alcoholic beverages have a bearing on the health of the people in any society.'

The evidence linking per capita consumption and alcohol-related damage is extensive and compelling. The examples cited below are but part of an array of data, and have been chosen to illustrate that the association between levels of consumption and problems persists over time and across different cultures.

(Throughout this chapter the statistics quoted have been culled from a variety of sources. In order to ensure a smooth flow in the text many references have been omitted. A bibliography is included at the end of the chapter which cites major sources.)

PER CAPITA CONSUMPTION AND PROBLEMS - SOME EVIDENCE
The British Experience

In 1982 each adult in Britain drank on average 9.2 litres of pure alcohol. As a nation we spend about £33 million on alcohol each day, and this expenditure on alcohol (1981 - £11,934 million) is greater than that on clothing (1981 - £10,131 million) or on the running of our motor cars (1981 - £10,150 million).

Such extensive use of alcohol is not a new phenomenon in Britain. Over the past 300 years marked fluctuations in consumption have occurred and several periods stand out as times of very heavy alcohol usage. Of these, the notorious gin era of 1730-50 and the period 1885-1915 were epochs of very heavy use which were characterised by cheap and easily available alcohol, with associated high rates of drunkenness and morbidity. The fluctuating course of per capita consumption and problems during the period 1885-1935 is well illustrated in Table 13.1. As may be seen, by the end of the nineteenth century per capita consumption had risen to 10.7 litres of absolute alcohol, and deaths from liver cirrhosis, delirium tremens and alcoholism exceeded 180 per one million inhabitants.

Table 13.1:   UK Annual Per Capita Alcohol Consumption and Average Annual Alcohol-Related Mortality Per One Million Population, 1885-1934 by Quinquennium

Quinquennium	Consumption in litres of pure alcohol	Deaths due to liver cirrhosis, dt's and chronic alcoholism per one million people
1885-9	9.7	154
1890-4	10.2	168
1895-9	10.7	182
1900-4	10.5	193
1905-9	9.2	156
1910-14	8.7	131
1915-19	5.9	81
1920-4	5.9	59
1925-9	5.1	55
1930-4	4.1	42

Source: WHO, Problems Related to Alcohol Consumption, Technical Report Series, WHO, Geneva, 1980.

The period of the First World War was associated with a marked downturn in alcohol consumption. The cause of this decline in drinking has been variously attributed, but the imposition of very restrictive licensing legislation and substantial tax increases upon alcoholic beverages played their part. The accelerated drop in consumption which occurred during the First World War saw a parallel marked downturn in alcohol-related mortality. Between 1900 and 1934 per capita consumption was halved and there was a five-fold drop in mortality.

If the period of observation is extended to 1950 the advantage of a diminishing per capita consumption is clearly shown. Between 1912 and 1952 the whole totality of alcohol-related problems declined. Offences of drunkenness fell from 60 per 10,000 population to 12 per 10,000, and the rate of liver cirrhosis deaths fell from 150 per million to 25 per million. These figures are of significance especially in the light of the events of the past 30 years. Between 1950 and 1980 there has been a doubling of alcohol consumption in Britain from 4.9 litres per adult to 10.4 litres. The result of this rapid increase in consumption is that our society is now experiencing alcohol problems of a very high order. Indeed, for the period 1952-82 convictions for drunkenness rose from 12 per 10,000 population to 24 per 10,000. Convictions for drinking and driving have, since 1968 and the imposition of 'breath tests', risen from 23,900 to 78,000 in 1980. In the past 30 years hospital admissions for 'alcoholism' and 'alcoholic psychosis' have soared from 512 to 13,916.

In the past decade, when the NHS in-patient provision of services for problem drinkers was static, admissions for 'alcoholism' doubled. Deaths from liver cirrhosis increased from below 1,500 in 1952 to over 2,750 in 1981. The rate per 100,000 inhabitants virtually doubled from 2.7 to 4.9.

Establishing the number of problem drinkers is notoriously difficult and available estimates do vary widely. The most authoritative recent reviews suggest that in England and Wales, some 750,000 - 850,000 people have significant problems (Donnan and Haskey, 1977; Taylor, 1981). Furthermore, one Scottish survey has indicated that 5 per cent of men and 1 per cent of women have serious alcohol problems (Saunders and Kershaw, 1979). If these figures are combined with the English and Welsh data it is possible to estimate that some one million people in Britain are experiencing serious problems related to their use of alcohol. In the early 1960s the most reliable estimates did not exceed 250,000.

The events of the past three years are also of considerable relevance. In the 1981 Budget the excise duty on alcoholic beverages increased sharply. This action, coupled with price increases imposed by the brewers, meant that for the first time in over 30 years the price of alcoholic beverages increased faster than the retail price index (RPI). Between 1978 and 1981 the RPI of alcoholic beverages rose by 61 per cent, the RPI of all items by 52 per cent and personal disposable income rose by 55 per cent. By 1981 alcohol was, in real terms, more expensive than in 1978. The impact of this event is of considerable interest. In the year 1981-2, for the first time in post-war Britain, per capita consumption of alcohol fell from 10.4 litres of pure alcohol per adult to 9.2 litres. This fall was associated with an 11 per cent reduction in convictions for drunkenness, an 8 per cent fall in drinking and driving convictions, and liver-cirrhosis deaths also fell by 4 per cent.

Thus, in the twentieth century, the British experience of alcohol consumption and alcohol-related problems clearly supports the statement made by the Royal College of Psychiatrists (1979) that 'per capita consumption and health damage go hand in hand, uphill and down dale'. This statement gains further credibility when the evidence from European countries is considered.

The European Experience

The association between per capita alcohol consumption and alcohol-related damage can be further examined by the use of cross-sectional data - that is, data from different countries at similar times. From a European perspective the conclusion from such analysis is clear cut: those countries with the highest per capita alcohol consumption have the highest levels of liver-cirrhosis mortality. The top six alcohol-consuming countries in 1979 were France (20.8 litres of pure alcohol per adult), Luxembourg (20.0), Spain (19.2), Italy (16.0), Austria (14.4), and Belgium (13.9). The liver-cirrhosis mortality league table is headed by Italy (34.8 deaths/100,000) and followed by Austria (31.2), France (30.4), Spain (27.6), West Germany (27.6), Luxembourg (27.0) and Belgium (14.4.). Thus, the top six 'drinking countries' also feature in six of the top seven places in the cirrhosis league table. Conversely, three out of four of the lowest alcohol-consuming countries - Norway (5.7 litres of absolute alcohol per adult), Sweden (7.1), the UK (9.8) and Ireland (10.0) - are also to be found at the bottom of the liver-cirrhosis mortality table, with Norway and England reporting a mortality rate of 4.2 per 100,000 and Ireland 3.6 per 100,000.

As may be appreciated, there is not an absolute, one-to-one relationship between per capita consumption and liver-cirrhosis mortality, but the correlation is very high, having been variously estimated at between +0.5 and +0.9 (e.g. see Schmidt, 1978). For naturally occurring social science data, this is a correlation of a very high order and is difficult to ignore.

An additional factor about the above figures is that there is also an association between being a high scorer in the mortality tables and having few controls over the availability of alcohol. Davies and Walsh (1983) have classified the countries of Europe in terms of the extent of alcohol-control policy that each nation has enacted. With regard to liver-cirrhosis deaths, five out of the top seven countries have low alcohol-control-policy status with the remaining two, Belgium and France, being respectively of 'average' and 'high' alcohol-control status. However, in the latter case, the imposition of a high level of controls has only recently occurred, and the appalling levels of damage caused in France by regular excessive use is a legacy of more liberal decades. It is apparent that the existence of an ad hoc and limited system of controls facilitates high levels of consumption, high rates of liver-cirrhosis mortality

217

and related physical morbidity. These cross-sectional data clearly show that the European experience of alcohol problems is one of low controls on alcohol consumption being associated with high consumption and high levels of problems. The converse is also true. High degrees of alcohol-control policy tend to be associated with low consumption and low levels of problems.

This conclusion is also evident from an examination of time-series data, that is, the study of different countries over time. The following examples of Finland, Poland, Spain, Luxembourg and Italy have been taken because they represent countries with different types of alcohol-control policy, yet they still clearly demonstrate the link between per capita consumption and harm.

The Finnish Experience

In 1950 per capita consumption in Finland was 1.7 litres of pure alcohol, and throughout the 1950s consumption remained at this very low level. The modesty of this level of consumption is made clear when compared to Britain, where the lowest twentieth-century annual per capita consumption figure was 3.5 litres (1934). In Finland the 1960s saw a gradual upturn in consumption with, by 1968, per capita consumption being 2.9 litres. At this time the Finnish government radically revised its long-established and very restrictive alcohol policy. The extent of this restrictive history can be judged by the fact that between 1919 and 1932 alcohol was prohibited, and even after the repeal of prohibition tight controls on the production and retail of alcohol were maintained, with all aspects of the production and sale of alcohol coming under the auspices of a State Alcohol Monopoly.

This monopoly curtailed the overall availability of alcohol by restricting the number of premises (especially in rural areas), the hours of sale, the type of beverages available and the amount of alcohol purchasable on any one occasion. Individuals were also required to hold a certificate to purchase spirits and fortified wine, which could be revoked for transgressions of alcohol-related laws and/or anti-social behaviour.

However, from the late 1950s a gradual liberalisation occurred which culminated in the 1968 Alcohol Act. The extent of this liberalisation is demonstrated by the following statistics: between 1950 and 1975 the number of monopoly liquor stores doubled from 83 to 194, licensed restaurants increased from 348 to 1,470, and the number of municipalities with a liquor shop increased from 59 to 134. In addition, opening hours were extended, the system of individual certificates of fitness to purchase removed, the legal drinking age was lowered and the real price of alcohol allowed to fall.

The result of this liberalisation surpassed all expectations. As examination of Table 13.2 shows, consumption of alcoholic beverages rose from 1.85 litres of absolute alcohol per head in 1960 to 6.2 litres by 1975. This three-and-a-half-fold increase in consumption was associated with a 60 per cent increase in arrests for drunkenness. Alcohol-related road traffic accidents increased by a factor of nearly 4, cases of drunk driving by a factor of 10. Liver-cirrhosis deaths more than doubled, and mortality relating to alcoholic poisoning and alcoholism increased by 275 per cent. In addition, between 1969 and 1975 male hospital admission rates for alcoholism increased by a factor of 1.7, admissions for pancreatitis doubled, as did admissions for alcoholic psychosis.

Table 13.2: Annual Per Capita Alcohol Consumption and Recorded Consequences of Drinking Per 100,000 Inhabitants in Finland in 1950, 1960, 1968 and 1975

	1950	1960	1968	1975
Per capita consumption in litres of absolute alcohol	1.73	1.85	2.88	6.19
Arrests for drunkenness	1668	2964	3185	5842
Alcohol-related road traffic accidents	20	28.5	44.9	75.1
Cases of drunk driving	37.5[a]	96.0	147.2	379.0
Deaths from liver cirrhosis	2.3[a]	3.3	3.6	6.3
Deaths from alcoholic poisoning and alcoholism	2.4	2.6	6.0	6.6

Sources: WHO, Problems Relating to Alcohol Consumption Technical Report, Series 650, WHO, Geneva, 1980.
    Makela, K. et al, 'Drink in Finland', in Alcohol, Society and the State, Vol.2, Addiction Research Foundation.

    a   1951 figure.

Not surprisingly, since 1975 the state liquor monopoly has been under pressure to curtail its liberalisation policy. Consequently, there have been some restrictions in opening hours, a total ban on the public advertising of alcoholic beverages, closer supervision of beer outlets and a fall in the number of licensed premises. Subsequently per capita consumption has stabilised and with it the level of alcohol-related damage. For a fuller account of the Finnish experience, Makela, Osterberg and Sulkunen (1981) is recommended, and it is salutary reading for those who consider per capita consumption of little significance in the etiology and prevention debates.

The Polish Experience
Between 1960 and 1975, per capita consumption in Poland increased from 6.2 litres of absolute alcohol per person to 10.6 litres, and in 1980 per capita consumption exceeded 11.0 litres. As may be

expected, this substantial increase in consumption was associated with an across-the-board rise in alcohol-related harm.

Between 1960 and 1975 liver-cirrhosis mortality increased from 3.4 per 100,000 population to 10.2 per 100,000; admissions to 'sobering-up stations' (a more accurate description of the equivalent of our 'detox' centres) rose from just over 100,000 per annum to nearly 300,000 each year, and admissions to psychiatric hospitals increased by a factor of 2.5 - from 9.4 to 23.9 per 100,000 population. Deaths from alcoholic poisoning were similarly influenced, up from 0.4 to 2.7 per 100,000 population.

Given that Poland has a long history of state alcohol control - and under the 1959 Prevention of Alcoholism Act the state was required to control per capita consumption - the recent events in Poland are of considerable interest. Between 1960 and 1970 the price of alcohol was maintained in relation to the average wage index and the increase in per capita consumption was modest, being in the five-year period 1965-70 approximately 14 per cent.

However, the early 1970s was a period of comparative affluence for Poland's expanding corps of industrial workers and the retail price of alcohol fell sharply. In the period 1970-5 consumption of alcohol rose by 43 per cent, from 7.3 to 10.6 litres of absolute alcohol per head.

In 1978, as a response to very evident damage relating to alcohol use, the government 're-established' the price of alcohol by increasing taxation on spirits by 38 per cent and the number of hours of opening of licensed premises were curtailed. These restrictions on availability were further extended in 1981 when, as a by-product of Poland's socio-political unrest, both the government and the Solidarity movement came to realise the desirability of limiting per capita consumption. In March 1981 the price of spirits was increased by 50 per cent and that of wine and beer was also increased, though by more modest amounts. The latest available figures show that in 1981/2 consumption fell by 24 per cent as compared to the previous year and, although no hard data on alcohol problems have yet been released, there is sufficient international evidence to predict that there will have been a substantial fall in the indices of alcohol-related harm.

The experiences of Finland and Poland are of interest because, in the former, liberalisation of alcohol availability was an intentional policy, whereas in Poland the upsurge in alcohol consumption occurred largely due to government omission - an apparent accidental and unintended liberalisation. Moreover, as per capita consumption increased, both countries experienced an appreciable upturn in alcohol-related damage. Both countries have subsequently rescinded their policy of making alcohol more available, and have focused their attention upon a reduction of per capita consumption as the most appropriate preventive strategy.

It is of course reasonable to protest that the examples of Finland and Poland, with their history of restrictive policies on alcohol availability, are atypical countries. It is possible that after a long period of restrictive alcohol legislation, liberalisation results in the population over-indulging, as a reaction to their past repression, and that some period of trial and error is necessary before the population learns to cope with its new freedoms and responsibilities. However, if one examines the data available from countries with a history of very limited or almost non-existent alcohol-control policy, then the same relationship between per capita consumption and levels of problems is evident.

The Experiences of Spain, Luxembourg and Italy

Between 1962 and 1979 per capita consumption in Spain rose from 14.7 litres of pure alcohol to 19.2 litres - an increase of 13 per cent. As was noted above, Spain ranks third in the European alcohol-consumption league table. Associated with this increase in consumption was a two-fold increase in the number of deaths from liver cirrhosis, up from 4,400 per annum in 1959 to an estimated figure of over 10,000 in 1980. The rate per 100,000 population has risen from 15 to an estimated 30.2, and this level of mortality is comparable with that of France and Italy. Davies and Walsh (1983), whilst commenting on the paucity of data on alcohol-related damage in Spain, note clinical impressions of recent increased rates of admission for alcoholism and alcoholic psychosis, as well as increases in public drunkenness and alcohol-related public disorder offences.

Similarly in Luxembourg, a state with negligible alcohol-control policies - for example, there are no restrictions on who sells alcohol, or on the number of outlets, opening hours or the advertising of alcohol - per capita consumption virtually doubled in the 30-year period 1950-80. This was an increase from 10.6 to 20.0 litres of pure alcohol per person, a level of consumption second only to France. Not surprisingly, alcohol-related damage is also high, with the rate of liver-cirrhosis mortality approaching 30 per 100,000 (1976), up from 23 per 100,000 in 1965. However, there are marked fluctuations in liver-cirrhosis figures for Luxembourg. (The size of the population, about 350,000, ensures that a rate per 100,000 is not the most reliable of indices.) On the other hand, other indices of alcohol-related harm, such as convictions for public drunkenness, drink and driving offences and alcohol-related morbidity, have all increased over the past three decades.

The Italian experience of problems and levels of consumption also supports the contention that a rising per capita consumption is associated with greater harm. Between 1950 and 1979 per capita consumption of pure alcohol increased from 12.5 to 15.9 litres per adult, though this latter figure reflects a fall from a peak of 18.8 litres per head in 1973. The latest liver-cirrhosis figures (1976) show that between 1953 and 1976 the rate of deaths per 100,000 rose from 14.1 to 34.8. Bonfiglio, Falli and Pacini (1977), reporting on hospital admissions for alcoholic psychosis in Italy, noted that between 1950 and 1962 (a period in which per capita consumption increased by over one-third) these admissions nearly doubled, up from 3.3 per 100,000 inhabitants to 6.3. Moreover, these admissions accounted for 6.7 per cent of all psychiatric admissions in 1950 and 9.8 per cent by 1962.

FALLING CONSUMPTION AND FALLING PROBLEMS

The data presented above are supportive of the contention that rising per capita consumption is associated with an increase in alcohol-related problems. From a prevention perspective, the interesting question is whether a falling per capita consumption is associated with a downturn in the indices of harm. A number of specific examples of sharp downturns in consumption and resultant decreases in damage have been recorded. One of the best known is reported from Denmark where, as a consequence of food shortages during the First World War, the price of aquavit was increased from 0.9 kronor to 11 kronor per litre, and at the same time beer prices approximately doubled. The impact of this swingeing increase was that within two years consumption of alcohol per person had fallen from 6.7 to 1.6 litres. At a stroke, the incidence of delirium tremens fell from 27 to 2 per 100,000, and the death rate for chronic alcoholism was similarly affected, down from 12 to 2 per 100,000 inhabitants.

As noted above, the First World War was also a time in Britain when per capita consumption and the incidence and prevalence of alcohol-related damage fell markedly. Similarly, liver-cirrhosis data from the city of Paris during both World Wars show that the restrictions imposed by the war upon the availability of alcohol resulted in remarkable downturns in the liver-cirrhosis death rates.

However, one of the most powerful examples of the benefits of a declining per capita consumption is the experience of France over the past two decades. As is well recognised, alcohol consumption in France is high, currently being about double that of the British population, whereas in 1960 French per capita consumption was five times that of the British. Since 1960 per capita consumption in France has fallen from 24.9 litres of pure alcohol per head to 20.8 litres in 1979. From a per capita consumption perspective, the most interesting finding is that alcohol problems in France have also declined in the past decade. Between 1970 and 1978 liver-cirrhosis deaths fell from 16,865 to 16,112, a drop in the rate per 100,000 inhabitants from 33.1 to 30.4. Similarly, admissions to hospital for alcoholism and alcoholic psychosis have fallen from over 4,000 to below 3,500, a drop in the rate per 100,000 population from 7.9 to 6.5.

The benefits of a declining per capita alcohol consumption can also be seen by examining the overall alcohol-related mortality rate, which is an accumulative index of death from liver cirrhosis, alcohol-related cancers, respiratory diseases, suicide, road traffic fatalities and other alcohol-related accidents (calculated each year by the French National Committee on Alcoholism). Between 1973 and 1978, when per capita alcohol consumption fell by 10 per cent, this alcohol-related mortality index fell from 41,826 deaths to 37,950, a fall of 9.3 per cent. Other indicators of harm were also reduced. Suspension of driving licences for drinking and driving fell from 16.8 in 1970 to 13.1 in 1975, and alcohol-related road deaths fell by 21 per cent in the two year period 1976-8.

An interesting recent development in France is that, despite the fall in per capita consumption and the associated decline in the indices of alcohol-related harm, a recent report on alcohol problems in France - known as the Bernard Report - has recommended that the damage accrued from the current level of per capita consumption is unacceptable, and that a further reduction in per capita consumption is necessary. Their appreciation of the significance of per capita consumption in the prevention area can be judged by the opening statement of their proposals:

> The Working Party's opinion is that an attempt must be made to reduce gradually the quantity of alcohol consumed by the French. The aim is basic. Without a substantial reduction in the consumption of alcohol, no improvement can be hoped for. (Bernard, 1980, p.29)

The intention is to limit per capita alcohol consumption by an increase in the price of alcoholic beverages, and to further reduce the levels of harm via specific prevention strategies relating to drinking and driving and education. The Bernard Committee recognised that although educational and other prevention techniques are valuable, they have limited impact and are unlikely to be of any influence if per capita consumption is increasing (Bernard, 1980).

THE PER CAPITA CONSUMPTION PHILOSOPHY - SOME COMMON CRITICISMS

As noted at the beginning of this chapter, the association between per capita alcohol consumption and alcohol-related problems, and the debate about the significance of this relationship in terms of preventive strategies, is not without the ability to generate some heat and acrimony. Indeed it is probably more accurate to use the expression 'the per capita brouhaha' and omit the use of the word 'debate'. It is relevant to consider some of the common criticisms of this model and reflect on the validity of the arguments presented by its opponents. In essence, such criticism usually revolves around four issues: (i) the contribution of Ledermann; (ii) the use of liver-cirrhosis data as an indicator of harm; (iii) the philosophical desirability of controlling the availability of a psychoactive drug; and (iv) the use of price as a mechanism for reducing per capita consumption.

The Contribution of Ledermann

In 1956 the French demographer Ledermann proposed a hypothesis about the distribution of alcohol consumption and its relationship to heavy drinking. He noted the link between per capita alcohol consumption and levels of harm, and drew upon data from various studies which indicated that the amounts people drank could best be illustrated by the use of a log normal curve. Such curves have mathematical properties from which Ledermann developed formulae to estimate the proportion of drinkers at any per capita level of consumption. An important feature of this model was that if per capita consumption increased then this resulted in a greater proportion of the drinking population passing over into the category of 'heavy drinker'.

As may be appreciated, this is a very mechanistic and rigid model. Indeed, the Ledermann hypothesis was an attempt to establish a scientific law about consumption levels and harmful drinking. It is important to realise that, once established, scientific laws have the property of being 'always true'. Thus, any single instance of disconfirmation means the rejection or at least reformulation of the existing law.

Not surprisingly, given the innovative nature and preventive implications of Ledermann's hypothesis, various researchers have tested out the working of his model. For example, Duffy in a series of papers (Duffy, 1977; Duffy and Cohen, 1978; Duffy, 1980) has authoritatively challenged some of the figures on which Ledermann based his original work, and has particularly criticised the accuracy of the estimates of heavy drinkers that can be obtained from per capita consumption data. However, it must be stressed that, whilst it is possible to attack the mechanistic, mathematical qualities of Ledermann, this does not of itself lead to the rejection of the association between per capita consumption and levels of harm.

The position taken in this chapter is that the link between consumption levels and harm is not one with the properties of a scientific law, but is rather one of statistical association. That is, the relationship is of an 'often true' nature, which is true more frequently than one might expect by chance. It is not an 'always true' relationship. Given the complex nature of alcohol-related problems, it would be remarkable indeed if, in all societies at all times, the amount consumed by the members of a society was the absolute and only cause of harm. As Skog (1980) has succinctly noted:

> Of course the relationship between per capita consumption and prevalence of heavy use is approximate rather than exact. Hence a moderate increase in total consumption may occur without being accompanied by a corresponding increase in the prevalence of heavy use ... However, it is difficult to find realistic examples where a substantial increase in overall consumption is not accompanied by an increase in the prevalence rate too. (p.144)

Thus, it is possible to make legitimate criticisms of Ledermann's work without disturbing his appreciation that per capita consumption and prevalence of problems are in some way linked. It is contended in this chapter that the per capita consumption of any given society is an important indicator, not because its numerical value will predict the number of 'heavy drinkers' or 'alcoholics' or whatever, but because per capita consumption is the barometer of a nation's drinking health. It is the fluctuations in this indicator, rather than its absolute value, which are of crucial importance.

It must be stressed that, because alcohol problems are determined by an interaction between the drinker, the drug and the social milieu of the actor, then different societies, with the same per capita consumption, will not necessarily have the same rate of problems. This is most powerfully demonstrated in the comparison between Scotland and England. Both have similar levels of per capita consumption, but the Scottish problem with alcohol is indisputably greater, with arrests for drunkenness, drink driving convictions, hospital admissions for alcoholism and deaths from liver cirrhosis all running at higher levels north of the border (Kilich and Plant, 1981). Yet rising per capita consumption in both countries has resulted in an increase in the indices of alcohol-related damage in both countries.

Liver Cirrhosis as an Indicator of Harm

A further charge made by the opponents in the per capita consumption debate concerns the use of liver-cirrhosis damage as an indicator of harm. Their argument is that liver cirrhosis is only reflective of a very small proportion of heavy drinkers, and that basing a prevention model upon such a skewed sample is theoretically unsound. A further comment is that liver cirrhosis takes years to develop, and short-term changes in per capita consumption do not affect mortality of this type.

In order to counter the first criticism it is necessary to clarify the manner in which alcohol problems are conceptualised. It is relevant to note that liver cirrhosis only reflects some types of alcohol-related damage, and this distinction is made clear by reference to what has become colloquially known as the 'three balls model of alcohol problems'. Thorley (1980) has proposed that the totality of alcohol problems is best conceived as consisting of:

(i)   those problems that relate to single session episodes of intoxication;

(ii)   those problems that relate to the regular, excessive use of alcohol;

and

(iii)   those problems that are associated with dependence on alcohol.

Thorley notes that at any time in a drinking career, individuals may experience problems in any of these categories. However the categories are not mutually exclusive, and thus it is possible for an individual to experience the various problems of intoxication and/or those related to regular excessive use and/or those associated with being dependent on alcohol. The importance of this model is that liver cirrhosis is very much an indicator of those problems that are caused by the regular excessive use of alcohol. As Schmidt (1978) has shown, liver cirrhosis correlates well with other physical and socio-economic problems caused by this regular type of drinking.

However, because people whose drinking is of a regular drinking type may not necessarily experience problems of intoxication or problems of dependence, the use of liver cirrhosis as an index of these problems is less strong. Nevertheless, as the evidence from Finland, Poland and the UK shows, it is possible to demonstrate that upturns in consumption and liver cirrhosis do correlate positively with increases in problems relating to intoxication and problems of dependence.

Another aspect of liver-cirrhosis mortality is that, even though such deaths are in numeric terms not high (in Britain in 1981 the rate was 4.9 per 100,000, or some 2,700 deaths per annum), any changes in this indicator are likely to be reflective of changes in a wide range of alcohol-related mortality and morbidity. It is recognised that the regular excessive use of alcohol contributes to a large number of general hospital admissions for conditions such as pancreatitis, digestive disorders, respiratory diseases, cancers, circulatory diseases and neuropathies (Taylor, 1981).

Obviously, the monitoring of the alcohol involvement in such conditions is not easily achieved, and thus the value of liver-cirrhosis figures, which do co-vary with these other conditions, is enhanced. Certainly, it seems reasonable to suggest that the liver-cirrhosis death rate is the most reliable of the indicators of the physical problems that accrue from the regular excessive use of alcohol and are likely to be reflective of a greater degree of morbidity and mortality than liver disease alone.

The final issue relating to liver cirrhosis is that some commentators dismiss such deaths as being due to long-term heavy drinking; as such they are not influenced by short-term fluctuations in per capita consumption. However, recent research refutes this criticism. Brenner (1975) and Saunders, Walters, Davies and Paton (1981), have shown that the time lag between per capita consumption changes and fluctuations in liver-cirrhosis deaths is short - between one and two years. In essence, it would appear that at any one time there is a pool of cirrhotics who are approaching the final stages of liver disease, but who are still susceptible to a raising or lowering of the alcohol waters. An increase in per capita consumption nudges such people in a direction of irreversible decline, whereas a fall pulls some of this group back from the brink. Thus, although the development of liver disease involves many years of drinking, the actual death rate appears sensitive to short-term changes in per capita consumption.

More Cruelty to Dead Horses

A third criticism of the per capita consumption model is that supporters of this preventive approach do not appreciate the value of alcohol to a society or the individual user. This objection is one of the most blatant examples of attacking straw men, tilting at windmills, or flogging dead horses that the alcohol studies field has yet produced. However, it is constantly repeated. The charge is that those who support some form of control upon overall consumption are 'neo-prohibitionists' who are motivated by some calvinistic trait of personality to deny people joy. In fact, the goal of a per capita consumption public policy is to enhance the well-being of the alcohol consumer (as well as the non-drinking neighbour) by ensuring that the maximum benefits are derived with the minimum of harm.

Essentially, society has to determine what level of damage relating to which level of consumption is acceptable. The public health perspective, which comes from an appreciation of the link between per capita alcohol consumption and damage, is about curtailing increases in per capita consumption and is not about orchestrating massive drops in per capita consumption. At the end of the day, the use of any psychoactive drug involves a balance between the benefits and the costs and, as the British and European data outlined above illustrate, rapid and unfettered increases in per capita consumption quickly tilt this balance so that a national 'debit' is attained.

A further comment is also warranted. This concerns the philosophy that pertains to the right of any individual to take drugs for non-medical reasons. If sovereignty of drug use is ascribed to the individual, such that the individual has the total freedom to use psychoactive drugs when and where he or she chooses, then at a stroke the entire basis of British drug-use legislation is removed. This may of course be no bad thing, but in Britain there has developed a consensus view that the use of psychoactive drugs is not a matter entirely for the individual to decide. From cannabis to cocaine, librium to largactil, magic mushrooms to morphine, the rights of the individual are curtailed. Indeed, the mere possession of some of these substances puts one at risk of long-term incarceration.

Given this stance, it is inconsistent and philosophically suspect to argue that only the use of the psychoactive drug alcohol should be a matter entirely of individual conscience. Within some of the intense and acrimonious debate that surrounds the per capita model are fundamental clashes about the philosophy of control. It is this author's contention that the per capita consumption model is well founded on the utilitarian principle of Bentham - that control is acceptable if it is aimed at ensuring the greater benefit for the greatest number.

Thus, the taunt of 'neo-prohibitionist' to those who support the per capita consumption model is vigorously rejected. As Davies (1983) has commented, such a charge is as legitimate as accusing those who argue for marital fidelity as being proponents of celibacy!

Price as a Mechanism for Reducing Per Capita Consumption and Problems

The criticism that is usually levelled at the proposal to reduce per capita consumption via manipulation of the price of alcoholic beverages is not that such tactics will not effect overall consumption - there is considerable evidence that alcohol sales are influenced by price (e.g. see Bruun et al., 1975; Moser, 1980; Maynard, Chapter 14) - but that such a strategy will not deter the heavy drinker. This criticism has been frequently cited and is repeated in that most insipid of government documents, Drinking

Sensibly (DHSS, 1981). Although the authors grudgingly conceded, and then ignored, that there was some evidence for a relationship between levels of consumption and indices of damage, they more enthusiastically endorsed the idea (with absolutely no evidence to support it) that:

> maintaining or increasing the real price of alcohol is not likely to influence many problem drinkers who will probably maintain their consumption by switching to a cheaper drink or reducing their expenditure on other items - perhaps to the detriment of their family. This suggests that increasing the real price of alcohol by increased taxation could play only a limited part in dealing with the problem of alcohol misuse. (DHSS, 1981, p.53)

In fact, there is evidence which clearly counters this unsupported conjecture and it comes from the work of Kendell, De Romanie and Ritson (1983). This team of Edinburgh researchers re-interviewed a representative sample of nearly 500 members of the public about their drinking and alcohol-related problems. The sample was first interviewed in 1978 and then in late 1981 and early 1982. It was found that, not only the sample's average consumption decreased (by 18 per cent) but that the number of reported alcohol-related problems had also fallen by 16 per cent. The significance of these findings was that the second wave of interviews occurred after the substantial rise in the price of alcoholic beverages that was brought about by the March 1981 Budget. The reason most frequently cited by respondents for cutting down their consumption was the increased price of alcohol. The most important finding of the study was, however, that the heavy drinkers and those suspected of being dependent on alcohol reduced their consumption as much as their more modest counterparts. As a consequence, their levels of problems and symptoms of dependence also fell. The message of this study is clear - in terms of alcohol-related problems, expensive alcohol is prophylactic alcohol.

CONCLUDING COMMENTS

Any use of psychoactive drugs induces costs as well as benefits. There is no safe psychoactive drug, and the essential problem is to achieve the maximum benefit with the minimum of costs. Thus the goal of public policy is the enhancement of consumer well-being - not the curtailment of joy. Yet the dilemma with alcohol is very clear. As we as a society drink more alcohol, so we experience more problems. The virtual doubling of alcohol consumption in recent years has resulted in an epidemic of alcohol-related problems which existing attempts at prevention or treatment have failed to modify. However well-meaning and conscientiously delivered, educational and counselling strategies have had no significant impact upon Britain's alcohol problems (see Chapter 6).

The question to be asked is, what level of per capita

consumption is acceptable? Compared to many European countries our level of consumption is low, but is it in the public interest to allow a further doubling or trebling of alcohol consumption and therefore a further increase in problems? At the end of the day, it is for society as a whole to decide what levels of consumption and harm are acceptable. It is, of course, of relevance that there has been a recent downturn in alcohol consumption in Britain and some indications of a subsequent fall in some types of problems. Unfortunately, such a trend is unlikely to be sustained. On this occasion it has been orchestrated by economic recession and the requirements of the Treasury rather than due to any consistent, long-term public health policy. Such a policy is urgently required to stem the epidemic of alcohol-related problems in our society. Based on the evidence of this chapter, it is considered that the essential core of any effective policy will have to be concerned with determining and then maintaining an overall level of alcohol consumption which facilitates public well-being and minimises harm. From the evidence of history and recent research, such a level of per capita consumption will have to be below that currently achieved.

Acknowledgement
This chapter has benefited greatly from the endeavours and help of Steven Allsop, Georgina Barr and Phil Davies. Their assistance is gratefully noted.

REFERENCES

Bernard, J. (1980) Alcoholism: A report to the President of the Republic by the Working Party chaired by Professor Bernard, Paris: La Documentation Française, (translated ASC Paisley College of Technology 1981)

Bonfiglio, G., Falli, S. and Pacini, A. (1977) 'Alcoholism in Italy: an outline highlighting some special features', British Journal of Addiction, 72, 1, 3-12

Brenner, M. (1975) 'Trends in alcohol consumption and associated illnesses: some effects of economic change', American Journal of Public Health, 65, 1279-92

Bruun, K., Edwards, G., Lumio, M., Makela, K., Pan, L., Popham, R., Room, R., Schmidt, W., Skog, O., Sulkunen, P. and Osterberg, E. (1975) Alcohol Control Policies in Public Health Perspective, Finland: The Finnish Foundation for Alcohol Studies

Davies, P. (1983) Personal communication
_____ and Walsh, D. (1983) Alcohol Problems and Alcohol Control in Europe, London: Croom Helm

DHSS (1981) Drinking Sensibly, London HMSO

Donnan, S. and Haskey, J. (1977) 'Alcoholism and cirrhosis of the liver', Population Trends (OPCS), 7, 18-24

Duffy, J. (1977) 'Estimating the proportion of heavy drinkers', in The Ledermann Curve, London: Alcohol Education Centre
_____ (1980) 'The association between per capita consumption of

alcohol and the proportion of excessive consumers', British Journal of Addiction, 75, 2, 147-52
_____ and Cohen, G. (1978) 'Total alcohol consumption and excessive drinking', British Journal of Addiction, 73, 2, 259-64
Kendell, R., De Romanie, M., and Ritson, E. (1983) 'Effect of economic changes on Scottish drinking habits 1978-82', British Journal of Addiction, 78, 365-79
Kilich, S. and Plant, M. (1981) 'Regional variations in the levels of alcohol-related problems in Britain', British Journal of Addiction, 76, 1, 47-62
Ledermann, S. (1956) Alcool, Alcoolisme, Alcoolisation, Données scientifiques de caractère physiologique, economique et social, Paris: Presses Universitaires de France
Makela, K., Osterberg, E. and Sulkunen, P. (1981) 'Drink in Finland: increasing alcohol availability in a monopoly state', in Alcohol, Society and the State: Vol. 2, The Social History of Control Policy in Seven Countries Single, E., Morgan, P. and de Lint, J. (eds), Toronto: Addiction Research Foundation.
Moser, J. (1980). Prevention of Alcohol-related Problems. World Health Organisation and Addiction Research Foundation: Toronto.
Royal College of Psychiatrists (1979) Alcohol and Alcoholism. London: Tavistock
Saunders, J., Walters, J., Davies, P. and Paton, A. (1981) 'A 20-year prospective study of cirrhosis', British Medical Journal, 282, 263-6
Saunders, W. and Kershaw, P. (1978) 'The prevalence of problem drinking and alcoholism in the West of Scotland' British Journal of Psychiatry, 133, 493-499
Schmidt, W. (1978) 'Cirrhosis and alcohol consumption: an epidemiological perspective', in Edwards, G. and Grant, M. (Eds), Alcoholism: New Knowledge and New Responses, London: Croom Helm
Skog, O. (1980) 'Total alcohol consumption and rates of excessive use: a rejoinder to Duffy and Cohen'. British Journal of Addiction, 75, 2, 133-45
Taylor, D. (1981) Alcohol: Reducing the Harm, London: Office of Health Economics
Thorley, A. (1980) 'Medical responses to problem drinking' Medicine, (3rd series) 35, 1816-22

BIBLIOGRAPHY
Armyr, G., Elmer, A. and Herz, U. (1982) Alcohol in the World of the 80s, Stockholm: Sober Forlags
Brewers' Society (1982) International Statistical Handbook, London: Brewers' Society
Bruun et al, (1975), Alcohol Control Policies in Public Health Perspective, Finland: The Finnish Foundation for Alcohol Studies
Central Statistical Office (1982) Annual Abstract of Statistics, London: HMSO

Davies, P. and Walsh, D. (1983) Alcohol Problems and Alcohol Control in Europe, London: Croom Helm

Makela, K., Osterberg, E. and Sulkunen, P. (1981) 'Drink in Finland: Increasing alcohol availability in a monopoly state' in Alcohol, Society and the State: Vol. 2. The Social History of Control Policy in Seven Countries, E. Single, P. Morgan and J. de Lint (eds), Addiction Research Foundation, Toronto

Moser, J. (1980) Prevention of Alcohol-related Problems, Toronto: World Health Organisation and Addiction Research Foundation

Williams, G. and Brake, G. (1980) Drink in Great Britain 1900-1979, London: Edsall & Co

Wilson, G. (1940) Alcohol and The Nation, London: Nicholson & Watson

World Health Organisation (1980) Problems Related to Alcohol Consumption, Technical Report Series 650, Geneva, WHO

_____ (1981) World Health Statistics Annual, Geneva, WHO

Chapter 14

THE ROLE OF ECONOMIC MEASURES IN PREVENTING DRINKING PROBLEMS

Alan Maynard

During the past five years a series of published and unpublished reports have described the problems arising from the large increase in per capita alcohol consumption during the last 20 years. During that period alcohol consumption has doubled, its real (inflation adjusted) price has declined substantially, and most of the alcohol-harm indicators have shown large increases. These trends were discussed in the report of the Special Committee of the Royal College of Psychiatrists (Royal College of Psychiatrists, 1979), and were analysed in detail in the report of the government 'Think Tank', completed in 1979 but not published (in Sweden!) until 1981 (Central Policy Review Staff, 1979). These manifestations of the policy problem have led to increased research interest (Social Science Research Council, 1982) and the reform of the alcohol-abuse prevention lobby by the government (Department of Health and Social Security, 1982).

The economic components of this renewed research and policy interest in the effects of alcohol abuse are not inconsiderable and continue to grow. A conference at Essex University (Grant, Plant and Williams, 1982) brought together for the first time in Britain a group of health economists and a group of 'alcohologists' to discuss socio-economic aspects of alcohol abuse. The Government Economic Service has published a report on the social costs of alcohol abuse (Holtermann and Burchell, 1981), which was part of the then unpublished Central Policy Review Staff (1979) Report.

Unfortunately, the interchange between economists and other researchers in the alcohol field remains limited. The purpose of this chapter is to make a small contribution to the reduction of this division of research activity into a common policy problem.

If, following the 'Think Tank' proposals (Central Policy Review Staff 1979), a conservative policy objective was adopted of maintaining per capita consumption at its present level, what advice can the economist offer? This question will be answered from two perspectives. In section one the conventional micro-economic theory of consumption will be set out briefly, and an attempt will be made to assess the effects of price, income and advertising on the demand for alcohol. This will be followed in section two by an outline of the political economy of the alcohol industry. Particular attention will be paid to how producer interests use the political mechanism to protect their trade.

CONTROLLING THE DEMAND FOR ALCOHOL
The role of alcohol taxation

The main prediction which is generated by the theory of demand is that, other things being equal, the quantity demanded is inversely related to the price of the product. The other things held equal are income, tastes and preferences and the prices of other products. From this the economist predicts that by adjusting taxation levels (either or both excise taxation and value added tax), it is possible to manipulate the level of demand for alcohol.

The state manipulates taxes for many reasons, only one of which is the control of alcohol consumption. The state seeks to raise taxation to fund Falkland adventures. It seeks to redistribute money to the poor via the Welfare State. It manipulates the economy by taxation and expenditure policies to achieve macro-economic targets such as low inflation, high unemployment and, in good years, some economic growth. The government manipulates taxes to push investment and consumption to levels consistent with these macro-economic goals. It is likely that most of these goals will be regarded as far more important than controlling the demand for alcoholic products. Typically, the Treasury is interested in macro-economic policy and tax revenues. Policies concerned with health which could, if prosecuted vigorously, reduce Treasury tax revenues, are unlikely to be adopted easily.

If such policies are adopted, the findings of economic analysis can inform policy analysis. Using time series regression analysis to investigate the relationship between income and price on the one hand and consumption on the other, it is possible to quantify the income and price elasticities of demand for alcoholic products. These rather esoteric economic terms have a very simple meaning. The price elasticity of demand is a measure of the responsiveness of the demand for a product when its price changes by a small amount. The income elasticity of demand is a measure of the change in the demand for a product when the income of consumers increases by a small amount. These measures can be estimated using time series data and the following simplified equation:

$$Da = x_1 + x_2\ Y + x_3\ Pa + x$$

Da = the demand for alcoholic products in logarithmic form and estimated separately for the different types of alcoholic product: beer, wine and spirits

Pa = the price of alcoholic products in logarithmic form, deflated appropriately to take account of inflation (changes in the retail price index)

Y = income in logarithmic form, usually proxied by consumption expenditure (i.e. capacity to consume)

x_1 = constant term

$$x_2 = \text{income elasticity of demand}$$
$$x_3 = \text{price elasticity of demand}$$
$$x = \text{residual term}$$

The equation merely indicates that demand is determined by price (Pa), income (Y) and a 'dustbin' variable, the residual term which accounts for the influence of all other factors. The quantity variable in this equation (Da) can be measured in expenditure or quantity terms. The method indicates the responsiveness of consumer spending with respect to changes in buyers' purchasing power (Y) and the price of the commodity (Pa). The quantity elasticity refers to physical volume consumed and the effects on it of changes in income and price.

The elasticities which are estimated in this econometric analysis must be interpreted with care. The estimated elasticities indicate the effects of <u>small</u> changes in price and income on the quantity of alcoholic products which are demanded. Such analysis does not inform the debate when the policy instrument being analysed is a large increase in the price of alcohol (Maynard and Kennan, 1981).

The elasticities may vary for large as opposed to small price and income changes because the slope of the demand curve at differing price levels is unlikely to be constant. For instance, a large increase in the price of legally produced and marketed alcoholic drink may induce both a significant increase in 'home brewing' and greater incentives for 'entrepreneurs' to indulge in the illegal production of liquor. Thus, prohibition was a form of social security or income redistribution which turned the Mafia into the capitalists they are today! Large price changes, therefore, may have large effects on the consumption of 'legal' alcoholic drinks with consequent significant reductions in the government's revenues and increased incomes for home brewers and/or the Mafia.

The economist is thus offering information about the effects of small price and income changes on the quantity of alcoholic drink demanded. The distinction made between price (P) and income (Y) is important because the respective elasticities enable us to distinguish between changes in consumption which can be related to changes in the relative price of alcoholic drink (P) (the substitution effect), and changes in consumption which can be related to alterations in income (Y) levels (the income effect).

Some estimates of income and price elasticities for the UK are given in Table 14.1. From these data it can be seen that price and income elasticities are relatively low for beer, higher for wine and at their highest levels for spirits. The estimates of the Central Statistical Office, which the government uses in its Budget calculations, indicate that a 1 per cent increase in the price of beer, wine and spirits will reduce the demand for each type of drink by 0.2, 1.1 and 1.6 per cent. Such measures linking price and consumption tell us little about the effect of consumption changes on various indicators of alcoholic abuse (e.g. road traffic accidents and alcohol-induced ill-health). Research on this relationship has been minimal in the UK, though Cook (1981, 1982) has shown that increases in the tax rate on spirits in 30 American states reduced both traffic accident and liver-cirrhosis mortality.

Table 14.1: The Price and Income Elasticity of the Demand for Alcoholic Drinks

| | | Elasticities | |
		price	income
Central Statistical Office (1980)	beer	-0.2	0.7
	wine	-1.1	2.5
	Spirits	-1.6	2.2
Duffy (1980)	beer	insignificant	0.8 to 1.1
	wine	-0.65 to -0.87	2.5
	spirits	-0.8 to -1.0	1.6

Sources: See the appropriate citations in References.

Another way of interpreting price elasticity is in relating price to revenue. If the price elasticity of demand for a good is equal to one, then expenditure on that good does not change as its price changes. The effect on expenditure of a higher price is just offset by the lower quantity bought. If the price elasticity is greater than one, the reduced consumption (quantity bought) offsets the rise in price and expenditure falls. Products with price elasticities less than one generate increases in revenue when prices rise with the small quantity effects being off set by the price effects. Thus, the Treasury prefers to tax products with low price elasticities (e.g. beer rather than spirits) because such policies minimise the chances of 'killing the goose that lays the golden (tax revenue) eggs'.

The freedom of the British government to fix taxation levels for alcoholic drinks is circumscribed by the Treaty of Rome. The European Community is seeking to create a Common Market in alcoholic drinks by removing internal barriers to trade, and is seeking to harmonise tax levels so that products are treated equally by the tax systems of the ten member countries. If the internal barriers to trade are reduced and competition increased, prices may fall for some products in some countries. The effects of such price falls (and consumption increases) on the alcohol-abuse problem are obvious in that successful competition policies in the EEC may increase the costs of alcohol abuse.

The harmonisation of the EEC tax systems will oblige Britain to reduce the relatively high levels of wine taxation (Maynard and O'Brien, 1982). The most likely way in which this will be done is to increase the taxation of beer, which has a low price elasticity, so that it can no longer be claimed that it is taxed at a low level relative to wine. Alternatively the wine price could be reduced. Whatever the price changes, the effects on consumption and harm should be monitored with care. The effects of implementing the Treaty of Rome will not necessarily reduce the costs of alcohol abuse.

The effects of price increases on the consumption of alcoholic drinks is complicated by income changes. From Table 14.1 it can be seen that a 1 per cent increase in income will, according to Central Statistical Office (CSO) data, increase beer, wine and spirits consumption by 0.7, 2.5 and 2.2 per cent respectively. Thus, the best way to reduce alcohol consumption may be to make people poorer! This conclusion is consistent with the UK experience in the inter-war period, and probably partly explains the stagnation of alcohol consumption, especially beer consumption, in the last few years.

The moral of these income elasticities is that if incomes (or consumption capacity) are rising and the policy objective is stability in the level of alcohol consumption, it may be necessary to raise the price of alcoholic drinks by an amount in excess of the inflation rate.

Thus, the income and price elasticities are smaller for the product, beer, with the largest market share but, according to CSO data, significant for all three products. Any policy-maker wishing to stabilise consumption has a policy instrument he can use, although in years of rising incomes the price increases needed to achieve the policy target will generally be in excess of the rate of change of prices. Furthermore, the elasticities may change over time if such a prevention policy were pursued, and the inevitable side effects of 'home brewing' and illegal production cannot be ignored. There is some scope to use tax-price increases to affect the consumption of alcoholic drinks, but it would be foolish to believe that alone they can remedy the problems associated with alcohol abuse.

The conclusion of this section is that there is some scope for using the price variable to control consumption. This policy is limited by the relatively small size for some of the elasticities (especially for beer), and has to be adopted vigorously if price increases are to compensate for the income effects of increasing affluence. Moreover, the use of the price (= tax) instrument is a delicate matter for the Treasury in that its vigorous use may affect deleteriously the government's tax revenues, and this not inconsiderable obstacle may make the enlightened efforts of the Department of Health come to nought. Furthermore, although economic research has investigated and identified the price-consumption links, the consumption - alcohol-induced-harm links are less certain. Statistical analysis of different income groups and for different harm indicators could perhaps throw more light on these interesting relationships.

The Role of Alcohol Advertising

In Britain we know little about the cross elasticity of demand for alcoholic drinks, for instance how a change in the price of beer affects the demand for wine, but the effects of advertising on demand have been investigated quite thoroughly.

Any discussion of advertising is inevitably emotional. The representatives of the advertising industry and their customers (the alcoholic drinks trade) argue that 10 per cent of expenditure on advertising has some effect on demand, but they cannot identify which 10 per cent. Furthermore, when pressed, they argue that advertising is concerned with market shares and has little effect on the size of the total market.

The research literature offers conflicting results, but generally the results show that the elasticity of demand with regard to advertising is low (see Strickland, 1982; McGuiness, 1982). Any attempt to control advertising expenditure would, it seems, have little effect on the demand for beer, wine and spirits. Furthermore, such controls, if successful, could reduce the costs of the companies and enable them to reduce their prices. Thus, paradoxically, if advertising were banned this might initially reduce consumption by a small amount (with elasticities of 0.15 to 0.3), but in the longer term the effect via lower industrial costs would be lower prices, inducing higher expenditure and increases in the consumption of alcoholic drinks.

Even if advertising were prohibited such a policy would be difficult to enforce (e.g. it might have to include sponsorship). Also, it would reduce the income of sports and the media, perhaps threatening their economic viability. The results of research indicate that crude control of advertising per se may not be 'a suitable case for treatment'.

An alternative policy is an advertising levy. Such a policy would increase the cost of advertising to the producer groups. To maintain advertising levels, additional (levy) costs would have to be financed, and this would increase costs, narrow profit margins and possibly lead to price increases with the associated potential consumption effects. To avoid these effects, the producers might reduce their effective levels of advertising by an amount equal to the levy, thereby reducing their financing of the media.

Such a policy has obvious characteristics. It increases the Treasury's revenues from the levy but, to the small extent that advertising affects demand, consumption may decline and tax revenues may be reduced as a result. Obviously, the levy is unattractive to the producers who will have increased incentives to finance non-levied advertising, e.g. sponsorship of sports, the arts and other worthy things. We know little about the effects of such activities on demand, but it is unlikely that the producers are acting out of mere altruism. With our present state of knowledge it is not possible to make precise estimates of the impact of an advertising levy. Like the tax-price policy, it is unlikely to be very attractive to vote-maximising politicians in the present environment.

Advertising is part of our culture and the life-cycle effects of this culture on preference formation have not been investigated adequately by economists. Strickland (1982) points us in the right direction, emphasising the effects of television in general, of which advertising is only one part, on the formation of preferences. Perhaps the psychologists could tell us more about the acquisition of preference over the life cycle. For example, do John Wayne's drinking bouts affect the subsequent consumption behaviour of our children more or less than the catchy tunes with which the brewers bombard our offspring? The appropriate research agenda would seem to be an analysis of preference formation over the life cycle and an appraisal of all aspects of the media on this process, not just advertising.

Another factor seemingly influencing demand is the number of outlets (see e.g. McGuinness, 1982). There is argument about the direction of causation; does increased consumption cause an increase in the number of outlets or does an increase in the number of outlets lead to an increase in consumption? There is a statistically significant link between these two variables, and this merits more careful investigation (to determine the direction of causation) than it has received from economists to date.

The effects of advertising, then, seem small and may be incompletely understood. It is possible that the control of the number of outlets may be a significant influence on demand and this influence merits careful appraisal.

CONTROLLING THE SUPPLY OF ALCOHOLIC DRINKS
The Political Economy of the Supply Side

Any policy, be it increased prices, reduced advertising or tighter control of the number of outlets, which reduces the demand for alcoholic drinks is likely to be opposed strongly by producer interests. The alcohol trade is a powerful lobby and its influence on policy formation is not inconsiderable.

The Central Policy Review Staff (1979) Report listed 16 departments of government which have direct interests in the alcohol trade. The Department of Health is concerned with the health affects of abuse; the Home Office controls licensing and the police who deal with the drunkenness, crime and traffic accidents arising from alcohol abuse; the Department of Transport is concerned with road accidents, whilst the Department of Employment is concerned with industrial accidents and absenteeism and their effects on output; the Treasury and Customs and Excise are concerned with tax revenues, whilst the Ministry of Agriculture, Fisheries and Food is concerned with the sponsorship of the alcohol industry; the Ministry of Defence is concerned with the effects of alcohol abuse on the military, and the Department of the Environment is concerned with football hooliganism and sports sponsorship by the alcohol industry.

The motives of these government agencies may conflict. The economist will argue that usually regulation favours the regulated, and government regulatory agencies will act in a way consistent with producer interests. Thus, the Department of Health may be opposed by a variety of departments, not the least important of which will be the Treasury, Customs and Excise, and the Ministry of Agriculture. The potential allies of the Department of Health, for instance Employment, Environment and the Home Office, tend to be difficult to mobilise because of their disparate interests and their physical separation. Thus there is a tendency for the government agencies of control to be fragmented and ill co-ordinated. No one in Whitehall village has the designated role, let alone the capacity, to mobilise and implement an effective alcohol policy.

On the other hand, the industry is well co-ordinated and capable of mobilising effective policies consistent with its interests. The market for beer is dominated by six brewing groups which control 80 per cent of the UK market. These 'big six' own about half of the UK's public houses. Furthermore, these groups are not single alcohol-product firms. For example, in 1980, Allied Lyons, Grand Metropolitan and Whitbreads, three of the 'big six' brewers, obtained 40, 20 and 11 per cent respectively of their profit from the sale of wines and spirits. Imperial, another of the big six, now gets only about 50 per cent of its profit from tobacco and is a major producer in the guise of Courage. All the brewers are diversified into food and leisure activities, and this diversification is increasing in the present period of stagnation in beer sales.

Forty per cent of the UK's wine distribution is controlled by eight companies. Four of these are 'big six' brewers and another two of them are the supermarket chain stores, Sainsburys and Marks and Spencers. Revenues from the export of Scotch whisky are a not inconsiderable component of the UK balance of trade. Seagrams and Hiram Walker of US have significant investments in UK productive capacity. The largest UK producer is the Distillers Company Limited, owning 45 malt distilleries and 5 grain distilleries in 1980. Whitbreads, the brewers, own 4 malt and 1 grain distilleries, and Grand Metropolitan and Lonrho also have significant holdings in productive capacity.

The links between these components of the market are extensive at the production, distribution and retailing levels. Furthermore, these trades have expanded in output and sales very rapidly so that by the late 1970s it was estimated that 750,000 were dependent on them for their jobs.

If it is assumed that each alcohol worker has at least two dependants above the age of 18, this means that there is a voting lobby of 2,250,000. Furthermore, local traders and others in Burton on Trent, Tadcaster and elsewhere have livelihoods directly dependent on these workers and their dependants. All in all, there is a not inconsiderable voting force which the producers can mobilise if need be.

This voting force of workers is supplemented by industrial lobbies working at the local and national levels. These lobbies have representatives in Parliament and elsewhere, and this is apparent in any public or private debate about the pros and cons of this trade.

The exact workings of these lobbies and the precise characteristics of the processes of policy formulation are not clear. Answers are required to questions such as, what are the limits of existing regulatory legislation? Is the full potential of this legislation exploited and if not, why not? The identification of producer interests and their links into the political system require elucidation. The impact of control policies on the likely economic performance of the industry (e.g. what will happen to employment and exports?) requires detailed investigation. Only if such research is carried out with care will it be possible to identify how the supply side of the alcoholic drinks industry affects formulation of public policy.

Any attempt to control alcohol consumption will affect the profits and employment of the drinks industry. Consequently, control will be opposed by producer interests which will use their intimate links with the political system to affect public policy to their advantage. Such opposition can be mitigated by appropriate public policies (e.g. subsidies or reduction of alcohol consumption) and is inevitable in any economy. Adam Smith, over 200 years ago, was familiar with the ways of industry and his insights remain apposite: 'People of the same trade seldom meet together, even for merriment or diversion, but the conversation ends in a conspiracy against the public, or in some contrivance to raise prices.' (Adam Smith, 1910)

CONCLUSION

The 'tool-kit' which the economist brings to bear on the problems arising from alcohol abuse offers insights into the behaviour of consumers and producers. These insights offer no panaceas to policy makers. There is no such thing as a free lunch as all policies have costs and benefits.

There is a role for economists to play in the analysis of the causes and cures of alcohol abuse. However, this role is limited and is best executed in a multidisciplinary environment. The economist must become a new brand of alcohologist prepared to work with clinicians, epidemiologists, sociologists, psychologists and statisticians who have research interests in alcohol abuse.

The conclusions to be derived from this brief review of the economics of alcohol abuse are modest. Prices do affect consumption, but the costs of vigorously using this policy may be unacceptable, e.g. lost tax revenues and illegal production of alcoholic drinks. Income affects consumption, as happened in the inter-war period. Advertising has small effects on consumption and is part of the larger culture which affects preference formation over the life cycle. The impact of an advertising levy on consumption and the effects of changed consumption, resulting from alterations in price, income or advertising outlays, on alcohol-induced harm are uncertain and merit fuller investigation by researchers. The political power of the producer interests is formidable and not well researched. Clearly, policy-makers and researchers must pay more attention to the political economy of policy formation if the effects of alcohol misuse are to be mitigated.

The complacency which accompanied the expansion of alcohol consumption between 1960 and 1980 is disappearing and the focus of research is sharpening. If these trends are to be maintained, all alcohologists will have to work hard in the years to come to follow Mao Tse-tung's advice: 'Complacency is the enemy of study. We cannot really learn anything until we rid ourselves of complacency. Our attitude towards ourselves should be "to be insatiable in learning" and towards others "to be tireless in teaching" .' (Mao Tse-tung, 1966, p.311)

REFERENCES

Central Policy Review Staff (1979) <u>Alcohol Policies</u>, Available from Dr Kettl Brunn, Institute of Sociology, University of Stockholm
Central Statistical Office (1980) 'A change in revenue from an indirect tax change', <u>Economic Trends</u>, March, 97-107
Cook, P.J. (1981) 'The effect of liquor taxes on drinking, cirrhosis and auto accidents' in M. Moore and D. Gerstein (eds), <u>Alcohol and Public Policy: Beyond the Shadow of Prohibition</u>, Washington: National Academy Press
____ (1982) 'Alcohol taxes as a public health measure' in M. Grant, M. Plant and A. Williams (eds), <u>Economics and Alcohol</u>, London: Croom Helm
Department of Health and Social Security (1982) <u>National Voluntary Organisations and Alcohol Abuse</u>, London: HMSO
Duffy, M. (1982) 'The effects of advertising on the total consumption of alcoholic drinks in the UK: some econometric estimates, <u>Journal of Advertising</u>, 1, 105-17
Grant, M., Plant, M. and Williams, A. (eds) (1982) <u>Economics and Alcohol</u>, London: Croom Helm
Holtermann, S. and Burchell, A. (1981) <u>The Costs of Alcohol Abuse</u>, Government Economic Service, Working Paper No. 37. London: Economic Advisers' Office, Department of Health and Social Security
Mao Tse-tung (1966) <u>Quotations From Chairman Mao</u>, Peking: Goverment Printing House
Maynard, A. and Kennan, P. (1981) 'The economics of alcohol abuse', <u>British Journal of Addiction</u>, 76, 339-45
____ and O'Brien, B. (1982) 'Harmonisation policies in the European Community and alcohol abuse', <u>British Journal of Addiction</u>, 77, 235-44
McGuinness, A. (1982) 'The demand for beer, spirits and wine in the UK, 1956-79' in M. Grant, M. Plant and A. Williams (eds), <u>Economics and Alcohol</u>, London: Croom Helm
Royal College of Psychiatrists (1979) <u>Alcohol and Alcoholism</u>, London: Tavistock
Smith, Adam (1910) <u>An Enquiry into the Nature and Causes of the Wealth of Nations</u>, London: Everyman

Social Science Research Council (1982) <u>Research Priorities in Addiction</u>, London: HMSO

Strickland, D.E. (1982) 'Advertising exposure, alcohol consumption and misuse of alcohol' in M. Grant, M. Plant and A. Williams (eds), <u>Economics and Alcohol</u>, London: Croom Helm

Chapter 15

USING NATURAL RESOURCES FOR PREVENTING DRINKING PROBLEMS

Fred Yates and David Hebblethwaite

Most of the documented work on prevention has been conducted within the health education tradition, constituted by small-scale alcohol education projects aimed at target groups or undiscriminating mass media campaigns. Few of these have been evaluated well enough for reviewers to agree on their effectiveness, and there has been some reluctance to draw any conclusions from the work because of methodological shortcomings (Blane, 1976; Cooper and Sobell, 1979; Staulcup, Kenward and Frigo, 1979). However, the evaluative investigations of both alcoholism education projects with small groups (Staulcup et al., 1979; Engs, 1977; Kinder, Pape and Walfish, 1980) and publicity campaigns using mass media techniques (Plant, Pirie and Kreitman, 1979; Cust, 1980; Wallack, 1980) have in general shown them to achieve a short-term penetration of their particular message and to be less successful in modifying general attitudes to drinking. A further, clearly negative outcome, reported across the range of evaluated preventive schemes, has been their failure to induce any change in drinking behaviour. This has been a consistent finding in primary prevention work and cannot be ignored, even though most of the studies measured behavioural effects only incidentally, taking knowledge of drinking and its related problems as their main criterion of evaluation.

Proponents of an orthodox position on health education would not accept this result as legitimate evidence against their work, since their official aim is to leave the client 'with total awareness of the range of behavioural options' (Tones, 1977) and does not extend to specific behavioural changes. However, widening a summary assessment to include drinking behaviour, the registered impact of conventional methods of prevention would seem limited to minor cognitive adjustments in target groups, leaving drinking patterns undisturbed.

THE INFLUENCE OF THE MEDICAL MODEL ON PREVENTION
Several key papers with a common theme have tried to explain this generally weak effect of preventive drinking measures and develop a new outlook on drinking problems. These views can be credited to at

least three authors (Room, 1974a, 1974b, 1981; Gusfield, 1976; Kalb, 1975) and are sufficiently distinctive in the critical debate on prevention strategies to have been referred to collectively (Edwards, 1975; Maloney, 1980). The essential argument against conventional methods is contained in a warning given by Room:

> A prevention programme is built on illusion if it assumes, as many proposals do, that the problems of alcohol in the general population are simply the problems of alcohol in the clinical population writ large. (1974a, p.16)

Room and others believe that prevention efforts have been misdirected because of an allegiance to a cluster of unwarranted assumptions based on a medical approach to prevention.

A fundamental error has been to extend the clinical perspective of those in treatment, together with the disease concept of alcoholism, to the general population of drinkers. Thus, disease-prevention strategies have been used to detect individual cases in the early stage of an alcoholic career when we know little about the aetiology of problem drinking (Kalb, 1975). Room and Kalb refer to general population longitudinal studies to argue against the equivalence of problems in general and clinical groups: 'Their general population data suggest that most people with the traditional warning signs of alcoholism do not end up with serious consequence.' (Kalb, 1975)

The other conceptual error identified by this group of authors has been to apply a public health model to drinking problems. Prevention campaigns have become preoccupied with the common agent of contagion, alcohol, and have fallen into adopting vague, over-ambitious goals directed towards a reduction in general consumption. These critics also give attention to the 'high ethics' of the public health office which promotes its own moral prescription for the sensible use of alcohol in a culture which is profoundly ambivalent towards it. Again, the inclination has been towards ill-defined propaganda activity against the substance itself. In addition, the group have questioned the implicit rationale of health education work generally, i.e. that an enlightened public or target audience will act sensibly to improve their health. That awareness of facts about alcohol or the consequences of heavy drinking are effective ways of producing behavioural change constitute two of the myths of prevention exposed by Kalb after surveying the evidence (Kalb, 1975). Preventive schemes, even the deliberately experimental ones (Staulcup et al., 1979), have almost all relied on unproven didactic measures to promote changes in behaviour. At worst, conventional methods may have succeeded only in the purveyance of superfluous knowledge.

This brief review cannot do justice to the careful scrutiny of underlying assumptions behind conventional programmes approached in individual ways by each author. There is agreement, however, that new thinking about prevention strategies has been impeded by an attachment to the medical model.

THE PROBLEM-PREVENTION APPROACH

The alternative programme of prevention offered by this group has been most clearly articulated by Room and referred to by him as a 'problem prevention' or 'disaggregative' approach (Room, 1981). It opens up a new area for prevention work by taking up a thoroughly pragmatic attitude towards particular, drink-related problems. Preventive strategies are to be judged on their practical merits to solve these concrete problems, and not on the evaluative and moral criteria of a suspect a priori model. A significant strategic consequence of this problem-based approach is that, instead of the individual and his consumption being the focus of preventive efforts, adjustments in the drinker's immediate environment become possible solutions. An interesting group of strategies are then made available which do not concern themselves with drinking per se. For example, one acceptable solution to street drunkenness would be to remove it from public view without altering consumption (Room, 1981). Safer vehicles and increasing the provision of taxi services are other ways in which the drinker's environment can be changed to insulate him from harm. A further novel category of measures would seek to reduce social reaction against drinking behaviour in contrast to orthodox health education work which, in broadcasting the dangers of alcohol, increases public sensitivities. Room points to the increased tolerance towards marijuana use and the change in professional and social attitudes towards masturbation which have reduced the magnitude of problems in other deviant areas (Room, 1981). Promoting alternative recreations to replace drinking and dismantling centres of heavy drinking would be the kinds of schemes most acceptable to traditionalists reviewing the list of proposals made by this group.

These are all practical remedies inspired by a shift of emphasis from the drinking to the problem itself. Gusfield (1976) summarises in extreme form this switch from conventional thinking on prevention: 'Instead of asking, "How do we adjust the individual drinker to his or her social functions?" it asks, "How do we adjust social functions so as to permit excessive drinking?".' Health education personnel and others engaged in the field of prevention would then take on a programme of concrete social engineering projects and move away from grand public health schemes.

In the critical examination of these ideas which follows we shall make use of the examples given in the key papers. We would resist the charge of mistaking illustrative material, which may have been chosen to stimulate new ways of looking at alcohol problems, for serious practical proposals. The assessment of a position which is openly atheoretical and problem-based can be made only from a consideration of the feasibility of the specific solutions offered.

A CRITICAL LOOK AT THE PARTICULAR REMEDIES
SUGGESTED BY THE PROBLEM-PREVENTION APPROACH

In general, we find few of the examples convincing as practical propositions for prevention. Reference to individual examples can best express our doubts. Is it realistic to expect employers to introduce more flexible working hours to reduce absenteeism caused through drinking, and is there not a danger that this release from set hours will be handled irresponsibly by some workers? Can some activity like meditation be judged a practical alternative to drinking behaviour? The precaution of fireproofing mattresses to reduce drink-related accidents is notable only for its triviality. Disregarding what may be insuperable technical difficulties, the installation of an ignition interlock system to obstruct the alcohol-impaired driver from using his car would surely be seen as a sinister form of technological control over personal freedom and would provoke widespread opposition.

Of course, these negative speculations have no empirical authority, but it is possible to compare the proposals with some longer-established schemes which could have been implemented. In particular, we refer to an authoritative work by Wilkinson derived from an officially appointed Co-operative Commission on the Study of Alcoholism (Wilkinson, 1970). It contains a number of interesting proposals to reduce heavy drinking practices which have been loosely placed within a socio-cultural model of prevention by other commentators (Blane, 1976; Whitehead, 1979; Popham, Schmidt and de Lint, 1976). Specifically, it is postulated that by breaking up deviant drinking conditions and encouraging the use of alcohol as a congenial accompaniment to other social activities, drinking problems generally would be alleviated. Room has referred critically to this social integration thesis as 'the innoculation hypothesis' (Room, 1971) but many of the specific recommendations bear a close resemblance to his own ideas and would be in the spirit of a problem-based approach. For instance, the recommendation to provide alcohol for young people in controlled family circumstances would presumably be approved by Room because it 'desensitises' parents to teenage drinking. Other liberalising measures proposed in the report, such as extending licensing hours, selling low-strength alcohol drinks in grocery stores and light food in liquor stores, and opening bars in leisure centres constitute a preventive programme of specific, operational schemes. The point of this comparison is that Wilkinson's proposals, as far as we are aware, have not been directly applied in practical preventive work, and we suspect that the provocative menu set out by Room and others has even less chance of being taken up by policy-makers with the power and resources to translate plans into action. Paradoxically then, we have found only improbable analogues in an approach which is avowedly practical. Other remedies derived from a theoretical position such as Wilkinson's Social Integration Model are at least as serviceable.

Our second objection is that this collection of isolated measures does not add up to an approach which has any programmatic unity. It does not settle the matter of how solutions to practical problems can be integrated so that they are not counter-productive, or offer any guidance on objective priorities. Room has acknowledged these general problems (Room, 1974a, 1981), but not appreciated that his exclusively problem-based approach actually magnifies them. For example, one class of preventive tactics suggested in his work has been the insulation of drinking behaviour from social reaction. Thus, the nuisance of public inebriates could be diminished by providing comfortable areas for drinking in municipal lodgings (Room, 1974a). But this solution conflicts with another general category of preventive measures offered in the same paper, 'The discouragement of worlds and locales of heavy drinking'. Again, 'desensitising' a wife to her husband's heavy drinking may be the answer to a marital crisis (Room, 1974b) but, because a moderating influence on excessive drinking is removed, other social problems like public drunkenness and the general health of the community may be exacerbated. The discrete preventive actions inspired by the problem-based approach are not organised around any superordinate or long-term policy on prevention which could resolve possible dissonant consequences.

In connection with this point, we note that the originality of some of their suggestions can be traced to the absence of the general principle upheld by nearly all other prevention planners, that a solution which increases alcohol consumption is unacceptable if only because of the risk to health. Room and his group may have been disinclined to isolate health problems for special consideration because of their disagreement with a medical view of prevention. But general physical deterioration, the aggravation of other health problems and those serious health hazards like cirrhosis most directly associated with long-term, regular excessive drinking remain legitimate causes for concern in practical prevention work, not at all discredited by their arguments. If an overall objective of a general reduction in consumption were taken up by the problem-prevention group then a number of their tactical platforms, like insulation of the drinker from harm and desensitisation of social reaction to problem drinking, would collapse. The 'item pool of innovative ideas on preventive strategies' attributed to the group by Edwards (1975) would then become rather shallow.

NATURALLY OCCURRING METHODS OF PREVENTION

Our serious point of dispute with Room's group should now be conspicuous. They are correct to criticise existing methods based on unsubstantiated or misconceived premises, but these are not reasons for regarding any general approach to prevention as mistaken. There may yet be a common foundation or guiding principle for prevention which is neither fallacious nor at risk of inspiring implausible schemes. In our view, the distinctive character of any preventive work is the central place it must occupy in the ordinary life of the community. By definition, prevention is pre-eminently concerned with social problems in their natural state before they become the responsibility of specialist services designated to identify and treat them. A primary source of usable material for the prevention strategist, then, will be the ordinary efforts of individuals, families, social groups and non-specialist agencies to absorb and repair those drinking problems which never emerge in a clinical setting. Yet these naturally occurring methods have not been the focus of empirical scrutiny, nor been conceived as a potentially useful resource in preventive work. Those few experimental projects which have taken up a community approach to drinking problems have been largely devoted to the education of community groups and agencies. The Maudsley Alcohol Pilot Project, for example, pioneered the Community Alcohol Team services to encourage and support primary workers in the detection and management of drinking problems within their own client groups (Cartwright, Shaw and Spratley, 1975). More recently, the California Prevention Demonstration included a community component of local alcohol discussion groups led by volunteers to reinforce a mass media campaign (Wallack and Barrows, 1981). To distinguish our position from other prevention projects which have used a community-based approach, we will provide some examples of the natural mechanisms to which we refer.

At the most simple level, every individual drinking act is organised around a shared pool of cultural restrictions and self-administered controls which can be conceived for our purposes as preventive activity. At least one study by a university-based marketing department has given attention to the 'consumer habits' of heavy drinkers and the real, everyday pressures which influence their drinking patterns in the design of a broad-based publicity exercise (Leathar, 1981). Recorded interviews with 40 young heavy drinkers in response to a specimen press advertisement on the dangers of alcohol were analysed. The test group were dismissive of the advertisement's conventional method of presenting objective facts about alcohol abuse and the advice given to keep consumption within prescribed safe levels. In their opinion, the message had missed the real factors influencing heavy-drinking practices in the target area of urban Scotland.

Regular social-drinking patterns were exceptional and the measurement of consumption was an alien notion in the drinking lives of young Glaswegians. The length of drinking sessions was the crucial factor which determined consumption, and various reasons were given for their termination - not wanting to miss work or forego other pleasures like eating and football matches; worry about spending too much money and not wishing to lose the respect of drinking companions by drinking to the point of insensibility.

As a consequence of this pilot work, a subsequent project to produce a television commercial used the key concept of 'maintaining priorities with one's own lifestyle'. Scenes were designed to depict the authentic consequences of problem drinking - the lonely figure of a problem drinker in a public house after his friends had left to attend a football match, for example. The study warns against the 'risk of promoting a correct message within an incompatible non-receptive context' - a mistake made in other campaigns which could be corrected by preparatory work to explore in detail the routine ways of coping with drink in the ordinary lives of individuals.

The preventive exertions of primary groups and significant others are also important, ranging from the well-meaning advice and lay help of close friends directed towards the drinker already known to have problems to the normal restraints on excessive drinking from within families. The wife who refuses to speak to her husband or cook a meal the day after a drinking celebration is demonstrating resourceful preventive action. It establishes a drinking norm between partners which may control future drinking occasions, but also allows drunkenness to take on the extra significance of a protest or rebellious act in marital disputes. These complicated, interpersonal factors surrounding drinking practices are overlooked in broad-based preventive work.

Finally, we should indicate those organised responses to aggregate drinking problems within the community which are on a scale nearer to the solutions contrived by Room and others, but with the crucial difference that they are natural adjustments in actual use. The examples given are taken from pilot work we have carried out in preparation for an extensive survey of drinking practices in two small towns in the north east of England.

A successful strategy taken up by publicans in one of the towns to protect their regular customers from the disruption caused by outsiders' heavy drinking on market days was to maintain a closed appearance after opening time, thereby discouraging casual visitors. The local police constabulary favoured pre-emptive measures to enforce the law against the sale of alcoholic drinks to those under 18 by paying random visits to public houses and cautioning bar staff and managers if necessary. Licensing magistrates in both towns were well aware of the late-night disturbances, increases in car thefts and petty crime attributable to nightclub activities in nearby areas, and guarded against the issue of regular late-night extensions in their own areas. The belligerence of late-night drunks arriving in hospital casualty areas was sometimes a problem, and the local hospitals protected themselves from ward disturbances by making routine overnight observation an exception for inebriated arrivals. Working Men's Clubs dominate the public drinking environment in one of the towns (Ashington), an active coalmining community, and could be expected to exercise a strong influence on drinking comportment quite different from public houses. These former institutions function as social clubs, organising old people's outings, raising money for charities and arranging members' entertainment as well as providing a drinking milieu. Committee members reported very little trouble on the premises resulting from drunkenness, and rarely had to invoke official club regulations on misconduct. Personal allegiance to the club and its social activities beyond the sale of alcohol probably discouraged the wilder, vandalistic acts of drunkenness despite high per capita consumption levels.

Officially appointed preventive efforts like health education could be placed at the very end of the continuum implicit in our examples. They represent the community's most sophisticated and least natural response to its drinking problems. We can agree with Room and other critics that these conventional preventive measures have been misconceived, but within our framework their effectiveness is limited by the fact that general public health messages or impersonal warnings about the potential hazards of drinking are very remote from the kinds of personal and community forces illustrated which actually control drinking behaviour.

We would like to see these natural sanctions made use of in organised schemes. The point of departure for an enterprise which locates drinking problems firmly in community life is firstly to accumulate a more precise and reliable knowledge of the drinking norms and behaviours out of which problems emerge. A detailed investigation of ordinary drinking practices would provide a rich chronicle of the natural controls which lie at the roots of preventive action. Of particular interest to preventionists should be the points at which these processes break down and are replaced by deviant drinking patterns. The housewife who drinks alone or the young all-male drinking gang with its own drinking rules have succeeded in isolating their drinking from community norms. With a better understanding of the interaction between these exiled groups and normal drinking sanctions it might be possible to deter their formation or devise ways of reinstating natural controls. Storm and Cutler (1981) have recently reported observational work carried out in public drinking places, and found large all-male drinking groups in beer parlours to be the heaviest drinkers. This is a significant detail which could be used to focus preventive work directly on those drinking groups most at risk in the drinking environment where the risks are taken. It would, for instance, be quite possible to promote public house entertainments and table games to compete for the time given to drinking by these all-male groups. The dartboard, dominoes and electronic games may have been underestimated as available, diversionary resources in preventive work. A long-sighted preventive measure to help those people who drink alone should be to return them to the company of others and the influence of public drinking standards. Local inducements which make unaccompanied entry into drinking places less forbidding, particularly for women, might be considered.

Whether these ideas can be translated into practical action will depend not only on a store of expertise about naturally occurring community resources, but also how far the goals of prevention correspond to existing community formulations of its drinking problems. In one of the towns we are studying there is a discotheque pointed out to us by magistrates as a local trouble spot which had led to court appearances. Disturbances were attributed to drinking amongst the young members encouraged by a late-night bar extension. The police had responded by making a presence at intervals throughout the evening. The manager of this discotheque attributed some of the trouble to older drinkers who came along to continue drinking after normal hours, and he had taken steps to deter latecomers. Because the discotheque was the recognised focus of a drinking problem, more extensive preventive work could expect local co-operation and be combined with existing measures which the community itself had initiated. The achievement for the prevention worker would be to demonstrate a single successful intervention which could be applied to other problem areas with community support. If broad policy aims on drinking problems can be reconstituted to reflect genuine community concerns, then natural controls become accessible to enhance planned action. The general aims of traditional public health measures, the dissemination of information, changes in attitudes, improvement in health are not seated in the ordinary community management of drinking problems, and there is a primary difficulty of convincing community members at risk or otherwise concerned about drinking of the relevance of such work.

This does not mean that attempts to tackle officially designated problems not recognised by the community must be abandoned, only that due account should be taken of how they are actually presented. For example, empirical study may suggest critical points of compliance when the impact of a health warning about excessive drinking can be most effective, perhaps in the general practitioner's surgery to patients with early signs of alcohol-related health problems. Returning to a drinking problem mentioned earlier, space over the alcohol-sales section of supermarkets could be the ideal location for a poster campaign to discourage solitary drinking.

We were able to obtain some impression of drinking problems as they exist in the lives of ordinary people from the results of a questionnaire survey we are carrying out in our two towns. So far, only the pilot results are available on 86 cases, but there is the suggestion that in Ashington drinking is more a troublesome feature of domestic life than in Bishop Auckland, where people seemed more concerned with the public disruption caused by drinking in their town. Drunkenness on the street and public transport were noted more often in Bishop Auckland despite the lower alcohol consumption for the area. Drinkers in Ashington were more likely to admit drinking more than they intended, to be criticised for their drinking and to argue after drinking, and Ashington respondents were also more likely to encounter drunkenness in the household and to ask some member to cut down or stop drinking. Community disapproval of drinking may then take different forms in the two towns. A campaign against public drunkenness would perhaps be more successful in Bishop Auckland, while preventive work in Ashington might be more effectively aimed at the effects of drinking on family life and relationships, where it is ordinarily perceived as a problem by the people of Ashington.

A final note of caution should be made about the style of prevention work we are supporting. The scale of organised community action must refer to identifiable communities, bounded by shared drinking norms and common resources. Organisers of the community component of the California Prevention Demonstration experienced considerable difficulties in co-ordinating agencies over a wide geographical area to arrange community meetings with disparate groups. Because their chosen study sites were communities 'only in a synthetic sense' they found no natural constituency to focus specific community ventures (Wallack and Barrows, 1981).

A preventive enterprise informed by these ideas cannot wander far from the 'terrain' in which drinking problems are ordinarily managed. It would be grounded on a thorough empirical understanding of a range of locally established community methods, giving some assurance of feasibility and efficacy which is lacking in the doubtful schemes submitted by Room and others. Informed by this knowledge, prevention schemes may be assembled so as to be relevant to problems located within a community and make full use of its own procedures of prevention to minimise them.

In the end, the empirical, community-orientated programme we are advocating does not radically depart from the problem-based approach. Prevention must be in the form of concrete projects, but the position of Room and his group does not look further than specific isolated problems at all levels, and this amounts to no more than an insistence that prevention work should be more pragmatic. It is presumed that we are already clear about the problems and possess the means to resolve them. We would extend their sensible advice, and recommend that the necessary preparation for future preventive work should begin with an ethnographic enquiry into ordinary community drinking practices.

It is the next stage of our work in the two towns mentioned in this paper to collect local material which could form the basis of an effective community strategy. This work has now been completed and is available at the moment as an unpublished report to the Health Education Council (Yates, Hebblethwaite and Thorley, 1984).

SUMMARY

There is now emerging a long-overdue recognition that preventive work in the area of drink-related problems has its own special responsibilities and is not simply adjunctive to the treatment of individuals with identified drinking difficulties. Upholders of this position (Room, 1974a, 1974b, 1981; Gusfield, 1976; Kalb, 1975) believe that preventive work should address clearly formulated concrete problems outside treatment and design specific strategies to deal with them. Although we agree that previous preventive schemes have been misconceived, we feel that an alternative movement should do more than submit an agenda of specific social problems to prevention workers. In this chapter we have expressed some doubts we have about the prevention of drinking problems as an exclusively pragmatic undertaking, and have tried to develop a more general theme based on the investigation of existing community responses to drinking problems.

REFERENCES

Blane, H.T. (1976) 'Education and the prevention of alcoholism' in B. Kissin and H. Begleiter (eds), The Biology of Alcoholism (vol. 4), New York: Plenum Press

Cartwright, A.K.J., Shaw, S.J. and Spratley, T.A. (1975) Designing a Comprehensive Community Response to Problems of Alcohol Abuse, Report to the DHSS by the Maudsley Alcohol Pilot Project, London: DHSS

Cooper, A.M. and Sobell, M. (1979) 'Does alcohol education prevent alcohol problems? Need for evaluation', Journal of Alcohol and Drug Education, 125, 54-63

Cust, G. (1980) 'Health education about alcohol in the Tyne Tees area' in J.S. Madden, R. Walker and W.H. Kenyon (eds), Aspects of Alcohol and Drug Dependence, London: Pitman Medical

Edwards, G. (1975) 'Alternative strategies for minimising alcohol problems', Journal of Alcohol and Alcoholism, 10, 45-66

Engs, R.C. (1977) 'Let's look before we leap: the cognitive and behavioural evaluation of a university alcohol education program', Journal of Alcohol and Drug Education, 22, 39-48

Gusfield, J.R. (1976) 'Alcohol and alcohol problems: new thinking and new directions' in W.J. Filstead, J.J. Rossi and M. Keller (eds), The Prevention of Drinking Problems, New York: Ballinger Publishing Company

Kalb, M. (1975) 'The myth of alcoholism prevention', Preventive Medicine, 4, 404-16

Kinder, W.N., Pape, N.E. and Walfish, S. (1980) 'Drug and alcohol education programs: a review of outcome studies', International Journal of the Addictions, 15, 1035-54

Leathar, D.S. (1981) 'Lack of response to health guidance among heavy drinkers', Working Paper MWP 81/20. Glasgow: University of Strathclyde, Department of Marketing

Maloney, S.K. (1980) 'Comment on "A review of federal primary alcoholism projects", and a reply', Journal of Studies on Alcohol, 41, 377-80

Plant, M.A., Pirie, F. and Kreitman, N. (1979) 'Evaluation of the Scottish Health Education Unit's 1976 Campaign on Alcoholism', Social Psychiatry, 14, 11-24

Popham, R.E., Schmidt, W. and de Lint, J. (1976) 'The effects of legal restraint on drinking' in B. Kissin and H. Begleiter (eds), The Biology of Alcoholism, (vol. 4), New York: Plenum Press

Room, R. (1971) 'Law and drinking behaviour' in J.A. Ewing and B.A. Rouse (eds), Drinking Laws and Drinking Behaviours: Some Past Experiences, Chicago: Nelson Hall

____ (1974a) 'Governing images and the prevention of alcohol problems', Preventive Medicine, 3, 11-23

____ (1974b) 'Minimising alcohol problems', Alcohol and Health Research World, Fall, 12-77

____ (1981) 'The case for a problem prevention approach to alcohol, drug and mental problems', Public Health Reports, 96, 26-33

Staulcup, H., Kenward, K. and Frigo, D.(1979) 'A review of federal primary alcoholism prevention projects', Journal of Studies on Alcohol, 40, 943-68

Storm, T. and Cutler, R.E. (1981) 'Observations of drinking in natural settings: Vancouver beer parlors and cocktail lounges', Journal of Studies on Alcohol, 42, 972-97

Tones, B.K. (1977) 'Effectiveness and efficacy in health education - a review of theory and practice', unpublished Ms, Edinburgh: Scottish Health Education Unit

Wallack, L.M. (1980) 'Assessing effects of mass media campaigns: an alternative perspective', Alcohol and Health Research World, 5, 17-29

___ and Barrows, D.C. (1981) Preventing Alcohol Problems in California: Evaluation of the 3-year 'Winners' Program, Contract A-A0345-8 from California Department of Alcohol and Drug Programs, unpublished report by Social Research Group, University of Berkeley

Whitehead, P.C. (1979) 'The prevention of alcoholism' in D. Robinson (ed.), Alcohol Problems, London: MacMillan

Wilkinson, R. (1970) The Prevention of Drinking Problems: Alcohol Control and Cultural Influences, London: Oxford University Press

Yates, F.E., Hebblethwaite, A. and Thorley, A. (1984) Drinking in Two North-East Towns: A Survey of the Natural Setting of Prevention, Health Education Council, 70 New Oxford Stret, London, WC1A 1AH

Chapter 16

THE ROLE OF MASS MEDIA CAMPAIGNS IN ALCOHOL HEALTH EDUCATION

Anthony Thorley

The mass media is one of the most seductive and compelling elements in our everyday lives, and it is credited with power and influences probably far beyond even its own wildest dreams. Consequently, everyone from politicians to potato-growers uses the media as a way of exerting social influence, and the alcohol health educator is no exception. Before proceeding to the contentious question of whether media campaigns in alcohol health education are effective, it is worth being quite clear from the outset exactly what we mean when we ask that question. If the effectiveness of health education is gauged in terms of its ability to educate people about health and disease, or impart knowledge about health risks, then the answer may be affirmative. On the other hand, if the effectiveness of health education is measured by its ability to prevent alcohol abuse, then the answer appears to be fairly gloomy. A number of reviews in the United Kingdom (Bell and Billington, 1980; Gatherer, Parfit, Porter and Vessey, 1979) and internationally (Kalb, 1975; Vuylsteek, 1979), have all found that the preventive influence of alcohol health education using mass media methods is minimal and barely worth the high levels of financial investment involved. However, mass media campaigns do appear to impart useful knowledge about alcohol and harmful drinking (Budd, Gray and McCron, 1983; Cust, 1980; Plant, Pirie and Kreitman, 1979), though there is little learning effect beyond three months in a general population. Moreover, the new knowledge rapidly wanes without further rehearsal, and no significant behaviour change is achieved.

The idea that alcohol problems in a society may be prevented by controlling the amount of alcohol consumed in that society (see Saunders, Chapter 13) has been a great stimulus to mass media campaigns aimed at the general public. Its shifting emphasis from 'you the alcoholic, me the normal drinker' to a conceptualisation in which anyone who drinks may experience alcohol problems has been particularly challenging to health educators. It is therefore no coincidence that in the late 1970s, against a background of Ledermann consumption dynamics, two major pioneering campaigns, heavily reliant on sophisticated mass media techniques, should have been carried out, one on each side of the Atlantic. One, lasting from 1977 to 1980 in the San Francisco East Bay area of California (referred to as the California study from now on) represents to my knowledge the most ambitious use of mass media in a prevention campaign in the USA (Wallack and Barrows, 1981). The other, piloted in 1974 and continued since 1977 in various stages in North-east England, represents the most extensive use of media in the United Kingdom to date (Budd et al., 1983; Cust, 1980). These two campaigns and their evaluative studies invite comparison, and indeed yield fascinating material and many lessons to learn. Much of this account will be concerned with making this comparison and using it in an attempt to rationalise a better use of media. But before proceeding to the campaign material, some basic assumptions must be examined.

EDUCATIONAL MODELS UNDERLYING ALCOHOL HEALTH EDUCATION

There must be a clear theory of education underpinning media material if it is to have any value. Most crudely, and usually described as such in most reviews on the matter, the underlying model presumes a relationship between knowledge, attitudes and behaviour. Taking the assumption that a behavioural change, for example an individual drinking less or avoiding an alcohol-related problem, is the objective of a preventive campaign, the classic and enduring approach has been that accurate and appropriate knowledge about, for instance, the harm of alcohol will lead to an attitudinal change towards, for instance, regular or heavy drinking, and that ultimately or inevitably this will lead to a behavioural change - less drinking or avoidance of problems.

In fact, as is well known and discussed more extensively elsewhere (Wallack, 1980; Gatherer et al, 1979; Schiøler, 1982), this model shows only minimal evidence of being effective, in particular when the unaffected or undiseased member of the general public is being asked to give up something pleasurable or hedonistic, such as drinking - or even getting drunk! Failure of this model to work in media campaigns on the use of car safety belts has led ultimately to coercion through legislation. A recent TV series in the UK on child-related accidents entitled 'Play it Safe' is judged to have been ineffective in reducing accidents (Williams and Sibert, 1983). An environmental approach, such as legislation to enforce safety standards of domestic equipment, is thought to be a more effective strategy. This environmental approach to domestic accidents has its parallels in the Problem Prevention approach to drinking problems advocated some time ago by Room (1981) and discussed in more detail in Chapter 15.

The processes between knowledge, attitudes and behaviour change are certainly very complex and barely understood in terms of general educational theory, and therefore extremely difficult to apply to the specific areas of alcohol use. Many authorities instance at this stage the similarities with tobacco use, but in truth there remain important distinctions. First, there is no convenient disease concept of smoking or nicotine addiction and therefore no way for the general smoking public to be in an 'us/them' distinction. This brings all adult smokers together as a target for media work. Secondly, whereas all cigarettes cause damage in degree, the same cannot be said about alcohol. Indeed, messages about alcohol are much more complex to give, and in the strained succinctness of a media jingle well nigh impossible. As I wrote in 1980:

> My impression is that advertising (e.g. T.V.) can only ask the public to do one thing: stop smoking, take more exercise, phone this number etc. The health message for alcohol is complex: a little may do you good and is a jolly nice thing, a little more might eventually put you in a coffin! Here is a real challenge for the advertising company engaged for health education. (Thorley, 1980, p.4)

The implication for alcohol knowledge, and drinking in general, is that the drinking threshold (i.e. upper level of safe drinking) should be defined as basic knowledge. As will be seen, the North-east England campaign eventually grasped this nettle in early 1981.

If this traditional model shows only modest success with smoking, and little or none with alcohol and other behaviours, why does it continue to hold the stage? One can ever be confident about giving unequivocal answers, but it is worth mentioning one or two hypotheses which may invite further debate. First, it is the fundamental model of passive education that most of us endure at school and college. It therefore dominates our thinking about all educational methods. Secondly, it is very non-threatening and non-intrusive to the individual and his liberty. We are only being told why it might be a good thing to wear a car safety belt or drink less; the final decision is ours. Thirdly, there is the more tenuous link with politics and propaganda in war and social crisis. Politicians and administrators see the knowledge/attitudes/behaviour-change model working very satisfactorily in crisis and during political campaigns. Here the media seem to make putty of men's minds. It is even possible in the space of a few short weeks or months to get people to change their political allegiance, or in the space of a few short hours allegedly to get the public to do most strange things in preparation for nuclear attack! It is not surprising that Governor Brown of California, convinced that his own political use of the media had won him State Governorship, should so enthusiastically advocate media coverage in the California campaign discussed below (Wallack and Barrows, 1981). What enthusiasts of this view overlook is that many people at election time, or in crisis, are not resistant to change or new ideas, but are actually open-minded and receptive to them!

A number of authors have drawn attention to the idea that enduring behaviour change is more likely when target groups are encouraged to first do something behavioural, to show some positive action. If this is coupled with knowledge, attitude change will take place and the whole process may proceed much faster than the time-scale, for instance, for reduced smoking or changes in seat-belt behaviour. At present though, there is not much evidence or experience on how to apply media resources with an 'action first' approach in alcohol campaigns, and the area deserves further exploration. As a consequence of these conceptual inadequacies the mass media approach can provide only a mere shadow of its popular promise when it is applied to health education. Budd and her colleagues (1983, p.5) have summarised the more persuasive model of media influence as follows:

1. That the media can disseminate messages quickly and efficiently to very large audiences.
2. That the media have a powerful capacity to persuade individuals to alter their behaviour.
3. That the power operates in a direct way on all individuals, largely irrespective of their social location, personality, previous experience, etc.

Budd et al. then remind us that 'with the possible exception of the first, these arguments are fallacious, and that there is little or no evidence to support the "direct effect model" of media influence'. As this model underpinned the North-east England and California campaigns, it would appear that both campaigns got off on the wrong foot from the start.

A final point to be reckoned with is the idea, so prevalent in our society, that commercial advertising works and is all-powerful (see Chapter 14). In the alcohol area in the United Kingdom, this usually takes the form of reminding the public of the apparent discrepancy between the annual sum the drinks industry spends on advertising and marketing, some £80 million - £100 million, compared with less than £1 million spent by the Health Education Council on combative alcohol-prevention campaigns. Somewhere, flying around in the preventionist's committee room, is the wild idea: 'Why can't we beat them at their own game?'! Again, this position presumes the power of advertising - using media methods when it is clear that the behaviour change produced by advertising is rarely more radical than brand or beverage change, or buying more of the same - essentially reinforcements of existing, socially approved and comfortable attitudes and behaviours. The advertising man from a nationally renowned company who silkily remarked to me in early 1978 that 'getting people to drink less is just like selling beans' had in fact got it very wrong and ought to have known better. Advertising may be practised in leading the public by the nose from one junk food to another but, in contrast, an alcohol-prevention campaign is the equivalent of asking the whole population to turn vegetarian.

What selling beans has succeeded in is turning the idea of a 'campaign' away from mere TV advertising to a complex, integrated structure of marketing, other forms of publicity, well-briefed sales people and staff on the ground, attractive packaging and so on (Budd et al., 1983). Here media use in an alcohol-prevention campaign may have a lot to learn.

Budd and her colleagues (1983) have shown that research in the mass communications literature is most relevant to any under-standing of the basic premises of a campaign. McQuail (1977) has outlined three main components of a mass communications campaign: the audience, the message and its source.

Audience
1. A large audience must be reached.
2. Appropriate numbers of that audience must be reached.
3. The audience should at least not be apathetic or resistant.
4. Success will be greater where the mass media is supported by a flow of interpersonal communication and a structure which provides supportive services.
5. The audience must perceive the message and understand it as intended by the authors.

Message
1. It should be unambiguous and relevant to the audience and is most likely to succeed if it reinforces existing beliefs.
2. Informative campaigns are more likely to succeed than those aiming to change attitudes or behaviour.
3. Subject matter which is more distant, and for which the audience has no competing sources of information, respond best to campaign treatment.
4. A campaign which permits or encourages some immediate responsive action is more likely to be effective.
5. Repetition is probably an advantage, although this is a commonsense rather than a scientifically proven view.

Source
1. The more channels carrying the message, the greater the probability of acceptance.
2. The status and authority of the source contribute to its credibility.
3. Some sources appear to create greater loyalty and credibility than others - although the evidence here is again sketchy. (Budd et al., 1983, p.8)

It remains to be seen how the North-east England and California campaigns match up to this basic outline.

THE NORTH-EAST ENGLAND CAMPAIGNS, 1974-9

In 1974 the newly formed Health Education Council approached local statutory health authorities and social services in the North-east of England to mount an experimental alcohol prevention campaign. The reasons for choosing the North-east remain obscure (Budd et al, 1983, p.8) and, possibly, were most arbitrary. However, without realising it, the Health Education Council had settled upon a region with some of the most entrenched drinking practices and, for males, the highest consumption levels in the United Kingdom. Two local alcohol treatment agencies made the prevention task a little more palatable. One was a new regional alcoholism treatment unit, Parkwood House, in a hospital in Newcastle which had been established in 1973. In 1974, the North East Council on Alcoholism (NECA), a non-statutory charity for counselling problem drinkers, was set up to coincide with the campaign. The campaign was strongly underpinned at a local level by an emerging team of highly talented health authority health education officers (AHEOs). Finally, and possibly most important, there was the existence of a local television station covering a fairly circumscribed North-east population of over three million people.

There was a number of agencies involved in the North-east campaign. The Health Education Council (HEC), funded by DHSS, was the initiator of the campaign and the client commissioning media work from a London-based advertising company. The North East Council on Alcoholism provided an administrative base for the campaign in Newcastle and, together with regional unit treatment staff and local AHEOs, a teaching team for multidisciplinary seminars in local community-orientated events. Evaluation of the campaign was limited to the media work and placed in the hands of a market research firm by the HEC. The National Council on Alcoholism, Medical Council on Alcoholism and the Teachers Advisory Council on Alcohol and Drug Education (TACADE), all national organisations in the alcohol control lobby, played a part in advising throughout the course of the campaign. Later, all the vested interests were to form into an Alcohol Education Working Party as an advisory committee meeting in London or Newcastle.

The aims of the pilot campaign were:

(1) To increase public and professional awareness of alcohol and its problems.
(2) To establish the feasibility of health education about alcohol and its problems (Cust, 1980).

Media work was commissioned for TV advertising, newspapers, bill board adverts and posters, and stressed: (i) some of the dangers of heavy drinking; (ii) signs and symptoms which were indicative of problems due to heavy drinking; (iii) where to get help. This material went out over five weeks from October to December 1974, and was supported by an active programme of seminars organised through NECA. These were not evaluated, and from the outset the campaign was centred on the media work. The campaign was designed as a piece of primary prevention, and yet most of its media material, described by the advertising company as 'anti-alcoholism' (Budd et al., 1983), was 'alcoholism-as-a-disease', orientated and, in fact, much closer to secondary prevention. Not surprisingly, a huge number of people responded in the North-east, over 900 enquiries for help were taken by the NECA, and yet only a handful gained counselling or significant assistance. The treatment agencies were overwhelmed and, consequently, professionally embarrassed.

Evaluation consisted of three surveys of 750 people in the North-east: a baseline before the survey started, one just after the campaign finished, and a final survey three months later (Cust, 1980). Controls were apparently not used. Evaluation showed that the campaign had good levels of penetration, that attitude change was slight and non-existent at three-months follow up, and that there were no significant changes in behaviour. The campaign had caused no lasting change, except an unevaluated increasing awareness amongst various professional groups involved. It had cost £88,000, mainly to pay for the media work.

Set against its specific aims this pilot was judged relatively successful. Cust (1980) reported that its lessons had been digested, and thus 'the HEC took up the difficult challenge of health education and alcohol again in 1977'. What emerges from the report prepared by Budd and her colleagues (1983, p.30) is that very little in fact had been digested and integrated into an improved media approach. There were many fundamental errors in 1974 but, one suspects, flushed with a kind of success at the novelty of the whole enterprise, a more extended campaign appeared worthwhile over three years from 1977. Two other influences made their presence felt: a personal interest by the Secretary of State (Ennals, 1977) and the Prevention Report of the Advisory Committee on Alcoholism (DHSS, 1977).

The 1977-9 campaigns were budgeted with a further £380,000, the structures pertaining in 1974 were used again, and the overall aims and objectives remained the same. Evaluation, but again only for the media work, was placed in the hands of market research. A control group was established somewhere in the English Midlands, but results of this evaluation remained most obscure and were never made available to the North-east Alcohol Working Party. The impression emerged that evaluation was hardly important compared with the raw presence of campaign activity, particularly on the media. More significantly, in the absence of evaluative data, it was virtually impossible to plan from one year to another.

This second stage of the campaign was a tangled mass of problems, mistakes and misperceptions. The media messages had shifted from a disease-orientated and secondary-prevention position to what was described as 'sensible drinking' and primary prevention. None the less, the pressure on treatment services rose dramatically in late 1977 and continued at that level for some years (Thorley, 1980). The slogan 'Everybody likes a drink, nobody likes a drunk' was criticised and misunderstood by many North-easterners. Not everybody does like a drink. People are not all agreed as to what a 'drunk' is. One man's 'sensible drinking' is another man's stupidity. The TV adverts, a series of playlets or vignettes, improved in quality and relevance to North-east culture as time went on, but they gave no clear message as to what anybody should actually do about their drinking. Perhaps because the adverts were no challenge to the audience, they were particularly and universally commended. The North-eastern drinker was being asked by the campaign to drink sensibly - but wasn't that what people were doing already? Later, in

1979, the agency abandoned this dubious slogan and replaced it with the equally unsatisfactory 'It's always the boozer who's the loser', a fascinating obverse of the California 'Winners' campaign described below.

The poster material was often ill-considered and poorly researched. The emotive face of a battered child in colour associated with the line 'Eight pints of beer and four large whiskies a day aren't doing her any good', became well known throughout the region, but a minority thought it was the girl who had been drinking! A beautifully manicured female hand reaching into a drawer for a bottle of vodka, suggestive of a female 'jet set' image, is hardly present in the working-class culture of the North-east. The famous 'Brewers Droop' poster (see Figure 16.1), which won an advertising prize for the HEC in 1979, always appeals to the middle-class educated media man. However, in the North-east, a vast majority of people had no idea at all what the symbols represented. One wit even queried whether it represented a crashed Volvo car! Irritation in the North East Working Party developed towards the distant central advertising agency that was generating this inadequate material.

Figure 16.1: The famous 'Brewer's Droop' advert

If you drink too much there's one part that every beer can reach.

Your health isn't the only thing which suffers if you over-drink. A night of heavy drinking can make it impossible for you to make love.
And even if you think your drinking isn't affecting you, have you ever wondered how it might be affecting your partner?
Put it this way. How would you like to be made love to by a drunk?

Everybody likes a drink. Nobody likes a drunk.

The Health Education Council Helping you to better health

Non-media parts of the campaign associated with multidisciplinary seminars, voluntary counsellor training, improved treatment facilities, better co-ordination of services and, in particular, work with industry were all proceeding relatively successfully but sadly, unevaluated (Budd et al., 1983, p.98; Thorley, 1980). Calls for more assistance in the community prevention field-work went largely unserviced, such that the personnel involved, especially the AHEOs, were stretched to the limit. Strains and tensions between the various interests began to show (Budd et al., 1983, p.72). By 1979 it was clear that the media work, now costing almost half a million pounds, was ineffective and increasingly embarrassing to all concerned. Many smaller publicity initiatives were also unsuccessful, but as there was no evaluation it was impossible to know exactly why.

Soon after the return of a Conservative government in 1979, the HEC appeared to develop domestic and financial crises of its own. For reasons which continue to be confused, the advertising for 1979/80 was suspended and, it was rumoured, used to finance another project at the HEC (Budd et al., 1983, p.36). Two other documents made very critical comment about the whole basis of the campaign, its use of media, its expense, its lack of valid or relevant evaluation, and its apparent relative failure to be effective in terms of primary prevention. One was an internal document prepared by the HEC's new research officer in late 1979 (Budd et al., 1983, p.56) and the other was prepared by myself (Thorley, 1980). The result of this pause was a complete change in direction during 1981, with media work fronted by the botanist and TV personality David Bellamy, so as to become known as the 'Bellamy' campaign. Before discussing this final stage let us examine the California campaign over the same period of time.

THE CALIFORNIA 'WINNERS' CAMPAIGN, 1977-80

In Calfornia in 1976 the situation was almost parallel to North-east England. There was no specific equivalent to the 1974 pilot campaign, but a collection of earlier media campaigns suggested to various parties in California that the time had come for a more concerted, longer-term campaign aimed at preventing the general public getting into drinking problems, rather (as had happened in England) than encouraging problem drinkers to recognise their problems and seek help (Wallack and Barrows, 1981, p.3). The process of generating this campaign involved State initiatives and interest, coupled with a well-developed academic presence centred upon the Social Research Group of the University of California. This academic involvement is in contrast to the United Kingdom campaign, and ensured from the outset a more sustained and valid strategy of evaluation. As Wallack and Barrows (1981, p.5) note: 'The academics who had been discussing prevention effects favoured an experimental design, such as had been used by Stanford Heart Disease Prevention Programme.'

The campaign was conceived in the form of three related programmes, much more clearly identified than their equivalents in

North-east England. One programme was to develop and show media messages, the second was to conduct a 'community education campaign', and third was to develop an overall evaluation. Some of the academics wanted the State to issue a single contract to one organisation which would develop all three programmes, as had occurred in the successful Stanford Heart Disease Programme, but, in the event, three separate contracts were issued. The Social Research Group was awarded the evaluation contract, a commercial firm the media development contract, and a local county authority the community education programme. Immediately this raised the problem of co-ordination and integration of effort of these three elements (Wallack and Barrows, 1981, p.6). Could academics, commercial executives, county bureaucrats, and State politicians all agree on overall aims and objectives? We are reminded here of the problems of overall campaign co-ordination in the North-east so excellently dissected by Budd and her colleagues (1983).

The overall aim of the campaign was: 'To prevent individuals from developing drinking behaviour that is detrimental to their health, or causes family, social or economic problems, or creates a financial burden upon the government.' (Wallack and Barrows, 1981, p.iv) There was a formal commitment to the knowledge - attitude - behaviour-change model:

> We are hoping for (but not necessarily confident of obtaining) significant changes within one year in public information levels about alcohol effects; we hope to get discernible changes in attitude towards alcohol within two years, and possibly some change in heavy drinking and drinking problems within perhaps three years. (Wallack and Barrows, 1981, p.12)

This is a very ambitious commitment and, as we shall see, totally unrealistic.

The campaign centred on three communities in the San Francisco Bay Area, and involved some use of scientific control groups. Communities in Alameda County received mass media (TV, radio, billboards), community organisation and development activities; communities in Contra Costa County received only the mass media messages; and those in a more distant city called Stockton received no special programme. The materials were supposed to be integrated between programmes and developed chronologically so as to optimise the knowledge - attitude - behaviour change effect.

Unlike the North-east campaign, some very basic pre-campaign anthropological work was carried out in all three communities to gain knowledge about normal values and drinking patterns. The communities were very heterogeneous and racially mixed and barely compatible in an experimental design (Wallack and Barrows, 1981, p.14).

Evaluation comprised three general population surveys of 600 people at each of the three sites, carried out over $2\frac{1}{2}$ years and consisting of a pre-campaign baseline, an interim sample and a post-campaign sample. This approach emphasised the academic Social Research Group's role and is far superior to the poor evaluation in the North-east study.

The media development centred on two rather contrasting slogans linked to a series of TV vignettes and related material for billboards. Central to the programme was a positive theme of 'Winners quit while they're ahead', in which winners of various games encourage moderation in drinking, rather than extra liquid celebration, by associating the desired behaviour with rewards and greater acceptance by peers. This runs counter to the more culturally approved idea that a winner can have an extra drink to celebrate! Indeed, the cultural impasse may have been a reason for the campaign foundering. The other slogan 'Caution: too much drinking can be harmful to your health and happiness', dropped later in the campaign, is very weak in that it says the obvious and means nothing until 'too much' is defined. Here are the slogans falling into the same pitfalls as in North-east England: too obvious to mean anything, or too distant from cultural norms.

Early in 1978 the State Governor, under pressure from certain legislators and the wine industry, deferred the launch of media material by four weeks. Some material which apparently suggested how much a person should drink was considered inappropriate for State sponsorship. This theme became equally controversial in the Bellamy campaign. Eventually the Governor's office selected two out of five films as being suitable, a clear example of political intervention.

The community prevention programme in Alameda County made valiant attempts to generate high community involvement and link with media material. This appears to be a more vigorous attempt than has ever been tried in North-east England and, although for a variety of complex reasons the community campaign was unsatisfactory, as in the North-east, it came to have most impact amongst committed professionals. Evaluation of this community prevention programme proved difficult and evidence of effectiveness was elusive (Wallack and Barrows 1981, p.34).

What did the evaluation show after three years work? First, there was insufficient processed material to feed into each new phase of the programme. Secondly, there was some increase in awareness and knowledge of alcohol problems. However, attitudes and drinking behaviours were unchanged. The programme had cost $2\frac{1}{2}$ million dollars. The final conclusion closely mirrors the situation in 1979 in the North-east England campaign: 'There are no clear-cut answers to the question of whether the demonstration on the whole succeeded or failed.' (Wallack and Barrows 1981, p.xvi).

THE 1981 BELLAMY CAMPAIGN AND ITS AFTERMATH

A series of events occurred in 1980 which caused major changes in a media approach for a new North-east campaign initiative in the Spring of 1981. These have been admirably identified and dissected by Budd et al. (1983, p.37) and include: (i) embarrassment over the apparent ineffectiveness of earlier campaigns; (ii) pressure from various sources to use a locally based advertising company more in tune with local culture; (iii) direct political interest at the DHSS effectively challenging the HEC to show that the media campaigns could influence the general public; (iv) pressure from the North-East Alcohol Working Party to give consumption guidelines to allow self-monitoring, i.e. to set drinking limits. This final factor proved controversial, just as it had in California. Although a great deal of compelling evidence was brought to bear with regard to limits by clinicians and the problem prevention lobby, the 'neo-prohibitionist' lobby argued that a daily safe limit, say of 10 units of ethanol, would in fact encourage people to increase their drinking up to that limit. Others argued over what a limit should be, or how it differs between men and women (Budd et al, 1983, p.41).

In the event, most of these pressures were acceeded to. A local advertising agency was commissioned and subsequently has worked most closely with planners of the campaign. For the first time in six years, really accurate culturally relevant material was developed, and a 5-pints (10 units) safe limit was adopted. Thus, a third phase was begun in Spring 1981 and had the following aims:

(1) To give guidelines as to what constitutes 'sensible drinking' and to relate the consequences of over-drinking to the individual's health and social life.

(2) To alert the individual to the fact that alcohol abuse is undermining and damaging to his/her community and therefore to that person.

David Bellamy, as a nationally known scientist and personality resident in the North-east, was chosen by the advertising company as likely to guarantee a universal reaction. The media material avoided proscriptive moralising and emphasised the good things that come from drinking, and an echo of 'a little may do you good and is a jolly nice thing' (Thorley, 1980) may have reappeared in the slogan, 'Why spoil a good thing?'. This was linked to material pointing out a 5-pints limit and emphasising the relationship between equivalents of beer (considered safe in the North-east) as compared with spirits (unlike Scotland, considered as very dangerous in the North-east) (see Figure 16.2). Related material was presented for TV, newspapers and billboards, and the campaign commenced in February 1981.

The positive effect was noticeable within a couple of weeks. Thus one irritated drinker phoned the NECA office to voice his disbelief in Bellamy's safe limit: 'It's a load of rubbish. Everybody in the pub says so!' In previous campaigns there was nothing like this to generate controversy and certainly nothing which occupied the whole pub. 'Two or three pints, two or three times a week. Why spoil a good thing?' got on to the tip of many people's tongues, and even became a children's skipping song! For the first time in the North-east campaigns, people were presenting at treatment

Figure 16.2: An Advert from the 1981 North-East England HEC Campaign

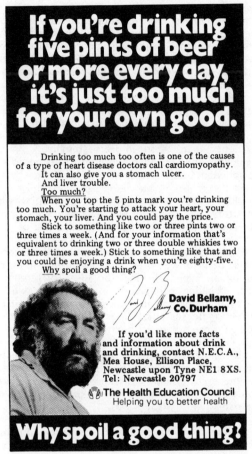

Drinking too much too often is one of the causes of a type of heart disease doctors call cardiomyopathy.

It can also give you a stomach ulcer.

And liver trouble.

Too much?

When you top the 5 pints mark you're drinking too much. You're starting to attack your heart, your stomach, your liver. And you could pay the price.

Stick to something like two or three pints two or three times a week. (And for your information that's equivalent to drinking two or three double whiskies two or three times a week.) Stick to something like that and you could be enjoying a drink when you're eighty-five.

Why spoil a good thing?

David Bellamy, Co. Durham

If you'd like more facts and information about drink and drinking, contact N.E.C.A., Mea House, Ellison Place, Newcastle upon Tyne NE1 8XS. Tel: Newcastle 20797

The Health Education Council
Helping you to better health

agencies not with drinking problems, but just enquiring about their consumption. At last it appeared as if the campaign was achieving some kind of primary prevention.

However, there were two very serious shortcomings. There was no poster material or media-related material for use in seminars and community prevention work and, more significantly, there was no evaluation other than very basic market research. This latter fact might sound incredible, but the HEC was still considering an evaluation proposal from the Centre for Mass Communications Research (CMCR) at Leicester University in early April 1981, nearly two months after the campaign had started. However, it was possible to discuss this evaluation omission with senior DHSS officials, and subsequently an evaluation of the second flight of

Bellamy material later in 1981, coupled with retrospective examination of the aims and achievements of the entire North-east campaign for 1974, was commissioned (Budd et al., 1983).

Although the Leicester CMCR evaluation team had no adequate pre-1981 baseline data, they were able to use a population in Leicestershire as a control group and carry out survey work which has shown some significant facts. Ninety-three per cent of the North-east sample had seen the campaign material and had positive things to say about Bellamy. When asked what they recollected of the material, 56 per cent mentioned that 'Bellamy compares beer and whisky/gives the equivalent of beer and whisky'. Twenty-three per cent were able to state that you should drink 'not more than 5 pints'. North-east drinkers were also more accurate in describing alcohol equivalents than those in Leicestershire. In short, the Bellamy campaign had succeeded in some of its basic objectives. Budd and her colleagues have noted:

> This level of penetration is certainly highly satisfactory, and probably beyond targets set by HEC staff. Moreover, in view of the aims of the campaign (i.e. to convey specific information about alcohol and alcohol use), it seems equally clear that the campaign may also be interpreted as being successful in meeting these aims. Even allowing for these differences in claimed drinking behaviour between those who had seen the campaign and those who had not, the evidence indicates that those who had seen the campaign were likely to have views about 'safe' and 'reasonable' limits for alcohol use which were more in line with those suggested in the advertising campaign. Further, these same people seemed, on average, to have more accurate assessments of the alcohol equivalent of different drinks - a key point conveyed in the campaign. (1983, p.153)

There is no evidence from this evaluation that the campaign had any influence on drinking behaviour, but it is increasingly accepted that such change can only occur after many years of presenting the same message. What is promising is that more recent market research evidence shows that the initial Bellamy campaign effect has been sustained, with only a marginal decline, for almost two years.

Here certainly is one lesson that has been learned in the North-east campaign: to make any significant impact on North-east drinking behaviour, alcohol campaigns in the widest sense must be continuously present for years and possibly decades. What emerges in the North-east since the success of the 1981 campaign is that its impact is hard to follow in subsequent media work. Does one plan more of the same, with or without a media front man such as David Bellamy? Does one try to lead a public with some inkling about alcohol equivalents into a more sophisticated use of this information, for example moving from beer/spirits to wines/fortified wines? Can one satisfactorily target more specific groups - women, younger people, those in the work place? Is it possible to design a logo instantly understandable, like the 'no smoking' logo, for an alcohol message which does not say 'don't drink' but something like 'why spoil a good thing?'. What do we really know about the developmental continuity of media material such that it will ultimately act in shaping a change in behaviour over many years? These are just some of the problems that are being grappled with in the North-east in the wake of 1981. My impression as a participant in planning current and future media and campaign work is that it is largely uncharted territory.

THE ROLE OF THE MEDIA IN FUTURE ALCOHOL CAMPAIGNS
If we return to our original question as to the role of mass media campaigns in alcohol health education, the North-east experience over ten years has much to say about a more subtle spin-off and influence. In order to compensate for its inadequacies as a social influence, as well as to complement its central thrust, there has been a massive amount of activity surrounding the media work of the campaign. The secondary prevention elements in the early campaigns were a spur to initiate or develop better services for problem drinkers, such that counselling services, hostels, day centres, dry clubs, shop fronts, dry holding units and community alcohol teams have all been established with a high degree of inter-agency co-ordination. The campaign's ground work over a decade has led to literally hundreds of seminars and lectures being given to professional and lay groups. Specific skills in alcohol health education as an adjunct to counselling have led to the development of 'Drinking Choices' (Simnett, Wright and Evans, 1983), a powerful experimental training module, now available nationally, which trains participants to be future trainers. Experience in formal training for lay voluntary counsellors and key professionals is being utilised in the establishment of a multidisciplinary diploma course in alcohol and drug-counselling practice at a local centre of higher education. Failure to have adequate anthropological and sociological data on patterns of North-east drinking before the campaigns has led to important prevention-orientated research initiatives, grounded in local cultural values, being made from the Centre for Alcohol and Drug Studies (see Chapter 15). To complement media messages on alcohol in the industrial setting with practical action, NECA has convened a most successful Industrial Working Party comprised of local firms who plan alcohol company policies, personnel training courses, and develop their own media material.

In contrast to the early direct efforts of mass media work, all these more peripheral activities are to be judged as broadly successful. In fact, they raise the question as to what is the campaign: the peripheral activities, or the media work, or both? Some of these activities clearly complement the knowledge - attitudes - behaviour-change process, whereas others (e.g. the Drinking Choices Module and the Industrial Working Party) utilise an 'action first' effect, suggesting that perhaps to be successful an overall campaign requires knowledge → behaviour and behaviour → knowledge processes occurring (in a planned way!) at the same time. Another potential and more successful use of an 'action first' approach in a media message would be if it followed the successful social integration of explanatory knowledge, so that when the person is challenged by the media to behave differently (e.g. to not drink and drive) and chooses to do so, he has compelling, adequate and easily memorised information for defending his action when challenged by critical peers. Such strategies require much further experiment.

The area where media campaigns have their most challenging effect has been with the general mass media themselves. Both the North-east and California experiences show that specific media campaigns in alcohol education are very expensive and only modestly successful in imparting knowledge. It appears that the more culturally and class-sensitive the material, the more effective the message. This largely rules out transferring regionally successful material over for national broadcasting, and would appear to limit work in the future at the level of regional initiatives. Is it likely that the vast expense of regional or national use of media, mainly TV at these times of limited resources, makes it hardly worth while to mount specific alcohol media work on a large scale again? The true answer may be simply, yes: that the media campaign, as an art or science, has become too costly for its purpose. Although both the contracted advertising company and the naïve health planner will always be keen to maintain campaigns on a large scale, the wise alcohol educator may wish to use the media in a more catalytic way.

Budd and her colleagues provide the key to an altered approach when they indicate that

> although ... the direct persuasive power of the media upon the individual can be shown to be very limited, the media do exert considerable influence in a highly complex indirect way, by structuring information and generally shaping the available perspectives for viewing the world. (1983, p.10)

Perhaps the true role of a specific and limited alcohol media campaign is to encourage and catalyse the general mass media to put alcohol problem prevention on their agenda and get accurate information across to the public. This approach gets the general mass media to become the media campaign - at no extra cost to health planners!

Some considerable progress has been made in this direction in the North-east of England campaign. Field workers have forged close and valued relations with local advertising agencies, newspapers and TV stations, in an area where 'Booze is always news!' Thus, newspaper articles on alcohol-related topics are positively encouraged and facilitated with interesting and topical information. Medical and biological information is demystified and simplified without distortion. Attention and care is given to the use of definitions and jargon, for so much else follows. The North-east campaign has recently run seminars for media men helping them to understand de-medicalised models of problem drinking, rather than emphasising alcoholism, by issuing explanatory glossaries to reporters and editors and enabling them to use specific publicity material produced by the NECA and the campaign effort. A local TV station has offered free public service announcements for counsellor recruitment and, in 1982, a more specific one-month campaign at peak viewing time as part of a regional magazine programme. The resultant 'That's the Limit' campaign offered over 45 minutes of prime television time spread over eight sessions, and covered many aspects of drinking behaviour. A complementary booklet was produced free by the company, and all the publicity and alcohol material was developed by Howe, Simnett and Thorley (1982) from NECA (see Figure 16.3 for a typical piece of this material). Although not formally evaluated, this campaign saved NECA thousands of pounds, complemented and developed existing media messages, and was judged by all concerned to be a very successful experiment, in that future 'free' media campaigns in North-east England are being planned.

The success and style of the North-east 'That's the Limit' campaign influenced the Health Education Council and the BBC in the development and production of a nationally networked 'That's the Limit' series of TV programmes on Sunday evenings in January 1984. This set of five, 10-minute programmes used a popular actor, Derek Griffiths, to present engaging and humorous material and a number of real-life drinking, self-help success stories, all based upon a nationally available 'That's the Limit' education booklet (HEC, 1984).

Projects like those in California and North-east England have blazed a trail. There is no reason for other regions, or other countries, to go over the same expensive ground. National awareness about alcohol and harm, safe drinking and health is much more developed than in 1974. The role for specific alcohol media work would appear to be to generate and amplify a more general, and ultimately more powerful, media effect. The time-scale for change is several decades, so alcohol educators have to become key initiators, consultants and advisors in general media initiatives, always maintaining topicality and interest. Let us not forget that, now 'Booze is news' all over the world, alcohol educators should be at the forefront of selecting that news and opinion and so influencing the general debate.

REFERENCES

Bell, J. and Billington, D.R. (1980) Annotated Bibliography of Health Education Research Completed in Britain from 1948-1978, Edinburgh: Scottish Health Education Unit

Budd, J., Gray, P. and McCron, R. (1983) The Tyne Tees Alcohol Education Campaign: An Evaluation, London: The Health Education Council

Figure 16.3: A simple guide to hangovers from the 1982 Tyne Tees Television "That's the Limit campaign.

Cust, G. (1980) 'Health education about alcohol in the Tyne Tees area' in J.S. Madden, R. Walker and W.H. Kenyon (eds), Aspects of Alcohol and Drug Dependence, London: Pitman Medical

DHSS (1977) Report on Prevention, Advisory Committee on Alcoholism, London: HMSO

Ennals, D. (1977) Speech at the Opening of the HEC's North-east Campaign on Alcohol Education, DHSS Press Release

Gatherer, A., Parfit, J., Porter, E., Vessey, M. (1979) Is Health Education Effective? Abstracts, Bibliography and Overview of Evaluated Studies, London: Health Education Council

Health Education Council (1984) That's the Limit: A Guide to Sensible Drinking, London: HEC

Howe, B., Simnett, I. and Thorley, A. (1982) That's the Limit! The Facts About Alcoholic Drinks and You, Newcastle: Tyne Tees Television and the North East Council on Alcoholism

Kalb, M. (1975) 'The myth of alcoholism prevention', Preventive Medicine, 4, 404-16

McQuail, D. (1977) 'The influence and effects of mass media' in J. Curran, M. Gurevitch and J. Woolacott (eds), Mass Communication and Society, London: Arnold and Open University Press

Plant, M.A., Pirie, F. and Kreitman, N. (1979) 'Evaluation of the Scottish Health Education Unit's 1976 Campaign on Alcoholism', Social Psychiatry, 14, 11-24

Room, R. (1981) 'The case for a problem prevention approach to alcohol, drugs and mental problems', Public Health Reports, 96, 26-33

Schiøler, P. (1982) 'Prevention - some principles' in P. Golding (ed.), Alcoholism: A Modern Perspective, Lancaster: MTP Press Ltd

Simnett, I., Wright, L. and Evans, M. (1983) Drinking Choices: A Training Manual for Health Educators, London: Health Education Council

Thorley, A. (1980) 'Alcohol education in the North East: some lessons learned from the HEC/NECA campaigns 1973-1979', paper presented to the Alcohol Education Working Party, HEC

Vuylsteek, K. (1979) Health Education: Smoking, Alcoholism, Drugs, Copenhagen: Regional Office for Europe, WHO

Wallack, L.M. (1980) 'Assessing effects of mass media campaigns: an alternative perspective', Alcohol Health and Research World, Fall, 17-29

____ and Barrows, D.C. (1981) Preventing Alcohol Problems in California: Evaluation of the Three Year 'Winners' Programme, San Francisco: California Department of Alcohol and Drug Programmes

Williams, H. and Sibert, J.R. (1983) 'Medicine and the media; Play it Safe', British Medical Journal, 286, 1983

LIST OF CONTRIBUTORS

Douglas Cameron Consultant Psychiatrist, Community Alcohol Services, Drury House, 50 Leicester Road, Narborough, Leicester, LE9 5DF

Alan Cartwright Principal Psychotherapist, Mount Zeehan Unit, St Martin's Hospital, Littlebourne Road, Canterbury, Kent CT1 1TD, and Lecturer in Alcohol Counselling and Consultation, University of Kent at Canterbury

Jonathan Chick Consultant Psychiatrist, University Department of Psychiatry, Royal Edinburgh Hospital, Morningside Terrace, Edinburgh EH10 5HF

Phil Davies Senior Social Scientist, Oxford Rehabilitation Research Unit, Nuffield Department of Orthopaedic Surgery, University of Oxford, Headington, Oxford OX3 7LD

George Gawlinski Senior Social Worker, Department of Psychiatry, Queen Elizabeth District General Hospital, Kings Lynn, Norfolk, PE30 4ET

Nick Heather Senior Research Fellow, Department of Psychiatry, University of Dundee, Ninewells Medical School, Dundee DD1 9SY

David Hebblethwaite Research Social Worker, Centre for Alcohol and Drug Studies, Parkwood House, St Nicholas' Hospital, Gosforth, Newcastle Upon Tyne NE3 3XT

Ray Hodgson Head, Department of Clinical Psychology, Whitchurch Hospital, Whitchurch, Cardiff CF4 7XB

Ron McKechnie Principal Clinical Psychologist, Department of Psychological Services and Research, Crichton Royal Hospital, Dumfries DG1 4TG

Alan Maynard Professor of Health Economics, Institute of Social and Economic Research, University of York, York YO1 5DD

Shirley Otto Independent Management Consultant, 79 Cold Harbour Lane, Camberwell, London SE1 3PW

Ian Robertson Principal Clinical Psychologist, Department of Clinical Psychology, Astley Ainslie Hospital, Edinburgh EH9 2HL, and Honorary Fellow, Department of Psychiatry, University of Edinburgh

Steve Rollnick Research Clinical Psychologist, Department of Clinical Psychology, Whitchurch Hospital, Whitchurch, Cardiff CF4 7XB

<u>Bill Saunders</u> Director, Alcohol Studies Centre, Department of Social Studies, Paisley College of Technology, 72 George Street, Paisley PA1 2LF

<u>Stan Shaw</u> Formerly Research Sociologist, Detoxification Evaluation Project, The Maudsley Hospital, Denmark Hill, London SE5 8AZ

<u>Tim Stockwell</u> Senior Clinical Psychologist, Community Alcohol Team, The 59 Centre, 59 Magdalen Street, Exeter, Devon

<u>Anthony Thorley</u> Consultant Psychiatrist and Honorary Director, Centre for Alcohol and Drug Studies, Parkwood House, St Nicholas' Hospital, Gosforth, Newcastle Upon Tyne NE3 3XT

<u>Fred Yates</u> Research Psychologist, Centre for Alcohol and Drug Studies, Parkwood House, St Nicholas' Hospital, Gosforth, Newcastle Upon Tyne NE3 3XT

INDEX

Note: in this index the abbreviation AD is used for alcohol dependence

Index